Political Discourses in African Thought

1860 to the Present

Pieter Boele van Hensbroek

 PRAEGER

Westport, Connecticut
London

Library of Congress Cataloging-in-Publication Data

Boele van Hensbroek, Pieter, 1954–
    Political discourses in African thought : 1860 to the present /
Pieter Boele van Hensbroek.
        p.   cm.
    Includes bibliographical references and index.
    ISBN 0–275–96494–9 (alk. paper)
    1. Political science—Africa—History.   I. Title.
JA84.A33 B64   1999
320′.071′06—dc21   98–44539

British Library Cataloguing in Publication Data is available.

Library of Congress Catalog Card Number: 98–44539
ISBN: 0–275–96494–9

First published in 1999

Praeger Publishers, 88 Post Road West, Westport, CT 06881
An imprint of Greenwood Publishing Group, Inc.
www.praeger.com

Printed in the United States of America

The paper used in this book complies with the
Permanent Paper Standard issued by the National
Information Standards Organization (Z39.48–1984).

10 9 8 7 6 5 4 3 2 1

To Roni Kuhl Bwalya, Daya Ariyawati, German and Felix Muruchi,
John Mulenga, Felicien Peries, Justine Katandika,
Gian-Franco Grompone, Arlindo Sitoe
and all those incredible international friendships
that belie much of our fashionable talk about "cultures"

Contents

Acknowledgements

I wish to thank some of the people who greatly contributed to the present book, first of all, Lolle Nauta for his unlimited dedication to my project and his critical and stimulating guidance. I also want to thank Martin Doornbos and Kwasi Wiredu for spending so much of their time, and for their superb ability to spot weaknesses in my presentation. A number of friends and colleagues shaped much of my philosophy: Gerard de Vries, the "philosophers club": Rein de Wilde, Sjaak Koenis, Pauline Westerman, and the research group in social philosophy of the Faculty of Philosophy of the University of Groningen. Others helped me to understand a little about how the world looks for an African intellectual: Roni Khul Bwalya, Ernest Wamba-dia-Wamba, Paulin Hountondji, my colleagues at the African journal of philosophy *QUEST*, and my bright, former students at the University of Zambia. I would like to thank the *Netherlands Organization for Scientific Research* for supporting this study with a five-year research grant, as well as the University of Groningen. Finally, I am most grateful to those who made it all possible: my parents, my wife and children, and the "Bureau Buitenland family."

1

Introduction

No account of any movement is complete that does not take account of the ideas, emotions, and even fantasies of its leaders—in short, the *idées forces* in the evolution of the Pan-African idea.[1]

J. Ayo Langley

This is a book of interpretation, not of fact. It studies the major discourses in African political thought throughout the last one and a half centuries, rendering new interpretations of a number of important theorists. Subsequently, this book analyzes paradigmatic models of thought that recur in precolonial, colonial, as well as post-colonial political discourses. This in-depth analysis allows for a critical inventory of African political thought at the close of the twentieth century.

The history of African political ideas is a neglected field of study. Investigations in African history, anthropology, and politics flourish, doing much in the last decades to eradicate a colonial, unhistorical, and stereotypical notion of Africa. The study of African intellectual creation, in particular political thought, however, remains quite marginal. No comprehensive history of Europe or the United States, for instance, would fail to discuss the ideas of Locke, Montesquieu, Jefferson, Dewey, or Marx, but when it comes to Africa apparently one can do almost without African intellectuals.[2] In those instances where African thought has been studied, expositions of metaphysical systems abound, whereas discussions of critical or theoretical thought belonging to individual Africans are quite rare.[3] Within Africanist scholarship the African intellectual remains an anomaly.

The present project requires a further "normalization" of the academic treatment of Africa. When it concerns any other part of the world, political philosophies are studied as distinct from proclaimed state ideologies. Then why should African political philosophy typically be equated with the statements of presidents or with the "traditional" African political system? Throughout the globe collective worldviews are studied as distinct from the philosophical reflections of individual thinkers (often going against the established worldview). Why then, in the case of Africa, should worldviews be the prime source for the study of ideas, and why should anthropologists act as amateur philosophers and philosophers act as amateur anthropologists?[4]

One of the results of this curious distribution of academic tasks, which seems to be uniquely reserved for Africa, is that interpretative histories with titles such as "Twentieth-Century African Political Thought" and "History of African Political Thought" cannot be found.[5] A number of excellent studies on specific authors or movements appeared in the 1960s and the early 1970s, such as those by Ayo Langley and Imanuel Geiss on Pan-Africanism. There are also a few good collections of classical texts, and classical works by African intellectuals were reprinted in that same period.[6] In the ensuing decades, however, there was practically no follow-up. Deficient intellectual historiography may also explain why one finds relatively little critical discussion of predecessors within African political discourses, resulting, not infrequently, in the reinvention of positions that were already excellently formulated by African precursors.[7]

There is much need, therefore, for "normal" studies in African intellectual history, in order to strengthen a tradition for the interpretation of African classics and a tradition of scholarly debate that forces theorists to stand on the shoulders of their predecessors.[8] The systematic research into African intellectual history of Ayo Langley should be continued.

FATHOMING CONTEMPORARY AFRICAN POLITICAL THOUGHT: HERMENEUTICAL, ANALYTICAL, AND CRITICAL TASKS

Hermeneutics

The central concerns for intellectuals in Africa have been socialism and development, for at least three decades. Today, new crucial issues take precedence on the agenda, such as democracy, civil society, a reorientation toward indigenous political forms, and the question of the nation-state. The present intellectual situation is not clear, however. On the one hand, there seems to be a remarkable consensus about political ideals, practically everybody values democracy, for instance. On the other hand, the way of shaping these ideals in the form of political conceptions is not always new. In many cases the new wine is poured into old paradigmatic sacks, creating an indistinct mixture of tastes. In order to gain a clear view of the present intellectual situation, therefore, an analysis of the various ways of framing conceptions, of the paradigmatic models of African political thought is needed. This book attempts to provide such an analysis. It aims, in short, to exhibit the intellectual armory that African political thought provides for attacking urgent present-day issues.

In order to achieve its aim, this study engages in three major exercises. It begins with a thorough historical review of discourses in African political thought, followed by a philosophical dissection of the key models of thought operative in these discourses, which finally results in a critical inventory of contemporary African political thought. The study, thus, involves three tasks: hermeneutical, analytical, and critical. Let me characterize each of the these tasks in more detail.

In the first place, the inventory requires a thorough interpretation of the history of ideas, in order to reclaim and chart the almost forgotten provinces of African political thought.[9] And there is much to be reclaimed. Even if, as in the present study, the attention is limited to the direct ancestors of the present-day political discourses of the French- or English-writing intelligentsia, a fascinating history presents itself. West Africa, in particular Sierra Leone, the Gold Coast (now Ghana), and Nigeria, has been the hotbed for the development of modern political thought in Africa south of the Sahara, much as France and Britain have been in Europe.[10] Not, as I will argue, because West African countries were the first to import European ideas, as is often said, but because they were the first to face the European confrontation and to produce a public space in which this encounter could be discussed.[11]

Initially, until the first years of this century, the colonial intrusion could be perceived as a temporary affair, soon to be overcome by a revitalized Africa. To highlight some conspicuous intellectual events, there were the optimistic state-building blueprints of Africanus Horton around 1870, the wide-ranging contributions to a philosophy of African regeneration by Edward Wilmot Blyden, and the sophisticated reconstructions of indigenous political and legal frameworks by John Mensah Sarbah and Joseph Casely Hayford around the turn of the century (see chapter 3 in this book).

In the first decades of the twentieth century, however, the colonial system appeared invincible and its discourse was hegemonic. There were only a few intellectuals who did not get entangled in this discourse. While the statement that Africans have the capacity for self-government was not exceptional around the turn of the century, it was considered to be a bold conjecture in the following decades. Colonialism determined that African politics had to take the form of an opposition movement operating within the colonial system. Opposition politics led to a restatement of African ambitions, such as in the case of important intellectuals like Kobina Sekyi, J. B. Danquah, Nnamdi Azikiwe, and Obafemi Awolowo (see chapter 4 in this book). *Emigré* communities in London and Paris produced more radical anticolonial voices (e.g., Lamine Senghor, Tiemoko Garan Kouyaté, George Padmore, Kwame Nkrumah), and African-American intellectuals infused the specific influences of Pan-African and black identity thought (e.g., Marcus Garvey, W.E.B. Du

Bois, Alain Locke).

The best known forms of African political thought, Négritude, African Socialism, and revolutionary theory, were the philosophies of the famous founding fathers of the new nations, such as Kwame Nkrumah, Sékou Touré, Julius Nyerere, Léopold Sédar Senghor, and Kenneth Kaunda. Political thought after World War II was much richer, however, than these obligatory examples. It included a liberal discourse on modernization and the forceful revolutionary thought of, for instance, Frantz Fanon and Amilcar Cabral. Marxist-inspired discourses dominated political thought in the 1970s and 1980s, before the movements for democratization during the 1990s directed political discourses to the issue of shaping an open political order and the rule of law in African countries.

Analysis

A history of ideas, as sketched above, can map discourses in African political thought, but it cannot uncover their architecture. For this purpose, we need a second type of exercise, an analytical exercise, that reveals the paradigmatic models of reasoning that structure discourses.

The need for analysis is demonstrated by the simple observation that political conceptions, despite an appearance of consistency, are usually "patched together" from different discursive sources and adjusted to suit the problem-agenda of the day. One cannot construct an intellectual building from nothing since the only building material available is the wreckage of previous discourses. Each discourse embodies a stock of concepts, dichotomies, metaphors, assumptions, and hopes about history and humanity. When new issues arise, we carry with us this inherited stock and adjust, rearrange, or convert it, while much retains its original form.

In this intellectual situation, gaining an understanding of a historical discourse involves a kind of archaeological analysis that identifies the discursive bits and pieces, the debris, from which the particular intellectual building is constructed. The archaeology also involves laying bare the (possibly ancient) ground plan and the foundationstones, tracing the practical functions for which the building was designed as well as those functions for which it is inappropriate.

A glimpse at contemporary discussions about democracy in Africa illustrates the conditioning of a discourse by its intellectual ground plan. Chapter 7 explores these contemporary discussions in more detail, but at this point I can highlight the fact that the turn toward democracy involved discourses that were tailored to deal with issues such as socialism or development planning. The discourses were reoriented toward the issue of democracy without changing their ground plan. In the case of Marxist discourse on democracy, foundational historicist assumptions had a high level of impact so that the issue of democracy became automatically conceived of as a struggle between major social actors (masses, classes, elites) within a historical process. In the case of those liberals, who perceive a fundamental separation between the private and the public while placing the seat of liberty on the side of the private, a similar conditioning of the view of democracy by the intellectual ground plan is evident. Democracy, in this view, primarily consists of defending the private from the public, for instance by underlining individual rights and parliament as the primary institution of controlling the government. Democracy tends to be conceived here in terms of a multiparty representation in parliament, not of the democratization of society within the private sphere (economy, culture, family, gender).

Critique

The previous section argued that a descriptive history of ideas needs to be complemented by an archaeological analysis that uncovers paradigmatic models of reasoning. If my inventory of contemporary African political thought is to be complete, however, even archaeological analysis fails to suffice. I still need to assess the abilities and disabilities of the intellectual armory at hand when dealing with the urgent questions of today. To complete the study of political ideas, therefore, a third type of exercise, a "critique of arms," is needed.[12] The roles of the hermeneutic and the analyst have to give way, finally, to that of the critic, thereby covering the full range of what philosophical study can contribute to the study of political ideas.

While moving from the role of the hermeneutic to that of the analyst and the critic, however, the philosopher becomes gradually more implicated in the results of the study. Hermeneutics, although unavoidably involving a *Vorverständnis* (preunderstanding) of the interpreter, implies a role that is largely invisible.[13] As an analyst, one already becomes more exposed: the uncovering of the basic aspects of an author's intellectual edifice that archaeological deconstruction and reconstruction aim to achieve is very much the analyst's "editing" of the available material. In the role of the critic, finally, the philosopher is fully involved; the critic becomes part of the debate and has to justify the criteria employed.

The present book, written by a non-African, is limited in its critical pretensions. The outsider has to strike a delicate balance between uncommitted and overcommitted attitudes. Those culturalist Westerners who fail to go beyond repeating the ideas of African philosophers out of sheer respect for the cultural "other" can be rightly accused of discrimination because they do not take their colleagues seriously as philosophers. Showing respect among philosophers is, after all, the act of giving critical attention. On the other hand, one has to avoid contributing to another long-standing European tradition, namely, that of providing well-intended, but unsolicited, advice to an African public.

Only the last chapters involve critical discussions. I employ the hermeneutical understanding and critical insights gathered in the previous chapters as tools for an interrogation of contemporary political discourses. My role can be compared to that of a parliamentary journalist: wellinformed and incisive while interviewing, but not attempting to take the seat of the parliamentarian.

THE ERA OF THE CONFRONTATION

The scope of the present study is limited. The main body of the book consists of historical and archaeological reconstruction. Its aim, however, as I explained above, is not to add to historical knowledge but to contribute to the interpretation of the contemporary African intellectual situation. This contemporary aim conditions the chronological limitations of the book. The demarcation of historical periods may often be somewhat arbitrary, but in this case it is not. Tracing the direct predecessors of present-day political discourses leads to a definite location, namely, the West African settlements, mainly Liberia and Sierra Leone, in the 1850s and 1860s.

The choice of this starting point does not derive from a preoccupation with the westernized elite in Africa, nor with a preconceived notion that only a Western type of thought can qualify as serious political reflection.[14] In the first place, the choice is determined by historical evidence. The types of discourse and vocabularies used in contemporary political thought in Africa actually trace back to that point. The origin in the West African settlements can, in the second place, be convincingly explained. The principal issue in African political thought throughout this era, namely, the issue of the confrontation with the powers and ideas coming from overseas, first arose in this location. It was on the West African coast, in a few small settlements, that actual colonial relations were first established, and so the problem of confronting the European challenge was originally experienced there.[15] As the front line of confrontation moved inland, it affected practically all African communities before the turn of the century.

African political thought has never been the same since this confrontation. Whether conceptualized as a confrontation with modernity, as in some discourses, or with Western culture, as in others, or with imperialist capitalism, it is always judged as a fundamental break. Even the situation before the break is hard to recapture in retrospect. The drama of the confrontation and the hegemonic power of the Europeans meant that the sophisticated indigenous traditions of politics became represented in a new way. They gradually became perceived, not in their own terms, but in the newly dominant ones, and not in their own right, but as different from European forms. In the new situation only, they became perceived as "indigenous," as "traditional," or even as

"African." Formulated in the dichotomous vocabulary that accompanied the European presence, one can say that indigenous Africa was a modern invention.[16]

The confrontation unavoidably produced a new political vocabulary. Introducing the idea of "traditional" African systems in contemporary political discourse was automatically recasting them in new words and conceptual schemes, giving them new meaning and political significance, and therefore practicing neotraditionalist reconstruction. Representing "what was there" in terms of "what came in" was thus not the malicious product of westernized, évolué culture, but an inescapable condition of African political thought in and after the confrontation with Europe.[17] This book reveals that the various restatements of African traditions were, in fact, quite potent hybrids. Reinterpreting the African past, whether as liberal, socialist, humanist, Pan-African, or democratic, has constituted one of the vital inspirations for political thought and action during the past century.

The correctness of a study's chronological limitations cannot be established *a priori*. They have to be proved by the result. Let me, therefore, set out on this venture, but not before I have critically selected my methodological vehicle.

NOTES

1. J. Ayo Langley, *Pan-Africanism and Nationalism in West Africa; A Case Study in Ideology and Social Classes* (Oxford: Clarendon Press, 1973), 13.

2. Some classical studies give African political discourses a place (e.g., D. Kimble, *A Political History of Ghana: The Rise of Gold Coast Nationalism, 1850–1928* [Oxford: Clarendon Press, 1963]; J. S. Coleman, *Nigeria: Background to Nationalism* [Berkeley: University of California Press, 1958]; C. Fyfe, *A History of Sierra Leone* [Oxford: Oxford University Press, 1962]; B. Davidson, *The Black Man's Burden: Africa and the Curse of the Nation-State* [New York: Times Books, 1992]; R. July, *A History of the African People* [New York: Faber & Faber, 1980]), but most otherwise excellent histories merely mention a few names (e.g., The Cambridge History of Africa; J. D. Fage, *A History of Africa* [1978; reprint, London: Routledge, 1995); R. Oliver & A. Atmore, *Africa since 1800* [1967; reprint, Cambridge: Cambridge University Press, 1994]). Among the few comprehensive works on African political thought since 1850 are R. July, *The Origins of Modern African Thought: Its Development in West Africa during the Nineteenth and Twentieth Centuries* (London: Faber & Faber, 1968); I. Geiss, *Panafrikanismus. Zur Geschichte der Dekolonisation* (Frankfurt am Mein: Europeische Verlagsanstalt, 1968); and J. A. Langley, *Pan-Africanism and Nationalism in West Africa*.

3. M. Fortes & G. Dieterlen, eds., *African Systems of Thought* (London: Oxford University Press, 1965); R. Horton, "African Traditional Thought and Western Science," *Africa* 34 (1967): 50–71, 155–187; I. Karp & Ch. S. Bird, eds., *Explorations in African Systems of Thought* (Bloomington: Indiana University Press, 1980); B. R. Wilson, *Rationality* (Oxford: Blackwell, 1979); M. Hollis & S. Lukes, eds., *Rationality*

and Relativism (Oxford: Basil Blackwell, 1982). Even among philosophers one of the main traditions is focusing on systems of thought. See (P. Tempels, *Bantou Philosophy* (1947; reprint, Paris: Présence Africaine, 1959); J. S. Mbiti, *African Religions & Philosophy* (London: Heinemann, 1969); O.E.A. Ruch & K. C. Anyanwu, *African Philosophy. An Introduction to the Main Trends in Contemporary Africa* (Rome: Catholic Book Agency, 1984).

4. Anthropological research on African systems of thought is highly interesting, but it does not concern creative, innovative thinking of Africans, not even in the best works (e.g., Karp & Bird, *Explorations in African Systems of Thought*; Horton, "African Traditional Thought and Western Science"; and R. Horton, "Tradition and Modernity Revisited," in Hollis & Lukes, *Rationality and Relativism*, 201–260). In the case of Robin Horton, who is not an amateur in philosophy, his comparisons of traditional thought and science hinge upon a standard "normative" critical rationalist image of science as being essentially critical and open. More empirically informed views of science, such as those produced in contemporary science studies, would not allow the same contrasts. As far as the philosophical study of African thought is concerned, this goes beyond amateur anthropology in a number of cases (e.g., B. Hallen & J. O. Sodipo, *Knowledge, Belief & Witchcraft: Analytic Experiments in African Philosophy* [London: Ethnographica, 1986]; H. O. Oruka, *Sage Philosophy* [Leiden: Brill, 1990]; K. Gyekye, *Essay on African Philosophical Thought: The Akan Conceptual Scheme* [Cambridge: Cambridge University Press, 1987]).

5. July, *The Origins of Modern African Thought*, a purely historical book, is the only exception to my knowledge.

6. Langley, *Pan-Africanism and Nationalism in West Africa*; J. A. Langley, *Ideologies of Liberation in Black Africa 1856–1970: Documents on Modern African Political Thought from Colonial Times to the Present* (London: Rex Collings, 1979); July, *The Origins of Modern African Thought*; H. S. Wilson, *Origins of West African Nationalism* (London: MacMillan; St. Martin Press, 1969); H. R. Lynch, *Edward Wilmot Blyden: Pan-Negro Patriot 1832–1912* (London: Oxford University Press, 1967); Geiss, *Panafrikanismus*; G. Shepperson, "Notes on American Negro Influences on the Emergence of African Nationalism," *Journal of African History* 1, no.2 (1960): 299–312; Y. Bénot, *Idéologies des Indépendences Africaines* (Paris: Maspero, 1972); and the always provocative works of Ali Mazrui. Collections of texts, such as G. C. Mutiso & S.W. Rohio, eds., *Readings in African Political Thought* (London: Heinemann, 1975); P. Sigmund, ed., *The Ideologies of Developing Nations* (New York: Praeger, 1963); and the Cass Library of African Studies, the *Africana Modern Library*, including reprints of classical works. Recently, for example, see Ph. Dewitte, *Les Mouvements Nègres en France 1919–1939* (Paris: L'Harmattan, 1985); and Davidson, *The Black Man's Burden*; and discussions of part of this heritage in V. Y. Mudimbe, *The Invention of Africa* (Bloomington: Indiana University Press, 1988) and K. A. Appiah, *In My Father's House, Africa in the Philosophy of Culture* (New York: Methuen, 1992).

7. The criticism of the idea of the single-party system in the early 1990s practically never referred to the criticism of that system formulated in the 1960s, when these systems were introduced. With hindsight, the critiques of the 1960s were far richer than those in the 1990s.

8. Historically informed studies are more common in discussions on specific African authors such as Fanon or Cabral. A tradition of interpretation, however, is hardly present. The sources for such work, in terms of classical texts, readers and journals, mostly have to be researched outside Africa itself, in European and American libraries.

9. Christopher Clapham, "The Context of African Political Thought," *The Journal of Modern African Studies* 8, no. 1 (1970): 1–13, rightly criticized the tendency to piece together disparate statements by African politicians and activists into ideologies or philosophies. It would be a mistake, however, to deny that elaborate expressions of a political discourse can be analyzed philosophically. The dominant tendency to study African political "facts" and interests at the expense of political discourse is even less correct: the political scientist cannot even start to grasp the perceived interests of political actors without entering into their universe of discourse.

10. Just like one can discuss Kant or Rousseau as contributors to a philosophical tradition without being accused of limiting the discussion to just Germany and France, the prominence of West African thinkers in this study can be legitimate. Philosophy concerns intellectual, not geographical, spaces and can freely focus on thinkers who are relevant for the topic and ignore those who are not. South Africa, for instance, produced a very rich political history; however, except for Sol Plaatje and the Freedom Charter, it does not seem to have left much sediment in the history of political thought up to now.

11. Shepperson, "Notes on American Negro Influences"; G. Shepperson, "External Factors in the development of African Nationalism, with Particular Reference to British Central Africa," *Phylon* 22, no. 3 (1961); G. Shepperson, "Abolitionism and African Political Thought," *Transition* 3, no. 2 (1964): 22–26; Geiss, *Panafrikanismus*.

12. I borrow the expression of "critique of arms" from the title of Régis Debray's famous text *La Critique des Armes* (Paris: Edition du Seuil, 1974), which critically examined revolutionary ideology and struggles in the 1960s. Originally, the expression comes from Marx.

13. See e.g. the discussion on H-G. Gadamer, pp. 51–65 in A. Giddens, *New Rules of Sociological Method* (London: Hutchinson, 1976).

14. Political and metapolitical reflection has not been absent, of course, in African societies from ancient Egypt to the kingdoms and empires in the nineteenth century.

15. Strictly speaking, European penetration into South Africa occurred earlier. However, the situation there was quite different.

16. Mudimbe, *The Invention of Africa*; Appiah, *In My Fathers House*. Maybe the less discursively structured forms of life, like music, family life, or dealings with the supernatural, could survive the confrontation relatively unharmed exactly because they could not be re-represented easily through the new vocabulary.

17. "The enforcement of Western discourse as the medium of exchange generates its own murky dispensations, often hard to track in terms of who is doing what to whom. The 'native' proves adept at using the symbols and signifying practices of the colonial in ways that fortify a 'newly marked' sense of indigenous difference," see A. M. Simone & E. Pieterse, "Civil Societies in an Internationalized Africa," *Social Dynamics* 19, no. 2 (1993): 59. Hybridity can be said to be the normal condition in a globalizing world, see Bauman, Z. "Modernity and Ambivalence," in M. Featherstone, ed., *Global Culture*, special issue of *Theory, Culture & Society* 7, nos. 2, 3 (1990):

143–169; Appiah, *In My Father's House*; Appadurai, A., "Disjuncture and Difference in the Global Cultural Economy," *Theory, Culture & Society* 7 (1990): 295–310); "purity" of intellectual traditions is mostly myth. See L. Keita on Mazrui in "Africa's Triple Heritage: Unique or Universal?" *Presence Africaine* 143 (1987): 91–100.

2

The Interpretation of Political Discourses

> History is the concrete body of a development, with its moments of intensity, its lapses, its extended periods of feverish agitation, its fainting spells; and only a metaphysician would seek its soul in the distant ideality of its origin.[1]
>
> *Michel Foucault*

Recovering the history of African political thought seems to be a straightforward task at first sight, involving a description of political ideas in the political context in which they were produced. A number of questions arise, however: Which are the appropriate concepts to use in the description? What is involved in order to understand the ideas correctly? How exactly are ideas related to the political situation in which they were developed? In any study of political ideas across boundaries of time or culture, there are several serious methodological issues to be considered. Without giving these attention, historiography risks being no more than a confirmation of our present views by making history into "a pack of tricks we play on dead men."[2]

A sensitive interpretation of discourses in African political thought requires an excursion into the theory of historiography. I will proceed here, first, by identifying key methodological problems. Subsequently, I propose to tackle these problems with the historical hermeneutics proposed by Quentin Skinner. Finally, I suggest an elaboration of Skinner's approach in order to forge a set of appropriate methodological tools for my archaeological reconstruction of African political discourses.

WRITING AFRICAN INTELLECTUAL HISTORY: TWO EXAMPLES

One of the most thorough and extensive studies of African political ideas is the book *Panafrikanismus* by Imanuel Geiss. Geiss's project was in fact broader than Pan-Africanism. He tried to grasp the various intellectual reactions in Africa to the sudden confrontation with Europe, often comparing Pan-Africanism with "Pan-movements" elsewhere in the world.

In Geiss's view, the basic issue for Africa in the nineteenth and twentieth centuries was the transition to modernity, which he perceived as an unavoidable historical process. Many people undergoing this process, however, experience the dislocations and pain that it causes and hesitate or try to escape. Pan-Africanism, in its various forms, is caught within this dilemma of modernization.

Geiss's detailed and insightful historiography stages historical events against the background of a squarely modernist view of the historical process. This modernist view consists of at least three elements: the notions "tradition" and "modernity," which define a basic polarity; the idea that tradition will eventually give way to modernity; and the appraisal that this process is all in all a desirable thing. Describing the historical material within this framework has several immediate consequences. African political thinkers become ordered as "modernizers," that is, those who have the courage to face the challenge of change, and "traditionalists," those resisting the trend of history and embodying the romantic reaction of the thinkers who "broke down" in the face of the requirements of the time and turned to folk tales, adopting African names, clothes, and traditions.[3] African history, as represented by Imanuel Geiss, thus becomes a battleground of great historical forces that are driving forward or restraining the historical process.

Another interesting interpretation of African history is provided by Jan Vansina. In *Paths in the Rainforest*, he retraces millennia of historical developments in the Congo-Zaire rain forests, which are often considered to lack history. Vansina also greatly contributed to the field of oral history. His article, "A Past for the Future," states his theoretical assumptions, especially the idea of traditions in African history. Vansina argues that various cultural traditions that define their own historical route exist. For the southern half of Africa, for instance, he identifies two major traditions: the Central African Bantu and the Eastern African Bantu, which "derived from a single ancestral culture developed in south eastern Nigeria in the third millennium B.C."[4]

Vansina explicates his theory of traditions and sociocultural evolution as follows: traditions are real things "out there" and they constitute the "pervasive fund of perceptions, beliefs, values, norms, expectations and practices common to the people within a community or a set of communities." A tradition has a core (or "preset framework") that "consists of collectively held principles about ultimate reality"; it constitutes a worldview. A tradition, then, "determines its own future, . . . as long as the societies which carry it retain their self-determination." This results, generally, in a basic continuity of traditions over long periods of time, interrupted by "short periods during which a major rearrangement of basic choices and principles is being made."[5]

From Vansina's idea of traditions follows an analysis of the present condition of Africa and its intellectuals. Africa suffered a catastrophic break in its major cultural traditions as a result of colonialism: "Each colony was conquered region by region, village by village against determined resistance. By 1920, the conquest had cost the lives of perhaps half the population of East and Central Africa and had ruptured the continuity of the old traditions."[6] In this way, the source of cultural and social continuity was destroyed, whereas the alternative European tradition did not become firmly established. The majority of the people live by the remains of the old African traditions, while the elite is Europeanized. To characterize this situation, Vansina typically uses an organic metaphor: "the social organism . . . rejecting a foreign organ transplantation."[7]

African nationalism and the building of nation-states became conceptualized in terms of Western notions, but these states could not overcome the "deep crisis of tradition." To manage such a state, divided between the westernized elite and the African majority, a system of clientism and control had to be worked out, which meant organizing society along indigenous African lines behind its official facade of Western-type institutions defined by formal law. According to Vansina, the preconditions for African development are not fulfilled unless the African leadership reconnects to the majority traditions and the general cultural dichotomy is overcome by the growth of stable "neo-African" majority traditions.

THE PROBLEM OF ANACHRONISM

In both Geiss's and Vansina's types of historiography, a particular conception of the historical process shapes the interpretation of African political thought. Geiss's conception of history relates political discourses to the question of modernization, whereas Vansina relates political discourses to the question of rebuilding vital African traditions.[8] Typically, the effect of these background conceptions is not only the ordering of historical discourses, but also their valuation. Geiss positions his values on a scale between courageous modernizers and regressive antimodernizers; Vansina suggests a choice between representing the majority tradition and supporting a foreign transplant. Their quite general convictions about what is at stake in modern African history thus entice historians to become, in a way, part of the discussions they study, even taking partisan positions in some cases.[9]

A historian unavoidably infuses an individual orientation in the presentation of the historical material, but there is more at issue here. My contention is that convictions about the historical process, such as the idea of modernization or of continuity of traditions, preclude understanding historical authors within their own frame of mind and within their own historical context. The historian, in such cases, enters the field with a prior substantial theory of history. Having some *a priori* knowledge about what this period in history "really" is about, the historian does not have to ask the historical actors what is at issue. The historian pretends to know beforehand the drama that they were enacting. The historiographer's task, then, is to document how the process unrolls and to identify the roles of specific political ideas and actors.

The possibility should be left open, however, that the people who are subject to historical study considered themselves to be actors in a different drama and that we are just burdening the past with the present by projecting our problem definitions upon them. There is some evidence that this actually happened in a number of interpretations of nineteenth-century African political thought. Can one, for instance, speak of "nationalism" when the actors concerned did not have the concept of a "nation" or were not primarily concerned with it? Can there be Pan-Africanists when the idea of an African identity had not been formulated?[10] Can there be modernists without the notion of modernity, and traditionalists without the idea that African societies were "traditional"?[11]

We are facing a general problem in the methodology of historiography, namely, that of anachronism. Fitting historical authors into twentieth-century categories is always a tricky affair. We run the risk of saddling a historical author with "a debate the terms of which were unavailable to him, and the point of which would have been lost on him." As Quentin Skinner suggested: "The key to excluding unhistorical meanings must lie in limiting our range of descriptions of any given text to those which the author himself might in principle have avowed."[12] In African historiography, for instance, we sometimes read that actors really were nationalists but did not realize that yet, so they were "cultural nationalists"; or they really were Pan-Africanists but did not express that idea fully, so they were "proto" Pan-Africanists. It is likely that these exercises in creative application of our own notions obscure our understanding of the theorists concerned rather than disclosing their thought.

A paradigmatic example of overcoming anachronistic historiography is provided by Thomas Kuhn's discovery of the idea of paradigms. In the preface to *The Essential Tension*, Kuhn described his failed struggle to discover the "prehistory" of Newtonian mechanics in Aristotle's *Physics*: "On a memorable (and very hot) Summer day the confusion melted as snow under a hot sun [when I] discovered a new way to read a series of texts," namely, by taking their own agenda seriously, by "learning to think like" the author.[13] Kuhn argued that the most accessible ways to read a text are often not the most appropriate ones in the case of historical texts. So Kuhn advised his students to look especially for the apparent absurdities in a text because making sense of these could lead to a proper understanding of the other passages.

For my present undertaking, Kuhn's lesson is clear. One cannot reduce historical African authors to the prehistory of late twentieth-century endeavors. Instead, we will have to suffer some "hot Summer days" to come to a more appropriate understanding of historical African discourses.

The curious situation that we face when studying African political thought spanning the last 150 years is that the historical process described is simultaneously the construction process of many of the notions used in the description. The notions of tribe, nation, race, identity, Africa, modernity, and tradition, as we know them, were in fact the **result** of the formation of groups, constellations of power, and the emergence of disciplines and discourses in the nineteenth and twentieth centuries. Unreflective use of these notions clearly involves the danger of disregarding the political and discursive situation of the very theorists whom we are trying to understand and thus of misunderstanding what they themselves were talking about.[14]

Let us consider the example of nineteenth-century political thinkers in West Africa. In the next chapter I will give a more comprehensive account of their discursive situation but some remarkable contrasts between their conceptual outfit and ours can be sketched here. "Africa" as a continent in the political sense or as a focus of identity did not exist as we know it today. The term "Ethiopia" was frequently used to denote the vast continent as perceived from across the Atlantic as well as a mythical identity and a God-given mission of black peoples. The notion of "Ethiopia" itself developed only within the Christian-eschatological tradition and is thus a recent phenomenon in African thought.[15] Within the abolitionist discourse in the nineteenth century that focused on missionary work, we also read of "Negritia."[16] As late as 1911, the prominent West African J. E. Casely Hayford, in his work *Ethiopia Unbound*, used "we from the East" when he talked about Africans, thus conceptualizing Africa within the vocabulary distinguishing the Orient and the Occident.[17]

Similarly, the notion of "race" was not used in nineteenth-century discourses in the way we know it. Cultural and biological issues were very much mixed.[18] In his fascinating study *The Image of Africa*, Philip Curtin recounts how the vocabulary of race-thought, with its categorizations and hierarchizations of races, the assumed essential characteristics of each race, and the specific political morale connected with all this, developed over a period of a hundred years. It solidified into a standard image in the 1850s and remained intact for the whole colonial period.

My examples of the notions of "Africa" and "race" show that using present-day concepts in historical descriptions may be inappropriate. The same problem may arise from the use of present-day general assumptions about humanity, culture, and history. The examples of Geiss and Vansina showed such instances. Some of these assumptions are so entrenched in our intellectual makeup that it is hard to even identify and question them. The idea of modernity, embracing a characteristic and powerful ensemble of science, the bureaucratic nation-state, individualism, and continuous advancement, is a case in point. More generally, the modernization idea involves distinct orders of society, like species constituting a functional whole.

The idea of modernity, as fundamentally distinct from previous types of human society, can suggest convincing and beautiful representations of African history. Traditional African cultures, it narrates, could not produce an effective response to modern science and technology with its superior armory and production capacity. Nor could they compete with the efficiency of modern formal political, administrative and military structures, as well as universalist religious and ethical systems. Africa's modernization deficit, in this interpretation, explains its subjugation to the European power.

The same idea is expressed in a moving story told in Maryse Condé's novel *Segou*. When the shadow of the French power approaches the city of Segou and a sequence of disasters strike the Traoré family, then the insight, clairvoyance, and powers of Koumaré, the medicine man and advisor, reach their limits. Koumaré had always identified the deeper meaning of calamity, sometimes only after the greatest exertion in meditation and hallucination, in the wrongdoings of an individual, the family, the king, or the whole Bambara people. However, the events accompanying the approach of the French are beyond his grasp, they were of a different order, a total drama, so that a *Götterdämmerung* evolved.

In many ways, the confrontation between African societies and the overseas powers presents itself as a confrontation between two different orders. The vocabulary of tradition and modernity presents itself, therefore, as the natural analytical tool for understanding this confrontation. It is worthwhile, however, to attempt to resist its charms and analyze the analytical tool itself. This leads to the conclusion that even some of our most general assumptions, such as the idea of modernity, may have to be avoided in historiography.

There is, for instance, a methodological problem with the idea of modernity. It serves to explain the almost constant revolutionizing of the world ever since the time of the scientific revolution and the establishment of the global hegemony of Western societies. There is a circularity here: Western hegemony is explained by its modernity, but when we ask what this modernity is, an (albeit idealized) description of the West is given. Strictly speaking, we have not acquired new information in this circular movement from the West via modernity to the West. We have a description and not an explanation. If Africa did not correspond with the modernity syndrome and in actual fact could not compete, we have stated two distinct facts. Theoretically, the possibility is still open that European victory was accidental and that Africa could have gone a different path, distinct from Western modernity. In that case, it was not Africa's nonmodernity but its less competitive system, or insufficient development of this system that should account for its loss.[19]

A nonanachronistic historiography requires that we should avoid describing the world of the people we study using, in an unexamined way, categories and concepts that we use to understand our world.[20] We cannot simply assume that the people we study were proposing different answers to the same problems that we see; they probably proposed different (or the same) answers to different problems. If, therefore, we want to understand their ideas, we need a hermeneutic approach, a positive historiographic program that finds out from the historical actors themselves what are the relevant problems, agendas, and concepts to understand their work. A methodology is required that involves a more empirical attitude toward African political thought than is common.

THE HISTORICAL HERMENEUTICS OF QUENTIN SKINNER: "WORDS ARE DEEDS"

Much of twentieth-century development of the theory of historiography, like that of many other fields, can be understood as the discovery of always new and more radical implications of Wittgenstein's *Philosophical Investigations*. Quentin Skinner is a case in point. The basis of his approach to the historiography of political ideas is a Wittgensteinian understanding of the intertwined nature of language and action. In the well-known words of Wittgenstein, meaning is constituted in "language games" that are embedded in "life forms."

An important consequence that can be drawn from these basic considerations about language, meaning, and action is that a language game is a conventional whole supplying the context in which individual statements make sense. The meaning of linguistic expressions, their implicit connotations, procedures for determining their truth value, and so forth, depend on this larger linguistic context. Language games are holistic and cannot, in a simple way, be proved or disproved by experience because we have no access to some nonlinguistically represented reality to provide an independent anchoring point.[21]

Because of this holistic and "floating" nature of language games, change is normally change within such a whole. "Retailoring a body of conventions," as Quentin Skinner calls this, still means that most of the discursive texture remains intact. Using the metaphors of Neurath and Wittgenstein, it is like "rebuilding a ship out at sea" or like "a river which adjusts its bed in the process of streaming." If one speaker would revolutionize his or her language too much, he or she would no longer be understood by the community. Influential political thinkers manage to "retailor" the discursive texture in which they operate, while leaving enough common ground with their public to remain understood.

A second consequence of the relation between language, meaning, and action is that linguistic representation of reality is an act; representation of political reality in political thought is a political act. A language game "creates a world" (as the constructivist jargon has it); it depicts the political problem situation in a specific way, suggesting key issues, possible solutions, and lines of action. Political thought is therefore political intervention that changes or solidifies current representations of political reality.[22]

Both points can be formulated more strictly in the terms of Skinner:

1. A political text is always a restatement or adjustment of a body of conventions (which thereby remains for the most part intact). Therefore, a political text is "an ideological manoeuvre."[23]

2. A political text is, however, also a directly "political manoeuver." The practical political aspect of a text is what Skinner calls its *pointe* and expresses the intention of the author: "the political theorist is responding to the political problems of the age" and "theories are about contemporary legitimation crises caused by shifting political relations." Skinner uses Wittgenstein's phrase: "Words are Deeds."[24]

This double aspect in the constitution of meaning, in being located in a body of conventions and in a field of action, is inherent to the use of language in general. Skinner refers here to Austin's analysis of speech-acts as both conveying a locutionary meaning (semantic reference of words and sentences) and having an "illocutionary force" (you *do* something in saying what you say, for instance, warning, promising, drawing attention to something or away from something). Understanding a speaker involves grasping both the locutionary and the illocutionary aspects of a speech-act. Understanding a text thus involves not just understanding the language of the text, but also tracing what the author was in fact doing by writing the text (its *pointe*, in Skinner's words).

At this point we have established the claim that language and action, or political text and political practice, are intrinsically interconnected, but we do not yet know what consequences it has for historiography, especially for the interpretation of historical political texts.

Skinner forcefully argues that interpreting texts only from the texts themselves (by reading them "over and over again") can never reveal the *pointe* of the text, that is, the specific intervention that it intends. On the other hand, only a "*con*textual reading" of political texts does not suffice for a good interpretation either. To explain a text contextually does not mean to understand it. Understanding always involves an interpretation of intentions that, because these cannot be observed directly, will always involve interpretation at the textual level.[25] Skinner's contention is that we can only understand the meaning of a text by grasping both the textual (ideological) intervention and the practical (political) intervention that it entails. This means that the interpreter should trace the standard ways of representing political reality in that particular time and understand the exact adjustments or reconfirmations of the standard that the text effects. Understanding their *pointe*, again, requires an analysis of the practical political intention of the texts.[26] Textual and social analysis should thus be combined. The concept of "discourse" is particularly useful here because it already combines these two dimensions, it indicates the use of language in concrete political contexts of action.[27]

Another consequence of Skinner's approach is that the contingent and contextually determined nature of political thought is highlighted. It does not make much sense to speak of "great traditions" of political thought reproducing themselves through the ages because, in fact, political thought is reconstituted again and again in new political circumstances. Old concepts acquire a new meaning as a result of their specific use. The contextually created character of political thought implies that we should trace concrete historical discourses rather than influences or traditions of thought.[28]

When discussing African political thought, this stress on the contextually created character of discourses can have a salutary consequence. Too often interpreters have "understood" African thought by tracing its origins to some European or American influence. However, the study of African political thought should concern, in the first place, concrete African political discourses in their specific historical situation.

EXEMPLARS IN POLITICAL THOUGHT

I can now take another step forward and enlarge the set of methodological instruments which Skinner provides us with. This is done by using Thomas Kuhn's analysis of the role of exemplars in scientific thought. The methodological approach thus prepared can guide the analysis of historical political discourses in the rest of this study.

It can be observed that the notions of body of conventions and language game share a similar reference with Kuhn's paradigm.[29] Skinner's "conventions" refer to "shared vocabulary, principles, assumptions, criteria for testing knowledge claims, problems, conceptual distinctions and so on."[30] The elements that Kuhn mentions for a "disciplinary matrix" (the notion that replaced the less specific term "paradigm" in 1969) are: basic symbolic generalizations, ontological or heuristic models, values about what are good explanations, predictions, theories and "exemplars", that is, the paradigmatic examples of good scientific work such as Newton's *Optics*.[31]

In 1969, Kuhn proceeded to identify in the paradigmatic example, or exemplar, the "deeper" sense of paradigms. The exemplar contains in condensed form the whole disciplinary matrix: "the components of knowledge [are] tacitly embedded in shared examples."[32] Learning and thinking organize themselves around these powerful heuristic guides, which contain the shared tacit knowledge of the community of discourse. If, therefore, we want to trace the heuristics of a scientific approach or model of thought, the exemplar is the key: "knowledge is not, without essential change, subject to paraphrase in terms or rules and criteria."[33]

The application of this Kuhnian idea to the analysis of political ideas is provided by the Dutch philosopher Lolle Nauta. Nauta suggests, arguing from the same Wittgensteinian foundations as Skinner and Kuhn, that in order to understand political concepts, we have to identify the specific examples that authors (and readers) had in mind when using these concepts: "it is impossible to get hold of abstract concepts like liberty, independence, and autonomy if we are not provided with examples. They are our guide, enabling us to apply the concept, teaching us how to use it. Without a context the life of a concept is left without oxygen; we are unable to decipher its meaning."[34] Nauta's claim concerns both the facts, namely, that concepts are shaped by the examples that people have in mind when using them, and our study of the facts, namely, that we cannot hope to understand a (historical) political thinker without grasping the concrete exemplary situations that were referred to in his thought.

This approach connects the advantages of both Kuhn's focus on exemplars and Skinner's analysis of the interconnections of textual-ideological and political-action domains.[35] In Skinner's terms, Nauta's claim is that a "body of conventions" is practically available in, and knowable through, its relevant exemplars. These provide us with a key to the interface of text, community of discourse, and context of action. They represent at once central political issues as perceived by the community of discourse and indicate the heuristics of the discourse, both the social roots and intellectual structure of the philosophical conception.

This double role of exemplars can be understood as follows:

1. Important political texts manage to represent political reality in such a convincing way that others recognize the validity of the representation. They do this by designing their representation around social situations or historical experiences that express real-life key experiences of the community of discourse. Hobbes exposition of the state of nature, for instance, can be seen as modeled on the early capitalist market; Marx's theory of history rests on the relation between propertied master versus propertyless worker; and Blyden's theory of African redemption is based upon the New World slavery experience (see chapter 3 of this book).[36] In all these cases, the convincing force of the representations derives from their references to social relations or key historical events that themselves are perceived by the public as fundamental to the whole social fabric.

It should be noted that in this way the connection between intellectual and social phenomena is not made by simply ascribing certain ideas to certain individual or group interests. In such an exercise the interpreter pretends to have independent access to both the meaning of the ideas and to the interests of the historical actor. The radical consequence of the Wittgensteinian conception of language and meaning, however, is that such access is impossible. Knowing ideas involves understanding their use in a specific context of application, and knowing (perceived) interests involves grasping the actors' interpretation of their interests.

2. An exemplar, however, not only represents political reality in a certain way, it also provides an organizing principle for the discourse itself. It suggests the key issues, the key metaphors, and the heuristic model for the perception of a whole range of secondary issues, in short, "certain specific situations at the back of the mind of social philosophers determine their way of problem-solving."[37] These exemplary situations provide the heuristic compass of the discourse. The Chinese revolution, for example, has provided a very influential exemplar for leftist political analysis in developing countries. The basic story of that revolution runs as follows: the cities, as centers of power, exploited the countryside, the periphery composed of the poor majority. Under the Communist party the peasant masses became united and organized and started an effective guerrilla war. By encircling the cities and cutting the links of unequal exchange between countryside and cities, the power of the cities, which was itself based upon these exploitative links, was broken and liberation was achieved. This story provides a heuristic model for center-periphery theories, suggesting both an analysis of basic relations of power according to the geographical metaphor of center and periphery, and for a strategy of liberation—reestablishing autonomy by uniting the periphery and delinking from the center. The core of that theory is contained in condensed form in the story of the Chinese revolution.

The key importance of exemplars within a text or a body of thought does not mean that they are easily recovered. To come to what the analyst suggests as the constitutive exemplar requires a process of distillation or of explication, of recognition of hidden patterns from images and examples. One could call it a process of textual psychoanalysis. Identifying an exemplar entails an *Aha-erlebnis* similar to what Thomas Kuhn observed about the discovery of paradigms.

CONCLUSION

The opening chapter defined the hermeneutical, the analytical, and the critical tasks of the present book. The methodology outlined in this chapter satisfies the needs of hermeneutics, by facilitating a non-anachronistic representation of historical discourses. It also provides methodological tools for the analyst by suggesting a way of practicing an archaeological reconstruction of African political discourses through excavating the constitutive exemplars and thereby the heuristics, the way of problemsolving, of discourses. Whether this method of reconstruction works satisfactorily can only be judged by the results. The following chapters, which reconstruct historical discourses and their exemplars, can be read as an attempt to test this approach.

Even for the limited critical objectives of this study, the proposed method can be of use. Tracing the heuristics of a discourse also involves examining what remains outside their scope, such as the questions not asked, the blind spots, the issues not thematized. As Nauta observes: "An exemplary situation is a kind of model and a model opens certain ways of seeing, but forecloses others as well."[38] Thus, Marx's exemplar of the master-slave dialectic was predisposed to a highly idealized conception of the role of the proletariat and to a deficient analysis of the variety of preconditions for moving from a state of alienation to one of autonomy.[39] Similarly E. W. Blyden's exemplar of the color line, as will be shown in the next chapter, let him see through the paternalistic, half-colonial relations on the West African coast in the 1860s and 1870s but prevented him from making a penetrating political analysis of the fully fledged colonial situations that emerged in the 1890s. Grasping the heuristics of a discourse involves recognizing its strengths as well as its weaknesses. This study has equipped itself sufficiently now to take to the field.

NOTES

1. M. Foucault, "Nietzsche, Genealogy and History," reprinted in P. Rabinov, *The Foucault Reader* (New York: Pantheon Books, 1984), 80.

2. Q. Skinner, "Meaning and Understanding in the History of Ideas," *History and Theory* 8 (1969): 3–53. Quoted from reprint in J. Tully, ed., *Meaning & Context. Quentin Skinner and His Critics* (Cambridge: Polity Press, 1988), 37.

3. I. Geiss, *Panafrikanismus. Zur Geschichte der Dekolonisation* (Frankfurt am Mein: Europeische Verlagsanstalt, 1968), 85, 162, 242.

4. J. Vansina, "A Past for the Future?" *Dalhousie Review*, 13. J. Vansina, "History of Central African Civilization" and "Kings in Tropical Africa," in E. Beumers & H-J. Koloss, eds., *Kings of Africa* (Maastricht: Foundation Kings of Africa, 1992), 13–26, also presents Vansina's ideas on the Bantu traditions.

5. Quotations from Vansina, "A Past for the Future?" 10, 11.

6. Ibid., 16.

7. Ibid., 20.

8. Vansina formulates the idea of traditions very clearly, although he himself did not write much about political thought.

9. In the case of Geiss, his excellent and comprehensive account is harmed by the tendency to pinpoint what he considers useful or harmful.

10. Note that the notion "African identity" was coined only in 1893 by E. W. Blyden.

11. The notion of "modernity" became prominent in early twentieth-century social science.

12. Q. Skinner, "Some Problems in the Analysis of Political Thought and Action," *Political Theory* 23 (1974): 277–303. Quotes from J. Tully, ed., *Meaning & Context. Quentin Skinner and His Critics* (Cambridge: Polity Press, 1988), 33, 102.

13. T. S. Kuhn, *The Essential Tension—Selected Studies in Scientific Tradition and Change* (Chicago: University of Chicago Press, 1977), 10.

14. "This special authority of an agent over his intentions does not exclude, of course, the possibility that an observer might be in a position to give a fuller or more convincing account of the agents behaviour than he could give himself. . . . But it does exclude the possibility that an acceptable account of an agent's behaviour could ever

survive the demonstration that it was itself dependent on the use of criteria of description and classification not available to the agent himself." Skinner, "Meaning and Understanding," 48.

15. See E. U. Essien-Udom, *Black Nationalism: The Search for Identity* (Chicago: University of Chicago Press, 1962) and F. N. Ugonna, "Introduction to the Second Edition," in J. E. Casely Hayford, *Ethiopia Unbound. Studies in Race Emancipation* (1911; reprint, London: Frank Cass, 1969), xiii–xxvi.

16. E. W. Blyden, *A Vindication of the Negro Race: Being a Brief Examination of the Arguments in Favour of African Inferiority*, with introduction by A. Crummell (Monrovia: n.p., 1857).

17. In *Ethiopia Unbound*, the word "Africa" is used but only in the geographical sense. See also V. Y. Mudimbe, *The Invention of Africa* (Bloomington: Indiana University Press, 1988).

18. Racist discourses today often practice that mixing of biological and cultural issues.

19. Further problems with the idea of modernity may be pointed out. It is an unempirical stereotype: the diversity of successful countries in the present world can hardly be reduced to one model. Finally, it conceals the much wider scope of possible alternatives, of different strategies and maybe of different modernities

20. They "impose . . . a deeply anachronistic sense of how to divide up the world." Q. Skinner, "Reply to my Critics," in J. Tully, ed., *Meaning & Context. Quentin Skinner and his Critics* (Cambridge: Polity Press, 1988), 248.

21. This does not exclude all possibilities of assessment. There can be convincing reasons to prefer one language game to another.

22. To have impact, the retailoring must be perceived as useful by a relevant public, it must fit social action, or changed social or political environments. See Tully, *Meaning & Context*, 23.

23. Tully, *Meaning & Context*, 10.

24. Quotes on Tully, *Meaning & Context*, 10, 13. Skinner discusses this issue in several articles, see e.g., Tully, *Meaning & Context*, 61, 83, 84.

25. Skinner, "Meaning and Understanding", 59–61.

26. Skinner's interpreter James Tully identifies five steps in the interpretative procedure of Skinner (Tully, *Meaning & Context*, 8–16).

27. For a clear comparison of the notions of ideology, paradigm and discourse, see P. N. Edwards, *The Closed World: Computers and the Politics of Discourse in Corld War America* (Cambridge: MIT Press, 1996), 30–41. Edwards describes discourse as follows: "discourse goes beyond speech acts to refer to the entire field of *signifying* or *meaningful practices*: those social interactions—material, institutional, and linguistic—through which reality is interpreted and constructed for us and with which human knowledge is produced and reproduced" (p. 34).

28. For interpreting a particular discourse, the inherited body of conventions is relevant, of course: after all some existing discursive texture is "retailored." However, the local circumstances will finally determine if conventions are maintained or not.

29. In his classical text "Meaning and Understanding," Skinner compares his work with Thomas Kuhn (on science) and Gombrich (on art) and uses the concept of *paradigm*. See Skinner, "Meaning and Understanding," 31–32.

30. Tully, *Meaning & Context*, 9.

31. T. S. Kuhn, *The Structure of Scientific Revolutions (2nd ed.)* (Chicago: University of Chicago Press, 1969), 182–187.

32. Ibid., 175.

33. Ibid., 175 for both quotes.

34. L. W. Nauta, "Historical Roots of the Concept of Autonomy in Western Philosophy," *Praxis International* 4, no. 4 (1985), 364.

35. There is a qualitative difference between Skinner's basic metaphor of change of discourse as "tailoring and retailoring textures," with Kuhn's metaphor of "Gestalt-switch" or "revolution." The first stresses gradual change in a network of meaning, while the latter stresses a break in traditions. There have been many discussions about Kuhn's idea of revolution, suggesting that, if studied in detail, every revolution involves a chain of smaller changes. See, G. Gutting, ed., *Paradigms and Revolutions* (Notre Dame: University of Notre Dame Press, 1980); I. Hacking, ed., *Scientific Revolutions* (London: Oxford University Press, 1981).

36. See Nauta, "Historical Roots of the Concept of Autonomy" for MacPherson's interpretation of Hobbes and his own analysis of Marx.

37. Nauta, "Historical Roots of the Concept of Autonomy, 365.

38. Ibid., 366.

39. Ibid., 370–373.

3

Confronting the European Challenge: Discourses in Nineteenth-Century African Political Thought

> And why should not the same race who governed Egypt, attacked the most famous and flourishing city—Rome, who had her churches, her universities, and her repositories of learning and science, once more stand on their legs and endeavour to raise their characters in the scale of the civilized world?[1]

The author who poses this rhetorical question is discussing the "progressive advancement of the Negro race under civilizing influence." In the preceding sections of the book he severely criticized the racist anthropological theories of his time and introduced the reader to his conception of Africa's future. In the following sections, he makes detailed suggestions about the political institutions that could create a series of independent states in West Africa. The book was published in the year 1868, and its author was James Africanus Beale Horton.

There is some irony in launching a study of African political thought with a quote from the African intellectual probably most criticized for being "un-African," "hypnotized," "irretrievably enchanted by Western culture," an "unrepentant Anglophile," "hybridized," and "transmogrified."[2] In view of the historical facts, there can be little doubt that Horton was in fact rather unrepresentative of African political thought of his age, namely the nineteenth century. His discourse, focusing on Africa's answer to the European challenge, can be considered representative of only a small circle of intellectuals in a few coastal enclaves on the West African coast in one particular decade.

But times were rapidly changing. A few decades after the 1860s, European domination expanded from the enclaves to engulf almost the entire African continent (see figures 3.1, 3.2, 3.3). What I termed earlier "the great confrontation" between Africa and the powerful West became the dominant political experience, and Horton's endeavor—to find an answer to the confrontation—became the principal problem for African political thought. Political thought in the enclaves constitutes, with hindsight, early examples of a discussion centered on a new theme. In fact, the various strategies for an African response to the European challenge that were proposed during these discussions reappeared in several forms throughout the more than hundred years that followed.

At first sight, the opening quote from Horton seems to betray a "modernist" bias of the present study. In fact, however, the quote indicates the study's specific historical focus on African political thought in the age of confrontation between Africa and the West. This chapter reconstructs the first generation of discourses, covering generally the period until colonial rule became fully established around 1900. For this purpose, the chapter sketches the particular historical context of the West African enclaves before providing a detailed reconstruction of the major variants of discourse.

Figure 3.1
The Pattern of Alien Rule in Africa, 1880

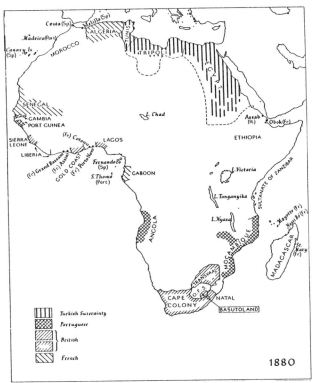

Source: J. D. Fage & M. Verity, *An Atlas of African History* (Second edition). London: Edward Arnold Publishers, 1978.

Figure 3.2
The Pattern of Alien Rule in Africa, 1891

Figure 3.3
The Pattern of Alien Rule in Africa, 1914

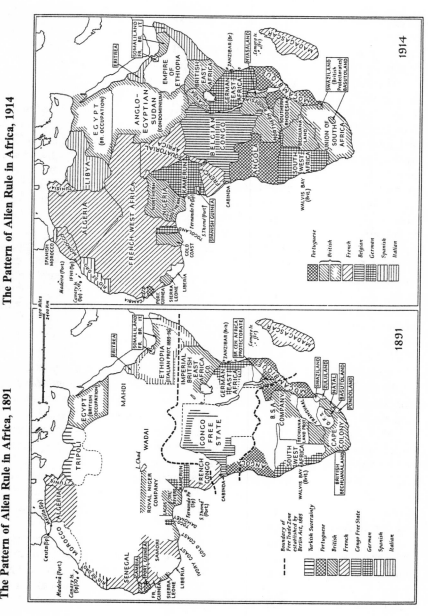

Source: J. D. Fage & M. Verity, *An Atlas of African History* (Second edition). London: Edward Arnold Publishers, 1978.

THE HISTORICAL CONTEXT OF THE WEST AFRICAN ENCLAVES

The nineteenth century was an exceptionally turbulent age in African history. The established political and economic structures were overturned, Islam and Christianity gained influence, and Western powers and ideas, which had remained in the margin of the physical and intellectual landscape at the beginning of the nineteenth century, occupied the center at its close.

The nineteenth century witnessed the clustering of a wide variety of smaller political units, such as kingdoms, into a limited number of states.[3] These included the Fulani empire of Sokoto and the Tokolor, Mandinka, and Asante empires in West Africa, as well as a number of large kingdoms in East and Central Africa. Such states, mainly deriving their power from control over trade routes and from the possibility of obtaining modern armaments, would be powerful trade partners that could not be challenged easily by European powers. Their intrinsic weakness, however, was the limited degree to which the tributary peripheral units identified with the power center.[4] This made it possible for a relatively small European military force to break them up and then confront and subjugate them.[5]

Western powers had occupied trading posts along the African coast, such as Saint Louis, Christiansborg, Elmina, and Goree, from the fifteenth century onward. Allied with the slave trade, with its height in the eighteenth and nineteenth centuries, these trading posts acquired great importance. The forts constituted the terminal stations of a trade line, involving strong inland African political units that had gained control over the hunting and trading of slaves. The areas where the slaves were finally taken from, however, suffered large-scale devastation.

From a global perspective, the slave trade was part of the South Atlantic System, which was a triangular trade carrying slaves to the plantations in the Americas, plantation products, especially sugar, to European markets, and arms and other products back to Africa again. This highly profitable trade, described by Marx as one of the main sources of Western European "original accumulation," was affected by the American War of Independence. The British lost their plantations and voices were raised to initiate a plantation economy on African soil, while simultaneously frustrating the slave trade in order to interrupt the supply of labor to the Americans, who were now competitors. Consequently, the disruption of the triangular trade inspired a new imperial interest in Africa, an interest in "legitimate trade" (nonslave trade).

Within the movement for the abolition of the slave trade, these imperial interests were combined with the humanitarian inspiration derived from the French revolution and from the evangelical revolution in the Church of England. Abolitionists thus became a strong and successful pressure group against slavery. Prominent public figures in Britain, such as Granville Sharp and William Wilberforce, were involved. The abolitionists were successful in Britain in 1807, in France in 1848, and in the United States in 1808 and 1865.

In 1833 abolition was extended to all British territories.[6] Several additional measures were taken as well, such as the stationing of a naval squadron to intercept slave ships and diplomatic action pushing countries to follow the British example in suppressing the slave trade.

Especially in the first half of the nineteenth century, this abolitionist or humanitarian movement was a major influence on British colonial politics and shaped the intellectual and political background of most Anglophone African theorists. The most tangible result, however, was the founding of the influential Sierra Leone colony, meant for the repatriation of destitute former black slaves from England. Despite the fact that almost none of the first group of black "resettlers" on the coast of Sierra Leone in 1787 survived, more arrived in the following years. Most notable were the "Nova Scotians," ex-slaves who had supported the British during the American War of Independence and had been moved first to Nova Scotia in America before being shipped to Sierra Leone. This large community, looking for liberty and constitutional government, represented the early beginnings of Western-type political activity in Sierra Leone.[7]

British policy towards West Africa remained indecisive for most of the century. The humanitarian lobby pushed for imperial penetration inland, but actual schemes were rarely successful, partly owing to the enormous loss of life due to tropical illnesses. West Africa gained the reputation of being the "white man's grave." Only in the third quarter of the century, after the use of quinine became common, and after the second Ashanti war (1874), did colonial expansion accelerate in this part of the globe. The increased competition between European powers due to their industrial expansion, which created the need for control over raw materials and markets, was the key background feature at this point. The Scramble for Africa and the Berlin Conference in 1884–85 left Africa almost completely under colonial domination by the turn of the century.

In the United States, the repatriation of free slaves was already being promoted by 1791. The first African American settlers arrived in West Africa in 1815.[8] Their settlement, called Liberia, adjacent to Sierra Leone, actually became independent in 1847. It adopted American political ideals and institutions. From the outset, marked differences arose within Liberia between the "tribal" Africans who originated in these areas and the immigrant ex-slaves. There were disputes over land, as well as cultural conflicts, partly resulting from the fact that the Christian, and often "whiter," immigrants felt far superior to the indigenous population.

During the nineteenth century, American-African relations remained limited to Liberia. The question of remigration to Africa was a subject of constant debate in African American organizations, especially because the American Colonization Society included white racialists who were interested in what they called "solving the Negro problem." The main inspiration of the various back-to-Africa movements, however, was the Pan-Negroist ideal, brought to Africa by such prominent African American immigrants as Alexander Crummell, Edward Wilmot Blyden, and Orishatuké Faduma (W. J. Davies). The actual number of black returnees to Liberia was limited and corresponded quite clearly with periods of intensified hardship for African Americans under American racism.[9]

The Recaptives

In Sierra Leone specific circumstances occurred. The British employed war vessels to intercept slave ships. When caught, such ships were taken to Freetown in Sierra Leone and the slaves, the "recaptives" as they were called, were set free to be received by the Church Missionary Society. In this way, after 1800, the black settlers from Britain and America were quickly outnumbered by Africans without the New World experience of slavery and racism, but with the traumatic experience of being caught (mostly by Africans) and liberated (by the British). The hard acculturation process under the Church Missionary Society invested the recaptives with a Western cultural background and its related personal and political ideals. In this way, Sierra Leone became a breeding place for a black, English-speaking, "Creole" intelligentsia, who, as skilled personnel in the colonial and missionary administrations, spread along the coast of West and Middle Africa for a large part of the nineteenth century. Sierra Leone, it was sometimes said, was "the leaven of the West African dough."[10]

The quick adaptation of the Creole community to "modern" culture and society, turning them into "black Europeans," moved them toward self-government, similar to that of Canada or Australia, a natural expectation. During the 1860s, the call for self-determination within the Creole community became louder. An interesting example involved the controversy about the handing over of church work to Africans.[11] Since the establishment of Sierra Leone, the British Church Missionary Society (CMS) controlled the center in public affairs. Under its honorary secretary, Henry Venn, however, there was a strong voice in the CMS for working toward an independent African church: a church for Africa, run by Africans. The Native Church Pastorate began operations in 1861, which meant that parishes were managed by Africans, under European church authorities. The Africans, especially those in the *Sierra Leone Native Association*, began demanding more African representation in the church in order to indigenize Christianity and change the church from within into an African church.[12]

The movement toward greater African control in Sierra Leonean affairs also resulted in a lively interest in African cultures and languages. The Creoles (or Krio), as English speakers, disclosed the sophistication of African languages and cultures and boosted the idea of Africa's own history and high culture. The issue of self-government arose in regard to a number of directly political issues as well, such as the case of the Fanti Federation.

A reverse development was taking place on the European side. In the second half of the nineteenth century, Africans were depicted as being essentially incapable of managing their own affairs, African cultures were presented as "primitive" and "savage," and a racial paradigm for the human sciences became established.[13] The Krio community in Sierra Leone was attacked for being an example not of the African capacity to become modern man, but rather one of "savages posturing as Europeans." The racist movement, in combination with the more aggressive stage of colonialism in the last quarter of the nineteenth century, put the Africanist movement on the defensive.[14] Educated Africans were pushed out of all influential positions in colonial and missionary administrations, bringing the period of mid-Victorian optimism to an end.

Not surprisingly, the first intellectuals to discuss the issue of confrontation with the West lived in the coastal settlements where the powerful European presence first became established. The settlements constituted a lively setting. Although European imperial rule was fully accepted, Africans challenged colonial and church paternalism, expressing great hopes of "Africa soon stretching her hands out to God" and aspiring for a greater degree of self-government. Interestingly, these hopes were combined with the anguish of seriously doubting their own newly shaped identities, aggravated by the premature deaths of eminent persons in their community.[15]

A number of the greatest African intellectuals of the nineteenth century, such as Africanus Horton, Edward Wilmot Blyden, and James Johnson, operated in this world. They were certainly not the only intellectuals on the vast African continent. With hindsight, however, they were the direct ancestors of the African political discourses in the century that followed.

My search for the dilemmas, proposed solutions, and models of political thought in the era of confrontation, does not start, therefore, in the great royal courts of African empires, nor "under the tree" where the council of elders met, but in the curious coastal spots of what could be called "proto-globalization." My source materials should not be the great repositories of indigenous knowledge, such as Ifa, but the profane political deliberations of individual Africans, expressed, for instance, in the speeches at Liberia's independence celebration, in the church politics of Sierra Leone, in public letters of prominent Africans to the British government, and in the program of modernization and self-government contained in the Mankessim declaration of the Fanti Federation. Political thought on Africa's future developed at the locations where confrontation was actually experienced.

THE DISCOURSE OF MID-VICTORIAN OPTIMISM:
AFRICANUS HORTON

In retrospect, at least three key events in the 1860s and 1870s stand out in West African history, namely, the proposals for African self-government in the 1865 report of a Select Committee of the British House of Commons, the so-called Fanti Federation of 1870, and the second Ashanti war in 1873–74, nearly won by the Ashanti but instead marking the beginning of massive colonial expansion into Africa. Africanus Horton involved himself with each of these events. One of the most prominent West Africans, son of a recaptive in Sierra Leone, and holding a doctorate in medicine from Edinburgh, he reacted to the Select Committee in his book *West African Countries and Peoples* (1868) and he defended the Fanti Federation in his *Letters on the Political Condition of the Gold Coast* (1870). An analysis of Horton's interventions can be a guide to understanding the discourse of mid-Victorian Krio optimism.

After the first Ashanti war of 1863, in which the British and Fanti armies were defeated by the Ashanti, the British contemplated a complete retreat from West Africa. In 1865, a Select Committee of the British House of Commons drew up a report on the future of the West Africa settlements, which was accepted by the House. This report proposed the gradual retirement of the British from West Africa. The policy "should be to encourage in the native the exercise of those qualities which may render it possible for us more and more to transfer to the natives the administrations of all the Governments, with a view to our ultimate withdrawal from all, except probably Sierra Leone." The expensive responsibilities in a part of the world so often described as the "white man's grave" would have to terminate.[16]

In Africa, of course, the perception of the Select Committee report was quite different from that in Britain. Horton was greatly inspired by the perspective, and heralded the adoption by the British of "that great principle of establishing independent African nationalities as independent as the present Liberian Government."[17] Horton wrote *West African Countries and Peoples* (1868), outlining possible political arrangements for new states in West Africa as a blueprint for actual implementation of the report's proposals.

The major political event in the aftermath of the Select Committee report was the establishment of the Fanti Federation in 1870, a political federation uniting the many units within the coastal region of what is now Ghana. Political turmoil around the exchange of trading forts between the British and the Dutch and the peril of the powerful Ashanti in the north triggered this political unity. The local British administration, however, saw the federation as an illegal threat to its authority and frustrated it whenever it could, even arresting and humiliating its leaders.

Horton intervened again, this time by publishing his correspondence with the Colonial Office in which he demanded recognition of the Fanti Federation (in his book, *Letters on the Political Condition of the Gold Coast*, of 1870).

Horton's immediate superiors in West Africa were furious and wanted him to be transferred, but he was protected by the London Colonial Office. However, Horton's (and others') pleas for recognition of the federation were not successful. The constant insults against mulattoes and educated natives, part of the racist propaganda of those decades, supplied easy justifications for distrusting the federation. Lord Kimberley, British secretary of state, suggested privileging the "hereditary chiefs only and endeavor[ing] as far as possible to govern through them."[18] Such a policy meant pushing out the mulattoes, West Indians, and educated Africans who were often prominently present in the administration. It also helped to create what later became a classical division in West African politics between educated elites and traditional rulers.[19]

The British presence in the Gold Coast could still have come to an end in the 1873–74 second Ashanti war. The Ashanti initially swept away the British loyal forces almost completely but failed to capture their main target, the Elmina Fort on the coast. The British could take revenge. They sent a purely white army force under General Worseley, which in record time penetrated north, destroyed the Ashanti capital Kumasi, and returned to the coast without even being attacked by the Ashanti army. This military operation was directly reported by the British and American media and boosted racist superiority sentiments. Any hopes for experiments such as the Fanti Federation had to be buried.

Horton participated in the Ashanti wars as an army doctor. In both cases, he was left with the black, partly West Indian soldiers at the Ashanti border during the rainy season. Neglected by the army command, he witnessed a record number of his soldiers die under these extremely unhealthy conditions before they were finally called back to the coast. While many of Horton's white military colleagues were specially decorated, his work was never rewarded.[20]

Africanus Horton's Life

The historical events recorded here provide a key to understanding the discourse of mid-Victorian optimism. Before turning to the discourse itself, let me consider one other aspect, namely the biographical one. The West African settlements created conditions for a number of Africans to advance rapidly. The rocketing careers of individual Krios, such as Samuel Lewis, Bishop Ajayi Crowther, Bishop James Johnson, William "Independent" Grant, G.G.M. Nicol, and Africanus Horton, shaped their views on the possibilities of African progress. The career of J.A.B. Horton showcases one of the most outspoken Krio biographies.[21]

James Beale Horton was born in 1835 from recaptive parents in the village of Gloucester in Sierra Leone. His father and mother had been set free from a slave ship. The recaptives were, as Horton perceived it, "on their arrival in

Sierra Leone, landed naked and in a state of abject rudeness and poverty, without the least knowledge of civilization."[22] Energetic missionary effort had Christianized and educated them. They had become part of "a nation of free black Christians" and a very successful nation at that.[23] In his sketch of the small settler village of Gloucester, the Nigerian historian Ayandele mentioned that by 1821 missionary efforts had been so effective that "500 out of a total population of 720 were able to read their Testaments," a literacy rate not easily matched by any other place in the world in the 1820s.[24]

In Horton's youth, African religious and social life forms became dominant again in Gloucester. The minority Christians called themselves the "righteous" and avoided all intercourse, even greetings, with the "nonrighteous." Horton's outlook was shaped by strict Puritanism. He was active in social affairs all his life, praised for his "urbane and suave disposition," but also practiced total abstinence from alcohol.[25]

After attending Fourah Bay College in Freetown, Sierra Leone, he was offered the exceptional chance of studying medicine in London in order to prepare for service in the British West African forces. When moving from King's College in London to the University of Edinburgh to take a medical doctorate, he added "Africanus" to his name. He was admitted into the British army as staff surgeon in West Africa, making him the highest-ranking African in British army service. Horton served at many places along the West African coast, acquiring extensive knowledge of the geological, economic, social, and political conditions in the coastal zone, and participating, as his position allowed, in political matters. After retirement, he resettled in Freetown, becoming active in the economic field by starting several companies and establishing the first West African bank, called the Commercial Bank of West Africa. Horton died suddenly in 1883.

A Philosophy of Universal Modernity

The details of Horton's biography and those of other prominent Krios and educated elites in his time are fascinating. At this point, however, I want to draw attention to only one distinguishing aspect of their lives, namely, that they represent rocketing careers. From humble backgrounds, with missionary help, and through educational advancement, they reached the top level of contemporary social and academic standing. Their careers refuted in the most concrete form contemporary racial prejudice and they were exemplary for what Africans and Africa could achieve within one generation.

Africanus Horton's body of thought should be analyzed against this background of hope for advancement, prosperity, and independence. It exemplifies in all its aspects the fiery and self-conscious discourse of a people who perceive themselves at the threshold of a new and better world.

Horton strongly believed in a universal conception of civilization and historical advancement, "that mankind, by the knowledge of metallurgy and other useful arts emerge from a primitive state of barbarism, and have gradually brought to themselves the benefits of a civilized life."[26] The torch of world-historical civilizational progress, however, is not always in the same hands. "Nations rise and fall; the once flourishing and civilized degenerates into a semi-barbarious state; and those who have lived in utter barbarism, after a lapse of time become the standing nation."[27]

The key example for Horton was Britain: at the time of the Romans Britain had existed in a state of hopeless barbarism, yet now it was the cream of civilization. Horton quoted Cicero, noting "that the ancient Britons went about scantly clothed; they painted their bodies in fantastic fashions, 'offered up human victims to uncouth idols, and lived in hollow trees and rude habitations.'"[28] Atticus advised a friend "not to buy slaves from Britain on account of their stupidity and their inaptitude to learn music and other accomplishments."[29] Relating this information to Africa, Horton immediately turned these quotations around to advance an argument against British racists: "And, in fact, if the comparison be made between the degree of improvement exhibited by the two countries, history informs us that the present degree of improvement exhibited by the liberated Africans under missionary influence far exceeds that of Britain under Roman influence during a similar period of time."[30]

Horton's universalist view of cultural development was based upon a practical concept of civilization. To be civilized simply means to be economically advanced, politically and militarily strong, and culturally sophisticated. He could, therefore, speak in one sentence of "the Christian and industrial regeneration of Africa."[31] Armed with such a concept of civilization, the task for Africa could be formulated in an equally straightforward manner:

to raise the nations of Africa from the debased and degraded state to which they have fallen, both morally and physically, to free them from the bloody and demoralizing influence of beastly superstition; from polygamy; from domestic slavery; from the paralysing effects, as regards productive industry, of customs and institutions which . . . prevent the creation of that capital by which alone the works necessarily attendant on civilization can be executed.[32]

Horton assumed that this task could never be accomplished without outside interference and help. To "make an onward step in the career of civilization" requires contact with already civilized nations.[33] Therefore, he could state, "I, amongst a great many others, appreciate any European element that enters Western Africa, whether in the capacity of merchants or pioneers of civilization, or in that of missionaries." As if to prove immediately that this was not a statement of servility, he added, "I will never permit any unjust abuse, any unfounded diatribe against the African race, to be ruthlessly lavished on them without repelling or exposing calumny."[34]

Horton's universalist conception of civilization made him the complete antidote to the racial theorizing of his time, which characteristically linked civilization with race. From what was considered a lack of civilization in Africa, the racists inferred the incapacity of the African race to civilize. Horton, on the contrary, pointed to environmental causes. He accepted, like the mainstream abolitionist thought of his time, the opinion that Africa was in a state of barbarism, far behind Europe. But he forcefully argued that "it is an incontrovertible logical inference that the difference arises entirely from the influences of external circumstances, **Truly**—*Natura una et communis omnium est*."[35] Such circumstances were, for instance, black Africa's isolation because of the Sahara from the mainstream of world cultural development, which was supposed to have moved from Persia, to Mesopotamia, Egypt, Greece, Rome, and finally the Western world.[36]

Blacks are, biologically and otherwise, as capable of civilization as whites. In view of the hardships they have survived, one could even say that they are physically fitter.[37] This unswerving attack on the biological assumptions of racist theory made Horton's an unusual antiracist argument for his time. Most contemporary defenses of the black man were religiously based arguments.[38] Horton, however, made full use of his biological knowledge and medical experience. His "The Negro's Place in Nature" (subtitle of part 1 of his *West African Countries and Peoples*) contains forceful and well-informed arguments in sections such as "Exposition of Erroneous Views Respecting the African," "False Theories of Modern Anthropologists," and "Some Anatomical Accounts of Negro Physique."[39]

Horton saw no obstacles to African advancement at the individual or psychological level. Many authors after him claimed to locate peculiar characteristics of the "African personality," which would be unsuited for capitalism, exact science, and individual ambition. Horton, however, quoted with approval:

If Adam Smith's theory is pronounced orthodox, that it is to the principle of parsimony we owe our capital, and again to capital we owe our comforts and enjoyment, we certainly have this desideratum in the African, who is for the most part a parsimonious citizen, ambitious to rise in the world, and consequently to save and amass.

And again:

They calculate figures in their memory to an extent which would surprise the most practised mathematician. . . . Some keep for years the debit and credit side of their account in their memory with great accuracy.[40]

According to Horton's analysis, neither the capitalist spirit nor the scientific spirit was absent from the African.

As Africans were perfectly fit for modernization, the issue for Africa was a practical one, namely, how to organize and stimulate the modernization process. With his practical turn of mind, Horton suggested a host of initiatives in the educational, economic, and political fields. He was well ahead of his time and was constantly stressing the need for a very active government policy in education, propagating compulsory education and the elevation of Fourah Bay College in Sierra Leone to a West African university. He greatly valued African entrepreneurship and started several companies himself, such as the Wassaw Light Railway Company Ltd. and the Commercial Bank of West Africa, which he managed himself during the last months of his life.

In politics, according to Horton, development depended on infusing "the true principles of civilized Government," including the election of rulers.[41] Without enlightened and modern government none of the modernizing policies that he considered essential would be possible. The "feudal lords" of the interior tribes did not promote development, neither did a hesitant and inconsistent British colonial policy. The core of Horton's vision was, therefore, the development of modern states in Africa, which he called "that great principle of self-government."[42]

His major work, *West African Countries and Peoples*, provides extensive descriptions of societies in various parts of British West Africa, combined with detailed suggestions for the institutional setup appropriate to each of the future states. He offered a complete plan, which the British would permit, supervise, and protect. It would create a number of dominions within the British Commonwealth in West Africa, each entitled to the same equal position as the white dominions, such as Canada and Australia enjoyed. Typically, Horton suggested the creation of Western-type political institutions. For Sierra Leone, for instance, he envisioned a

constitutional form of government [that] must form the basis of his administration, consisting of a House of Assembly which should be composed of men elected by the people, as it will be difficult for his Government to stand without popular confidence, and the only means by which that can be secured is by giving the people the power to elect one branch of the Legislature. . . . Each member should have landed property, be over the age of twenty-two, and be properly educated.[43]

He also outlined the need for a senate. In other countries Horton recommended a house of chiefs. The head of state, whether a monarch or a president, would always be elected by general suffrage.[44]

The ground plan for modern African government in the form of independent African states had to be implemented by active and benevolent British intervention. Horton, therefore, joined forces with the British humanitarians and philanthropists on the issue of the need for a consistent and active British policy for West Africa. He frequently published in the *African Times*, the monthly publication of the African Aid Society, which was the main defendant in the 1860s and 1870s of the humanitarian case in Britain.[45]

Two Interpretations of Horton

The various elements of Horton's thought constitute a comprehensive and remarkably consistent philosophical conception about Africa's condition and future. However strongly one may disagree with his views, it is fair to accept that Horton was much more than the alienated "Black Englishman" or elite ideologist whom some commentators present.[46] In fact, I would argue that these charges result from a faulty historiographic methodology, and, in some cases, themselves betray a Eurocentric bias.

Let me first look at Horton as a so-called "Black Englishman." Ayandele states that he was one of

a new species of African—hybridized, transmogrified, and passionate borrowers of Western values, ideas, norms, mores, thought-patterns, religion, and cosmology; deserters of their fatherland's cultural heritage; revellers in the white man's mental world; worshippers of the white man's education; apostles of political, social, and cultural aspirations completely at variance with the aspirations of the rest of the continent.[47]

Is it correct to state that Horton represented an alien European discourse? Horton was an Anglophile; he identified with the abolitionist position and admired its British protagonists, particularly his mentor, the secretary of the Church Missionary Society, Henry Venn. Horton was also immersed in the *African Times* and other British magazines. For Horton, however, these commitments did not exclude being fully involved in a West African rather than a European project.[48] The perception that Horton was alienated from Africa can appear only to the observer who thinks in terms of fundamental differences between the African and the non-African. According to Horton's universalist view on civilization, however, no such fundamental differences exist. Propagating Christianity, science, and middle-class values is not "deserting the fatherland" but working for its modernization.

When it came to concrete choices, it is clear that Horton was not an apostle of foreign political schemes. The discrepancy emerged, for instance, on the issue of the exchange of forts between the British and the Dutch on the Gold Coast, which was much resented in Africa. The *African Times* welcomed this move because it could facilitate a more coherent trade policy. Horton, however, fulminated against the exchange, as it was arranged without the involvement of the Africans concerned and was considered harmful to their interests.[49]

Rather than imitating a European discourse, Horton embodied a quite consistently developed and actively militated discourse on Africa from a particular West African point of view. The discourse only concerned the political struggles of a few small groups situated in a handful of peculiar spots on the coast, but it discussed issues that became a concern for the whole of

Africa.[50] To overlook the specifically African roots of Horton's discourse results from a preoccupation with European intellectual history rather than with the particular West African condition in Horton's time. Non-Europeans are assumed to imitate European standards if they sometimes hold the same views as Europeans.

The interpretation of Horton's ideas as voicing elite interests encounters similar problems. Let me first examine the elite. The educated elite were a rapidly rising class consisting of businessmen, church pastors, and local government employees, and later including lawyers and journalists. Education was the main avenue of progress for this elite, and mission schools (Fourah Bay College in Freetown and the Wesleyan Boys School in Cape Coast) were breeding places for the rising intelligentsia. In the coastal cities there was an animated social life following British examples; for instance, there were debating clubs. From a sociological point of view, the educated elite were intermediaries between the Western powers and the indigenous leaders and peoples. They were ambassadors of Christianity and modernization, as well as protagonists of African interests.[51] The position of the elite became endangered toward the end of the century, when whites could survive better in Africa due to improved medical knowledge, thus reducing the need for African brokers. The growing influence of the racist ideology even cultivated an outright disdain among the British colonialists, introducing such malign expressions as "hybrids," "trousered niggers," and so forth.

Horton's ideas exactly reflected the period in which the educated elite had its highest hopes, namely, the time following the 1865 Select Committee report when there seemed to be an option of actually gaining the leadership of independent African nations. Horton expressed educated elite interests, but more than that, he formulated a political alternative in that particular historical situation.

Both interpretations of Horton, as being alienated from African realities, a "Black Englishman," and as ideologist of the educated elite, share the serious flaw that they do not derive their interpretation from the texts and the specific historical circumstances. Rather they develop conjectures about lines of historical influencing, or advance interest theories, and then ascribe ideas to "sources" or to "interests." However sophisticated the historians' ideas and theories may be (which they are often not), the objects that they have to explain, that is, the texts themselves, have to be grasped first. Texts are only comprehended when we understand the meaning of the words, ideas, and acts involved. Hermeneutics precedes explanation.[52] At this point, I will provide a basic, hermeneutical understanding of the optimistic Krio discourse.

The Recaptive as Exemplar for African Development

The drive and message of Horton's ideas is brought to life when his texts are read as part of the collective experiences, the hopes and fears, images and ambitions shared by the Krios in the West African coastal enclaves during the 1860s and 1870s.[53] The key collective experience of the Krio community was that of the success of the recaptives. Horton epitomized this experience in the following words:

Fancy a lot of slaves—unlettered, rude, naked, possessing no knowledge of the useful arts—thrown into a wild country, to cut down the woods and build towns; fancy these ragged, wild natives under British, and consequently, civilized influences, after a lapse of a few years, becoming large landowners, possessing large mercantile establishments and money, claiming a voice in the legislative government, and giving their offspring proper English and foreign education; and dare you tell me that the African is not susceptible of improvement of the highest order, that he does not possess in himself a principle of progression and a desire of perfection far surpassing many existing nations—since it can not be shown in the world's history that any people with so limited advantages has shown such results within fifty years.[54]

The recaptive story embodies in a nutshell Horton's whole conception of African advancement from a "barbarous" starting position, under civilizing influence, to civilized, rich, politically articulate nations. The individual rocketing careers exemplify what the continent as a whole can achieve. The vision of a "modern" African future was not an abstractly constructed possibility nor a cheap import from Britain. It had a concrete meaning for those whose collective political memory was marked by this recaptive experience.

Here, we have an exemplar as discussed in chapter 2. Core political concepts are coined by the way they are used in the exemplary story (in the case of Horton, the Krio success story). This exemplar is not an abstract idea, since the story refers to a key real-life situation or collective experience. This social reference provides the exemplar and its concepts with political and emotional fuel. The exemplar plays a constitutive role in the discourse by representing, verbalizing one could say, key collective experiences. The recaptive success story is precisely such a discourse-animating exemplar.[55]

The first methodological gain of this analysis is that the discourse is not simply ascribed to (assumed) interests. The keys to understanding a discourse are literally read from the text. My reading can, therefore, also be criticized by drawing from textual analysis. Horton recounts the story of the recaptives of Sierra Leone at several points in the text as proof of the possibility of rapid African advancement.[56] "Within a short period of time, they [the missionaries] have brought up a race of men for whom destiny has mapped out an important mission in Africa." Later in the book he again recounts the recaptive story at length.[57] Here the recaptives are

landed naked and in a state of abject rudeness and poverty, without the least knowledge of civilization . . . they begin slowly to throw off their air of serfdom. . . . [Their children] seek after and obtain justice; preach loudly the Christian ethics . . . buy up the former abodes of their European masters; carry on extensive mercantile speculations . . . look out for a better form of government administration.[58]

A second revenue of my reading of Horton through the recaptive exemplar is that a number of curious details of his views begin to make sense. Horton's quite positive image of Britain, even in the face of contrary evidence is often explained by invoking the allegation that Horton was an unrepentant anglophile. The recaptive exemplar, however, shows that the idea of "Britain the civilizer" is constitutive for the discourse. The recaptive success story already includes the benevolent outside civilizer (Britain). The impending advancement of Africa as a whole requires such a civilizing agent. The model of Horton's whole conception resembles that of a chemical reaction where "barbarous" Africa is transformed into "modern" Africa. This reaction only works under the influence of certain catalysts, such as Christianity, Western education, a modern developmentalist state, trade, communication, and industry. All these elements were embodied in Horton's Britain.

The place of Britain in the optimistic Krio discourse, as the world-historically appointed catalyst of African progress, explains why Horton maintained his "platonic conception of British presence in West Africa," as Ayandele complains, rather than making a realistic assessment of the British role.[59] Horton's Britain was essentially what it had to be in his conception of African development. When the British behaved differently from what Horton's theory required, this could not simply be accepted as a fact by Horton so it was turned into a moral issue, namely, that Britain was "forgetting its world-historical mission." The discursive role of Britain in the Krio discourse can be compared to the position of the proletariat in Marxist theory: the proletariat is given certain properties and tasks in the theory. The fact that the actual proletariat acted differently did not, for Marxists, refute the theory, but was turned into a moral and political problem of the proletariat not taking up its "real" historical task.

Another peculiar aspect of Horton's thought, namely, his negative view of contemporary indigenous African societies, can also be understood in terms of the exemplar. These societies were by definition barbarous, backward, and weak, and were seen as the raw material that had to be civilized and strengthened. Just like the case of the exemplary recaptives who made their "great leap ahead" through an external missionary activity, Horton envisioned transforming traditional societies through an infusion of European civilization. Consistent with this view, he considered the nature and details of indigenous traditions quite irrelevant for development.[60] Horton believed in Africans but not in African cultures.[61]

The final advantage of analyzing the Krio discourse through its exemplar, the recaptive success story, is that it can clarify its limited presence in African history. To which groups did the discourse appeal? Why did this appeal suddenly disappear so completely that Horton was quickly forgotten and not even quoted by the next generation of African intellectuals?[62] This exemplar of recaptive success expressed the particular historical situation of the coastal elites in the 1860s and 1870s. With the establishment of Western powers on the coast, they could have great hopes for the future, namely, by creating wealth, by gradually Africanizing the whole state administration, and by taking over from the whites, who could not survive the African climate. The leadership of modern African societies would be the task for the educated elites. "Buy up the former abodes of their European masters; carry on extensive mercantile speculations; seek after the indulgences of civilized life, and travel in foreign countries to seek after wealth . . . look out for a better form of government administration."[63] These specific historical roots also explain the rapid decline of the optimistic Krio discourse in the 1870s. In the last three decades of the nineteenth century, the British were clearly more interested in colonial expansion than in their so-called civilizing mission. Racist assumptions became dominant and these, among other things, resulted in discriminating against educated Africans and even eliminating them from higher positions in government, administration, and missionary organizations. In fact, the negative attitude of the British toward the Fanti Federation, the Native Pastorate controversy in the early 1870s, and the forcing out of the first African bishop, the Yoruba recaptive Ajayi Crowther, were early instances of conflict between the educated elite and the colonial administration. Resentment among the educated elites grew steadily. In such an atmosphere, the optimistic Krio discourse lost appeal and it became completely obsolete following the subsequent actual colonial rule throughout most of Africa.

Lacking an outside benevolent civilizer, only two options concerning African development remained by the end of the nineteenth century. First, to forget the whole dream of a "modern" Africa and strive for an authentic indigenous Africa—this is the road proposed by Edward Wilmot Blyden. Second, to accept the modernization ideal, but try to find resources for modernization in African traditions and social life itself—this idea was developed later by intellectuals such as John Mensah Sarbah and Joseph E. Casely Hayford. Let me now turn to these intellectual options.

THE DISCOURSE OF AFRICAN REGENERATION:
EDWARD WILMOT BLYDEN

In visions of the future, I behold those beautiful hills—the banks of those harming streams, the verdant plains and flowery field, the salubrious highlands in primeaval innocence and glory, and those fertile districts watered everywhere as the garden of the Lord: I see them all taken possession of by the returning exiles from the West, trained for the work of rebuilding waste place under severe discipline and hard bondage. I see, too, their brethren hastening to welcome them from the slopes of the Niger . . . Mohammedans and Pagans, chiefs and people, all coming to catch something of the inspiration the exiles nhave brought . . . and to march back hand-in-hand with their returned brethren towards the sunrise for the regeneration of a continent . . . raised from the slumber of the ages and resqued from a stagnant barbarism. "Ethiopia shall suddenly stretch out her hands unto God."[64]

Edward Wilmot Blyden

The proud republic of Liberia, founded in 1817 and declared independent in 1847, was rather less idyllic than Blyden's vision suggests, expressed on a mission to stimulate American blacks to return to Africa. Liberia's capital, Monrovia, was a small settlement living in near-constant antagonism with the inland African population, and its internal politics were marked by a new colorline between lighter- and darker-skinned Liberians.[65]

The arrival of Edward Wilmot Blyden in 1851, only a few years after independence, infused Liberian life not only with a flamboyant public figure but also with an intellectual of much more than Liberian, or even West African, stature. For decades, this self-made and self-educated man became the most prominent West African ideologue opposing dominant European paternalism. Blyden's biographer H. R. Lynch called him "the greatest nineteenth century black intellectual" and the historian A. A. Ayandele termed him an "African celebrity." Blyden was admired by the next generation of African intellectuals, yet he provoked quite negative valuations as well.[66]

Blyden was born into a family of free, educated blacks on the Danish Caribbean island of St. Thomas in 1832. He went to the United States for studies in theology, but could not enter a university there because of racial discrimination and so decided instead to go to the free "Negro" republic of Liberia in 1850. Blyden began teaching at the Presbyterian Alexander High School in 1854 and was ordained a Presbyterian minister in 1858. He taught himself Latin and Greek (to read the scriptures), later Arabic as well, and devoured contemporary popular and political writings.[67]

Blyden expected African Americans never to attain equal status in America and strongly supported the call for a return to Africa.[68] He visited the United States twice on Liberian government missions to attract immigrants.[69] Within Liberia, Blyden, being very black, sided against the "mulatto" ruling caste in often bitter struggles. In one of these, Blyden's friend Alexander Crummell aspired to become Episcopal bishop of Liberia, but was effectively blocked by the American mother church and Liberian mulattoes. Another issue that divided blacks and mulattoes in Liberia was the position of native Africans. These Africans held no citizenship rights (unless "acculturated") and were discriminated against in various ways. Crummell's and Blyden's church work among indigenous Africans taught them to respect indigenous cultures. In addition, they saw the complete integration of "natives" in educational and missionary efforts as central to the Pan-Africanist and Pan-Negroist movements that was to spread from Liberia to the rest of Africa.

Blyden was involved in the election of the black president Roye and held high political offices, but he had to flee to Sierra Leone when Roye was overthrown and killed in 1871. In Freetown, Blyden established his newspaper *The Negro* and made several official government missions into the interior, always urging the British government to expand its influence. He also became involved immediately in the Native Pastorate controversy.[70]

Back in Liberia Blyden was appointed Liberian ambassador to England for several years and president of the Liberia College. He ran for the presidency of the republic in 1885 but lost and mostly lived in Sierra Leone for the rest of his life. However, Blyden traveled frequently, exemplified by his visit to the United States in 1889 where he was celebrated by conservative whites as "the heaven-appointed medium for helping to solve the (Negro) problem."[71] In 1890 Blyden visited Lagos which was quickly becoming the most important center in West Africa. Blyden was received with much honor "as the highest intellectual representative and the greatest defender and uplifter of the African race" and he preached on relations with Muslims, on the need for an African institution of higher learning, and on an independent African church that would appoint Bishop Crowther, an African, as its head. Laymen founded the United Native African Church that same year.[72]

Blyden remained a highly respected man with contacts among most of the important political figures in West Africa, yet he was practically penniless when he died in 1912 in Sierra Leone.

Blyden's Development

It is tempting, at this point, to assemble Blyden's views into one coherent position. Such a position would then be termed "antiracist racism" or "nineteenth-century Négritude" (expressions used in interpretations of Blyden). Typically, however, such terms refer to twentieth-century intellectual events and may result in an anachronistic interpretation. I want to stay closer to the actual situations in which Blyden operated and to reconstruct Blyden's discourse as an event in African intellectual and political history. An additional advantage of analyzing Blyden's discourse in this way is that important shifts in his position can be revealed. Rather than presenting one paradigmatic position, Blyden radically changed his ideas during his long life, which shows the remarkable force and originality of his thought.

When Blyden arrived in Liberia, "for love of his fatherland" and to serve the Pan-Negroist cause, his frame of mind fully expressed Christian abolitionism. He preached that *Negritia* should "stretch out her hands unto God."[73] In the divine plan for the rebirth of Africa, the civilized, Christianized, and educated ex-slaves from the Americas played a primary role. Slavery itself was considered to have been part of this divine plan, because it was through the New World slavery experience that "the sons of Ham" could absorb Christianity in order to effect the regeneration of the continent. In the political field, this divine plan involved the Republic of Liberia, as well as the attempts of European powers to penetrate into, and Christianize, Africa.

Next to being an abolitionist civilizer, Blyden was a Pan-Negroist from the very beginning. Pan-Negroism, the idea that all black people in the world are essentially one and should reunite, had quite a different origin from abolitionism. It derived from the African New World slavery experience, involving the colorline and a self-definition "as blacks." Within Africa itself, a person's identity would generally derive from belonging to a particular people, culture, or language group. People of African descent in the Americas, however, could mostly trace their ancestry only in a general way to Africa, which was seen as the home continent or the fatherland of the black people. This idea of "Africa" was based on color or race, rather than on the actual hundreds of cultures and peoples inhabiting the geographical space of Africa. The Pan-Negroist "Africa" was conditioned by the social situation from which it derived, a racial self-definition as the counterpart to the white oppressor.

This particular self-definition "as blacks" was initially brought to Africa by Pan-Negroists such as Blyden and Crummell. Pan-Negroism, as well as abolitionism, is a view of Africa from a position outside of Africa. In both cases Africa and Africans are positioned in grand dichotomies, namely civilized-primitive and black-white respectively.

The abolitionist and the Pan-Negroist discourses do not automatically conform, however. The early Christian Pan-Negroists, such as Blyden and Crummell, aligned the two in an interesting way by applying the civilized-primitive dichotomy within the black race, namely, between the New World "exiled brethren" who were "trained for the work of rebuilding waste place under severe discipline and hard bondage" (that is, the civilized) and the indigenous Africans who had to be "raised from the slumber of the ages and rescued from a stagnant barbarism" (that is, the primitive). The intellectual framework of Blyden and Crummell thus consisted of a peculiar combination of a Pan-Negro discourse on African identity and an abolitionist discourse on civilization.

The most remarkable achievement of Blyden's intellectual career was that he managed to gradually distance himself from almost every aspect of the Christian abolitionist discourse. The key to the development of Blyden's thought was that he actually sought exposure to African life and cultures. Blyden participated in hurch work among indigenous communities in Liberia, traveled inland, studied African cultures and history, learned Arabic, and traveled to Egypt. This firsthand knowledge of Africa corrected his negative idea of African cultures. Thus, a constitutive element of the Christian abolitionist discourse (which needed a negative idea of African culture in order to justify the claim that this culture should be replaced by Christianity) was undermined. In fact, Blyden gradually developed a very positive view of African culture. African culture should not be replaced by Christian, "civilized" culture but be protected against this "alien" influence. Blyden contended that, in its own way, African culture was superior to Western culture.

Blyden thus challenged a core element of the abolitionist-humanitarian "civilizers" discourse, and created the possibility of a new, what can be called an "Afrocentric" or "African regeneration," discourse. This new discourse of racial and cultural self-consciousness could become a vehicle for a critique of the missionary (and in principle also the colonial) establishment in West Africa. It could define a separate African position.

A Philosophy of Racial Identity

The idea of a basic difference between cultures or races was central to Blyden's new African regeneration discourse. Every race is a natural unit, having its own "home" continent, character, and mission. The idea of race in Blyden's discourse was not simply the modern biological concept.[74] For Blyden race had a number of references: biological, cultural, and religious, all of which established racial identities as God-created units of humanity. The specificity of races should unfold, each developing in its own way, complementing the other races and thereby shaping the complete creation according to the dictates of providence.

Each race is endowed with peculiar talents, and watchful to the last degree is the great Creator over the individuality, the freedom and independence of each. In the music of the universe, each shall give a different sound, but necessary to the grand symphony. There are several sounds not yet brought out, and the feeblest of all is that hitherto produced by the Negro; but only he can furnish it. And when he furnishes it in its fullness and perfection, it will be welcomed with delight by the world.[75]

As a consequence of his view on race, Blyden saw nothing wrong with the term "Negro." He even insisted on writing it with a capital "N" and made it the title of the journal he founded in Freetown. According to Blyden "Pride of race" was essential for Negro progress, a dictate of nature as well as a divine commandment. The great challenge for the self-conscious Negro was to bring out, discover, and develop this specifically African mode in all aspects of life. This would mean developing African religious expression, African education, African social organization, and African political order. Blyden found many succinct expressions for this idea, such as "Be yourselves . . . if you surrender your personality, you have nothing left to give the world," and "the African must advance by the methods of his own. He must possess a power distinct from the European."[76]

The more radical implications of this view were developed later in Blyden's life, such as the idea of a specifically African personality. The African personality is defined in contrast to the European one, which is identified as harsh, individualistic, competitive, combative, nonreligious, and materialistic. Africans are by nature softer and more cheerful, they have sympathy, a willingness to serve, and are spiritual. Their orientation is toward agriculture, not industry.[77] In a letter to Booker T. Washington, Blyden wrote:

The spirit of service in the black man is born of his spiritual genius. . . . [T]he supple, yielding, conciliatory, obedient, gentle, patient, musical spirit that is not full of offensive resistance—how sadly the white man needs it! . . . Let him fight the battle of government on the stump, at the polls and in the legislative halls. Our kingdom in America is not this world. We cannot compete with the Anglo-Saxon. He is so dreadfully determined, so intolerant and self assertive, intent upon carrying his point at all hazards, having good in view of course; but the wheels of his mind and understanding need oiling sadly with the oil of African good nature.[78]

The contributions of the Negro toward world culture would therefore be that of peacemaker and conserver of the spirituality of the world.

Thus, Ethiopia and Ethiopians, having always served, will continue to serve the world. The Negro is, at the moment, the opposite of the Anglo-Saxon. Those everywhere serve the world; these everywhere govern the world. . . . And in the light of the ultimate good of the universe, I do not see why the calling of the one should be considered the result of a curse, and the calling of the other the result of special favour. The one fulfils its mission of domination, the other of submission. The one serves mankind by ruling; the other serves mankind by serving. The one wears the crown and wields the sceptre; the other bears the stripes and carries the cross. Africa is distinguished as having *served* and *suffered*. In this, her lot is not unlike that of God's ancient people, the Hebrews. . . . The lot of Africa resembles also His who made himself of no reputation, but took upon himself the form of a servant.[79]

Consistent with Blyden's idea of cultural difference, Christianity, as a Western religion, could not be the universal norm. His contention that Christianity was not fit for Africa shocked his contemporaries, both black and white. "The so-called Christian public are not yet prepared for such a catastrophe to their enterprise, which nevertheless, so far as Africa is concerned, is hopeless."[80] Although originally ordained as a Presbyterian minister, Blyden became increasingly critical about the role of the Christian mission on the coast. Simultaneously, his esteem for Islamic culture grew. For some time Blyden appears to have considered Islam as preparatory for what he considered "in essence the highest form of religion," namely, Christianity.[81] It is unclear whether Blyden ever really abandoned the ideal of a Christian Africa and converted to Islam. Mudimbe maintains that "in spirit Blyden was a Muslim."[82]

In any case, Blyden saw Islam as better suited to the needs of the African continent because it could civilize Africa while respecting its traditions. Islam could bind tribes together, suppress savage practices, as well as promote egalitarianism and abstination. Islam also had not resulted in "Moorish" domination over Africans. Great African warriors have expelled the conquerors and adjusted Islam to accommodate the social peculiarities of the people.[83] Blyden claimed that he had not experienced discrimination during his travels throughout the Muslim interior and the Middle East and that he observed full black participation in the administration. For his practical endeavors, however, Blyden continued to depend on financial support from British and American Christians. Even if Blyden was not a Christian anymore, he could not have afforded to stress this openly.

The shift to a new discourse on African regeneration evolved parallel to changing views on the remigration of African Americans. Originally, Blyden's Christian abolitionist and Pan-Negroist orientation made him strongly favor remigration. Shedding his abolitionist missionarism, however, made him more reluctant. Blyden even developed an aversion to accepting mixed bloods, mulattoes, as full Negroes (or indeed as full humans).[84] Such discriminatory views severely complicated Blyden's dealings with the black leadership in the United States, where persons of mixed blood were prominently present. In fact, Blyden did not accept the common definition of "Negro" as someone having Negro blood. To qualify as a Negro Blyden required majority—or even pure Negro descent—hence his use of notions such as "pure Negroes," "genuine Negroes," and "half-casts." In his later life Blyden even favored the prohibition of interracial marriages.

Such discrimination is consistent with Blyden's theoretical framework. His concept of race suggests that the divine mandate for the authenticity and the purity of African culture also involves the purity of race. For Blyden, biological and cultural issues (which—in the late twentieth-century—are considered quite separate things) were mixed from the beginning.[85]

In educational matters, Blyden's ideas worked out clearly, too. He favored a curriculum specially designed for African students to be taught in indigenous institutions by Africans. Blyden's idea of an African curriculum, included the study of Arabic and African culture and history, as well as that of the Greek and Roman classics (sic!). Since African students should not be distracted from their own "racial instincts" the study of later European culture should be excluded. Toward the end of his life, Blyden increasingly stressed the appropriateness of the industrial arts for African students.[86]

The political views involved in the new African regeneration discourse were ambiguous. On the one hand, they stressed Negro self-assertion and unity. In Blyden's view, the world of his lifetime developed according to the logic of racial identities, which he saw as a great support for African liberation.[87] Regaining African historical and cultural identity and developing indigenous institutions could help to constitute the regeneration of Africa. On the other hand, a consistent elaboration of Blyden's philosophy of racial/cultural difference implied the idea that Africans should leave politics to the race that excels in this area, namely the Europeans. "The one serves mankind by domination, the other by submission. The one serves mankind by ruling, the other serves mankind by serving." Especially toward the end of his life, Blyden drifted toward a philosophical position that denied the relevance of political power for Africans (even proposing white governance for the free black state of Liberia) and called for British colonial expansion inland.[88] Whites, according to Blyden's racial framework of ideas, could not settle permanently on the African continent so that colonialism was considered by nature to be only temporary. At the same time, according to the providential scheme of things, the British had a historical task in Africa to facilitate education, trade, and the creation of a great unified West African state. Every care should be taken, however, to ensure that throughout this process the basic African social system would remain intact.[89]

The political logic of the African regeneration discourse allows, ultimately, two alternatives: either proceeding toward an outspoken anticolonial ideology around the idea of "Africa for the Africans," or becoming an ideology of resignation on account of the African's special personality and "lot to serve." The first option was expressed by Marcus Garvey in the United States after World War I. Blyden gradually developed a version of the second option. In his quite long-term view, Africans could benefit from colonialism. Blyden neither believed that political action was appropriate nor that Africans were ripe for political leadership.[90]

The exemplary text for Blyden's conservative position toward the end of his life is the book *African Life and Customs* (1908), originally published as a newspaper series in Sierra Leone.[91] The book is a superbly elegant, idealized presentation of "the" African way of life, covering its various aspects one by one, and clearly showing its intricate balance, wisdom, and perfect adaptation to the African situation. Most of what has been written on "the" African in the framework of African Socialism, or Ethnophilosophy in the twentieth-century pales in comparison to Blyden's *African Life and Customs*.

Blyden's long journey from abolitionist cultural imperialism to cultural nationalism came to its consistent conclusion in *African Life and Customs*. His philosophy developed from a view of Africa as still having to acquire everything to a view of Africa that, in principle, has everything already, shifting from a profoundly evolutionary discourse to an essentialist discourse. The style and structure of Blyden's texts also inverted. His early texts represent a standard narrative of an outsider preaching to Africans ("Christianize!" and "Civilize!") while he turned toward a standard narrative of an African preaching to outsiders ("We Africans") later. The external aim of *African Life and Customs* is shown in the text itself since every paragraph begins with an exposition of problems in European (British) society, before presenting the African way as the perfect alternative. This strategy reveals Blyden's creative polemical mind at its best: he inverted the roles so that Europe is not exemplary for Africa, but rather Africa is exemplary for Europe.

The Exemplar of the Colorline

The foregoing presentation of Blyden's development suggests an internalistic interpretation. It maintains that Blyden's views consistently developed toward one of the logical conclusions allowed by a discourse based on the idea of race. Such an interpretation, however, ignores that Blyden was very much part of the intellectual and cultural developments of his time. He was well read, participating in contemporary debates and arousing great enthusiasm.[92] In terms of Quentin Skinner, one could say that Blyden's "retailoring" of the paradigm of scientific racism had a specific political meaning and aroused strong sentiments in his time. As I hope to show here, in order to understand Blyden's African regeneration discourse, it is essential to trace its place throughout the ideas and the politics of the last decades of the nineteenth-century.

The African regeneration discourse builds on an intellectual heritage of nineteenth-century scientific racist theory, as much as on an understanding of the world in terms of ethnicallybased nationalities, which was shared by the contemporaries.

Within the last thirty years, the sentiment of race and of nationality has attained wonderful development. Not only have the teachings of thinkers and philosophers set forth the importance of the theory, but the deeds of statesmen and patriots have, more or less successfully, demonstrated the practicality of it. The efforts of men like Garibaldi and Cavour in Italy, of Kossnuth in Hungary, of Bismarck in Germany, of the Ashantees and Zulus in Africa, have proved the indestructible vitality and tenacity of race.[93]

Blyden perceived himself to be part of a grand global process of peoples, nations, and races reclaiming their legitimate place in this world: "The feeling is in the atmosphere—the plane in which races move. And there is no people in whom the desire for race integrity and race preservation is stronger than in the Negro."[94]

The intellectual tradition in which Blyden's views were shaped was the discourse of scientific racism, but he altered the discourse to suit his agenda. While accepting its key concepts (race, instinct, natural order), dichotomies (black-white), and theories (on the "serving" nature of blacks, the natural home continents of races, the degenerating effects of mixing of races), he toppled, as it were, the structure of racist discourse by replacing a hierarchical order of races with an order of difference. The modern reader will be astonished by Blyden's quotations of the crudest racists. According to Blyden's own intellectual framework, however, these racist theorists were not mistaken about the facts (racial differences) but about the interpretation and valuation of these facts (a hierarchy of races).

In order to understand Blyden, it is necessary to recognize the political context in which the African regeneration discourse functioned. Blyden, it was felt by his contemporaries, explicated the essence of their historical situation with striking accuracy. The last decades of the nineteenth-century not only had the "sentiments of race and nationality" as a "feeling in the atmosphere," they were also the time when the colonial "empires of race" were actually being established. For the African educated elite the establishment of colonial rule meant segregation and eviction from all but the lowest ranks in colonial and missionary administrations. Blyden's African regeneration discourse expressed these experiences of segregation and feelings of race, as much as it helped to interpret the experience of colonial subjugation in terms of race.

Blyden's key instrument to represent the emerging colonial situation was the exemplary idea of the colorline, suggesting a basic opposition of a white master and a black slave. From the very beginning, Blyden's Pan-Negroist thought embodied a key historical experience, namely that of New World slavery. This experience suggested the exemplar of the colorline as a mold for understanding every other aspect of the world. Its psychology revolved around the idea of alienation and authenticity. Its geography suggested that continents "belong to" races. Its history suggested that blacks were originally in their natural state of togetherness, became caught in the diaspora, a passing, abnormal state, but would be reunited as a race.

When Pan-Negroism was transferred from an American to an African context, in the early period of Liberia, it landed in quite a different environment. The division between lighter and darker Liberian citizens (expressed in two political parties and in anti-elite struggles) could be described as some kind of colorline, which may include the divide between immigrants, Christian citizens, and indigenous noncitizens as well. Outside of Liberia, the idea of a colorline failed to be relevant, however. There the issue of color was not "charged" with social and political meaning to establish it as foundational and inspirational for a discourse.

The historical situation in Africa changed rapidly, however, with the rise of colonial racism in the last three decades of the nineteenth-century. Colonial expansion and scientific racism created "empires of race." The African educated elite especially suffered from discrimination. The idea of the colorline thus acquired new relevance, expressing, not slavery-related racism, but colonial racism.

The nature of the colorline was different, however, in both cases. For example, in the African situation the black side of the colorline was less tainted with extreme pain, violence, and alienation than in the American situation. After all, the experience of being black in Africa did not belong to a battered minority, but rather to a self-conscious and resourceful majority. Even visual appearance reflected the difference in division between black and white on the two continents. In Africa (except for South Africa) white areas would appear as tiny, isolated, and vulnerable. Because Europeans were poorly adapted to the African environment physically, the European presence tended to be perceived as a temporary arrangement. As noted earlier, in Africa identity referred to specific African cultures, whereas the New World colorline tended to shape the black identity as a "negative," or a negation of the white identity.

Probably, in the African case the idea of the black-white divide has always been more of a cultureline than a colorline. Blyden's thought itself, although consistently framed in a terminology of race, can support such an interpretation. If Blyden's notion of race is translated into present-day concepts, it tends to have at least as many connotations of culture as of biology. If one would consistently replace Blyden's word "race" with a general concept of "culture," then his argument would remain basically unchanged.

It is, thus, important to note that the new African regeneration discourse in Africa in the 1880s and 1890s was not simply a return to a Pan-Negroist position. The latter expressed a New World experience, while the former expressed an African experience (an experience, at least, that was, within a few decades, shared by the whole continent). Blyden's new African regeneration discourse itself did much to make the educated elite interpret their collective experiences in terms of grand racial and cultural oppositions. Their thinking turned toward positions that were much more race, color, and culture conscious than during the previous decades. For instance, many took African names, the African Dress Society was formed, and African cultural, religious, and political systems were studied. The African regeneration discourse was very much an African discourse.

The interpretation of the African regeneration discourse in terms of the elites' experience of a colonial colorline can explain the loss of appeal of the regeneration discourse around the turn of the century. Blyden's forceful positions on such issues as an African church, an African curriculum, an African personality, history, and high culture, as well as his ideas on race pride and nonacculturation, were striking at the heart of paternalistic rule in the proto-colonial enclaves on the West African coast between 1870 and 1900. However, when colonialism became established around 1900, when fully fledged administrative, legal, military, and economic structures were being imposed, then the political rather than the cultural aspects of colonial rule became the primary issue. Blyden's grand ideological warfare was still inspiring but did not really address the most urgent problems of the day, namely, the enforcement of colonial rule and the issue of representation of African interests within the new system.

THE DISCOURSE OF INDIGENOUS SELF-RULE: THE PROTECTION SOCIETY AND CASELY HAYFORD

There was a theoretical policy and a practical one, the latter having as its aim such a shaping of circumstances as would for ever make the Ethiopian in his own country a hewer of wood and a drawer of water unto his Caucasian protector and so-called friend.[95]

Casely Hayford

The division of Africa and the imposition of colonial rule around the turn of the century created new conditions for political thought. The Berlin Conference, which decided about the division of Africa, took place in 1885. Actual occupation of the assigned territories was concluded only around 1900. For political thought in Africa, the hard fact of absolute colonial rule put an end to the nineteenth-century view that overseas colonial powers and indigenous rulers, despite their differences in power, could in fact negotiate, sign treaties, and expect to be respected as equal partners. This harsh message was, however, not received without protest. It gave rise to an interesting political discourse that formulated a grand (although aborted) option for Africa's future.

By focusing on the movement of the Aboriginals Rights Protection Society (ARPS) and its struggles in the Gold Coast around 1900, this third type of political discourse, different from the optimistic Krio and African regeneration discourses, discloses itself. The discourse represents the end of the old nineteenth-century political horizon, which was "open" in the sense that it left room for African aspirations "to work out our own salvation." At the same time, however, the discourse absorbed several fundamental assumptions that betray its tribute to the colonial situation, and it can thus be said to represent the beginning of a new type of political discourse. I will now try to unravel the intricacies and contradictions of this highly interesting answer to the question of "Whither Africa?"

On the shop floor of history, a number of changes took place around the turn of the century. Within the realm of British power in West Africa the importance of Nigeria, as compared to that of Sierra Leone increased. The Gold Coast remained of great importance intellectually. A further shift could be seen in the rising importance of the press. A multitude of newspapers appeared in Nigeria, the Gold Coast, and Sierra Leone. Some of them, like *The Lagos Weekly Record* of John Payne Jackson, remained for some fourty years a strong advocate of nationalist interest. Most of the leading political figures were themselves active journalists. The westernized elite had grown in size. In urban centers, such as Lagos, Accra, and Cape Coast, there was an animated social and public life with debating clubs and societies in the British style.

The major players in African politics were the educated elite and the traditional rulers. It has been habitual to judge negatively about the elitist or Westernized educated class because of their alleged alienation from the people and indigenous rulers.[96] These cleavages should not be overstated, however. The educated were, for the most part, closely attuned to their home areas, and with their traditional rulers. Furthermore, they cannot be taken as a homogeneous group. The ARPS paper, *The Gold Coast Aborigines,* of 8 Feb. 1902, for instance, stated: "We want Educated Fantis not europeanized natives. We simply want our education to enable us to develop and to improve our native ideas, customs, manners and institutions."[97] Similarly, *The Times of Nigeria*, in an editorial, differentiated between "two categories of African educated natives: the sophisticated ones who were losing touch with their indigenous systems and betraying their fellow Africans (and these abounded in Lagos) and those who were patriotic, inwardly agitating."[98]

The Aboriginal Rights Protection Society

A historical need for such patriotic, inward agitation presented itself in the Gold Coast in the 1890s with the issuing of colonial land laws that declared, among other things, that wastelands were crown lands. Educated elites and traditional rulers alike realized that these laws affected the heart of traditional systems of rule and they rose up to "defend both land rights and the social structure based upon them."[99] The Aboriginals Rights Protection Society, which was established in 1896 to fight this cause, was in fact an early example of a "modern" political movement in Africa.

The ARPS revived the spirit of the Fanti Federation of twenty-five years before.[100] The old confederationists joined the younger generation of intellectuals such as John Mensah Sarbah, Joseph Casely Hayford, and Kobina Sekyi. From his deathbed, King Gartey IV of Winneba, who had been elected the first president of the Fanti Federation and continued to be one of the most important traditional rulers of the Gold Coast, confirmed the historical link between the ARPS case and the Fanti Federation.

Now that the big struggle before us *re* the Land Bills &c. the history past, present and future call with one loud voice for Loyalty, Unity of purpose, and perseverance in actions. . . . Hopefully therefore I fall in this battle field with many wounds fresh and old and deep scars of the defunct Fanti Confederation. Kindly convey my last farewell to all true patriotic native kings and friends of the countries cause, here and elsewhere and to the Aborigines Society in England. Be constitutional. God bless you, our Country and the Queen. Amen.[101]

The society was constitutional and successful. After active agitation and a deputation to London, the laws were withdrawn. This victory, however, could not stop the process of gradual usurpation of African sovereignty. The Gold Coast was declared to be a crown colony in 1901, and the Native Jurisdiction Law of 1910 legalized the inferior position of traditional rulers.

In fact, the Land Laws signified, within the Gold Coast context, the harsh awakening to the realities of colonial subjugation. The agreement of the famous Bond of 1844 that the indigenous rulers and the British (at first the merchant Captain George Maclean) would sit together as equals "to administer the affairs of the country and dispense justice" was over.[102] As the Gold Coast intellectual J. B. Danquah's subtle analysis showed:

The Gold Coast people and their natural rulers were gradually reduced from the relation of independent states friendly with the Queen-Empress to the level of subject states in a Crown Colony, the inhabitants of which can only seek for a share in the government of their own country at the hands of red-tape Governors "on the spot," who live in Castles and Forts[103] and demand loyalty from the people and their rulers, like conquered vassals in the palace of the Great Mogul.

The age in which an independent national consciousness dawned upon the Gold Coast people came to an end in 1897, but it was natural that the great reaction that set in should have resulted in a period of sustained and organized criticism of British intentions and good faith, of dissatisfaction with the new regime, a constitutional and standing protest against the flagrant departure from the Bond of 1844. The aim of the new policy tended gradually to encroach upon the rights and liberties of the Gold Coast people, to close their courts, to seize their lands, and to curtail the inherited independence of the native states in the continued enjoyment of which neither the people nor the natural rulers had divested themselves, either by conquest, cession or sale to the British.[104]

The ARPS is not only interesting as a case of successful constitutional agitation against a colonial power but even more so for the ideas that carried this movement. "West Africans felt cheated of their land, deprived of their right of self-government, defrauded of their economical resources and stripped of the very essentials of their culture and way of life."[105] The political thought of nineteenth-century Africans, however, did not provide a useful tool to transform this frustration into effective political action. The Horton-type modernizationist optimism would be anachronistic, even a form of collaboration in this situation.[106] Blyden's cultural conservatism was popular, expressing African frustrations with colonial paternalism and racism, but his political conservatism, especially in his later years, was a poor tool for effective political action.

The nineteenth-century ideologies suggested a choice between moderniz-ation and African tradition, while neither provided a forceful framework for political action in a situation characterized by enforced colonial penetration. The way out was shown by ARPS intellectuals such as Mensah Sarbah and Casely Hayford. They suggested that there is no contradiction between tradition and modernization. African traditions, they argued, are perfectly able to adjust in their own way to modern times, if only given the chance. It is this fair chance that was denied to them.

The reasoning of the ARPS intellectuals located the key issue, and therefore the focus of the struggle, in the political sphere. Whereas for Horton economic and technological modernization was the key to Africa's future, and for Blyden it was cultural authenticity, for the ARPS the key issue was political, namely, the liberty of "working out our own salvation" as a people.[107]

The ARPS aimed at the concrete political option that the British should "confine themselves more to external administration, leaving the internal government of the people to develop upon the natural lines of their own institutions."[108] The Japanese, while facing the threat of modernized Europe, revolutionized their own culture under Méidji rule. In the same way, the ARPS intellectuals wanted to renovate indigenous political traditions as the basis for an indigenous path to modernization.

This grand ideological option of modernization-from-indigenous-roots involved a statement of the vitality belonging to indigenous traditions that is reminiscent of Blyden. Blyden, in fact, was very popular among the ARPS intellectuals. When looked at more carefully, however, their own argument was quite different from that of Blyden. Rather than affirming a general African identity as different from the European one, the ARPS intellectuals wanted to show the vitality of specific Fanti and Ashanti traditions as a basis for actually organizing social and political life on the coast. "Going Fantee" in names, clothes, religion and language, including the propagation of traditional political institutions, was a political program. Whereas Blyden was making a cultural statement (in a broad sense), the ARPS intellectuals were formulating a political alternative.

Blyden invited his contemporaries to admire the African tradition and follow the logic and instincts of their race, but he did so using the English (or Arab) language exclusively and wearing only the best British suits, often having a British audience in mind. Blyden's much younger admirer Casely Hayford praised the specific Fanti-Ashanti tradition while frequently wearing neotraditional garb, quoting indigenous songs and sayings, while occasionally, in brackets, signing his African name Ekra-Agiman.

Ethiopia Chained—Ethiopia Unbound

Joseph Casely Hayford was an exemplary representative of the ARPS discourse. Hayford was a journalist, Cambridge-trained lawyer, and an important politician, the "uncrowned king of West Africa" during the first three decades of this century. Beyond being a political leader, Casely Hayford was probably the most comprehensive and representative political theorist of these decades in British West Africa: eloquent, sophisticated, witty, and, where necessary, he made extensive reference to historical fact. He wrote, among other works, *Gold Coast Native Institutions* (1903), *Ethiopia Unbound* (1911), *The Truth about the West African Land Question* (1913), and *United West Africa* (1919). After the World War I he shifted to a more pragmatic and Pan–West African position, which will be discussed in the next chapter.

Hayford's *Gold Coast Native Institutions* described the highly sophisticated Ashanti and Fanti political procedures, with their own checks and balances and mechanisms that promote thorough political deliberation. Typically, Casely Hayford gave an enthusiastic description of the role of the "linguist" (or "speaker"), especially in the Ashanti system. "The Linguist is the most important personage of the Native State. He is in some cases more influential than the Chief. . . . He is generally the repository, or, if you like, a walking encyclopedia, of all traditional knowledge . . . his knowledge embraces the political history of the whole State, as well as of sister States."[109] His speeches sparkle with humor. He is the master in "the art of linguistic oratory" and creative in guiding the discussion to reach a balanced conclusion. Casely Hayford's inspired representation suggests that the educated were not outside the traditional system and competing with it, but right at its center. Thus, he welded together the two major forces in indigenous politics in one model. For the "educated son of the nation" there was an important role "to serve his countries cause" as councilor, advisor, or linguist.[110]

In a second way, Casely Hayford's *Native Institutions* effected a skillful integration of different political forces. Whereas John Mensah Sarbah, his senior contemporary, titled his famous scholarly study *Fanti Customary Law*, Casely Hayford used the general title *Gold Coast Native Institutions*. Old divisions, such as those between Fanti and Ashanti, were suppressed in favor of the new encompassing unit Gold Coast. Casely Hayford's description is in fact a nationalist construction, namely, a conscious attempt to establish a national Fanti-Ashanti tradition.

Whereas *Gold Coast Native Institutions* provided the scientific proof for the existence of an indigenous Gold Coast political heritage, the appeal for Africans to actually turn to this heritage to create their future was expressed in Casely Hayford's magnificent fictional and partly autobiographical work *Ethiopia Unbound*. The main character of the story, traveling to England and through his home country, proves at every point that his indigenous background and inspiration is more humane, natural, sensitive, and logically consistent than the British-Christian influences. When it comes to practical achievements in administration, the foreign tradition is criticized as disastrous for the Gold Coast. Casely Hayford's conclusion was clear: there is no alternative for the Gold Coast except to build on the indigenous tradition. There is "no healthy growth except from within."[111]

This healthy growth, however, was blocked by colonial administration. The colonial power claimed to have a civilizing mission. Casely Hayford, however, showed that this mission consisted instead of the suppression of civilization, of indigenous civilization. For Casely Hayford, "Colonial Africa was . . . Ethiopia chained. His political theory was that with Africans assuming control of their own affairs and developing their indigenous institutions, fettered Ethiopia would be unbound and eventually emerge as a giant among other nationalities."[112] The price of not taking this course would be costly: the people of the Gold Coast would forever be "hewers of wood and drawers of water in their own country."

Although far from a revolutionary, Casely Hayford was convinced of the essential illegitimacy of colonial rule. This is illustrated dramatically in *Ethiopia Unbound*, where the narrative recounts how Kwamanka is teaching his son about the "Black Peril," the "Yellow Peril," and the "Russian Bear." The boy asks, "But why don't you expose these things, Dad?" The father, giving "vent to some utterance from the very recesses of his soul," answers, "The hour has not yet come. Pray for thy father, that when it comes, he may be found strong and faithful."[113]

Modernization-from-Indigenous-Roots

Taken together, the ARPS discourse as represented by Casely Hayford's ideas, constitutes a remarkable and consistent alternative for development. This alternative of modernization-from-indigenous-roots, summarized in my own words, runs as follows: We are a nation, we have always ruled ourselves, and we will rule ourselves again. We have our own civilization and our own set of political institutions. These can be revived and modernized to cater to the needs of today in an African way, analogous to the Japanese modernizing in a Japanese way. Our problem is shortsighted and biased British governors and politicians who fail to see that our natural place is that of a free nation within the empire.[114]

In the days of the ARPS movement, this idea of modernization-from-indigenous-roots was not simply a theoretical conception. Several concrete exemplary situations fixed the idea in contemporary historical consciousness. In Fanti history itself, the idea could be traced back to the inspiration of the abortive Fanti Federation. Internationally, it had its great examples in Japan and Ethiopia. Japan had avoided becoming "chained" by colonialism through a strategy of modernization-from-its-own-roots. Its power was proven by Japan's historic victory over the Russians in 1904. The state of Ethiopia had preserved its independence by beating the Italians in the equally historic battle at Aduwa in 1896.[115] These actual examples of a successful strategy to escape colonial subjugation and to identify an indigenous path of development gave social meaning to the idea of an unbound Africa. They shaped the political horizon of the ARPS and their success stories are thus the exemplars of the idea of modernization-from-indigenous-roots.

In my discussions about the optimistic Krio discourse and the African regeneration discourse, I showed that exemplars are important references in the texts themselves. This is also the case for the inspiration of the Fanti federation and the success story of Japan. These were frequently invoked by Sarbah and Casely Hayford in arguing the ARPS case. Danquah, later, expressed the same view by saying that King Garthey "tried to do for the Gold Coast in 1867 what Meiji did for Japan in 1867."[116]

The grand metaphor that is the title of Casely Hayford's book *Ethiopia Unbound* already expresses the whole idea of modernization-from-indigenous-roots. First, Africa embodies an old and superb civilization, that is, it is Ethiopia; second, it is bound, or chained, that is, it is fettered not by natural but by human factors so that the issue is political liberation; third, once unbound it will flourish: "prosperous cities will grow up . . . vast wealth will be created . . . and between the races there will be mutual respect."[117]

Proud as the idea of modernization-from-indigenous-roots may be, it was probably already an illusion by 1900. The rapid political developments increasingly made irrelevant the option of escaping from colonialism and successfully reclaiming the historical rights of traditional rulers, as in the Bond of 1844. As Danquah stated in 1932: "the age in which an independent national consciousness dawned upon the Gold Coast people came to an end in 1897."[118] The ARPS was a last upsurge of this assessment of colonial expansion, which Danquah called the "historical school" in African thought at the time.[119] From then on political struggle would necessarily occur from a position as a colonized people.

The Gold Coast people had effectively become part of the Empire, and for weal or woe, what they could best do to foster the national cause and liberty was to work from within the British constitution itself for a liberal recognition of our right and capacity to direct our destiny within an Empire of free nations and not as a subject Colony forming the "pocket borough" of the English Parliament.[120]

In a similar vein, the historian David Kimble stated that "the form of government and the peoples under its rule had changed beyond recognition during the few years 1897–1902," while, in terms of the ARPS, "its leaders hardly realized that power was slipping away from them, in favour of those who were more concerned with a fundamental change in the colonial relation than with the preservation of traditional rights."[121]

In a peculiar way, however, the ARPS discourse was not only the grand end of an era of essentially precolonial rule. It was also the beginning of a twentieth-century discourse of nationalist liberation. It was a swan song, so to say, but already largely in a musical notation of the new era. The way in which the indigenous alternative was presented, the notions used and the arguments advanced were new. It was a discourse in terms of countries, nations, constitutions, rights, and so forth. The Gold Coast nation itself, which should be "unchained," was a product of the colonial power uniting, among others, Fanti and Ashanti, peoples with a history of mutual strife. In *The Gold Coast Nation*, the journal of the ARPS, Atto Ahuma cried out in capitals, "WE ARE A NATION," and added: "If we were not one it was time to invent one."[122] "We are all one, and natives of the same colony."[123]

Again, like in most historical cases, national consciousness basically arose out of the struggle itself. The ARPS statement, "we are a nation having its own tradition," is the product of the specific historical situation in which the threat of colonial subjugation forced this Gold Coast nationality upon the people. As in many other historical cases, however, this consciousness came too late to raise a political power strong enough to resist further colonial subjugation.

The ARPS discourse also pays tribute to the new colonial situation in the arguments used to defend African rights. For instance, the ardent nationalist and editor of *The Gold Coast Chronicle*, Atto Ahuma, stated: "we are being welded together under one umbrageous Flag. . . . The Gold Coast under the aegis of the Union Jack is the unanswerable argument to all who may incontinently withhold from us the common rights, privileges, and status of nationality."[124] It was the Union Jack that provided the argument for national liberation! This was not that strange if we look at the specific political actions that Ahuma's statement supports: namely, petitioning the governor, representing grievances within the Legislative Council of the colony, and going to London, while declaring over and over again that they were strictly constitutional, which meant adhering to the constitution of the colonial empire. In fact, the form of action taken by the ARPS was already similar to that of a nationalist opposition movement within the colonial system.

My point here is that the message of the ARPS is to escape colonial usurpation of native power, which entails a precolonial-rule political horizon, as explained above. On the other hand, the wording and much of the actual political action of the ARPS made it a nationalist liberation discourse and an early example of anti-colonialism in a colonial situation.

This interesting ambiguity in the ARPS discourse also explains its fate in history. The inspiring message that there is an indigenous road to modernity, as a national enterprise based on the Gold Coast native institutions, could be formulated only toward the end of the century when the Gold Coast as a unit actually came into being, that is, when a colonial administration also became established in the territories outside the vicinity of the coastal forts. The establishment of colonial rule and the formation of a national consciousness went hand in hand. A quarter of a century earlier, in 1874, the Fanti Federation could not yet rely on such a national consciousness; when their leaders were arrested, the population did not emerge to rescue "the nation."

On the other hand, the appeal of the discourse aimed at reestablishing indigenous self-rule could not last long. Concrete political issues in the colony required political organization within the logic of that system: "for weal or woe, what they could best do to foster the national cause and liberty was to work from within the British constitution itself," as J. B. Danquah wrote. At the same time, the colonial administration incorporated the chiefs in this administration, but on its own terms. The alternative of rebuilding indigenous political institutions thus became quite a theoretical one. De Graft Johnson's *Towards Nationhood in West Africa* is a case in point. This book probably provided the most complete proposal for adjusting indigenous institutions to the format of a modern nation-state.[125] However, it did so in 1928 and, despite its sophistication, it remained an intellectual exercise lacking political importance.

In the first decade of the twentieth-century, the ARPS could not attain much. There was a need to fight using more effective political organizations, and to confront the system on its own ground. This is the context of the next phase of political struggle, for instance in the African National Congress (ANC) in South Africa, or the National Congress of British West Africa (NCBWA), established in 1920 as the first transnational and Pan–West African organization in that era.[126]

CONCLUSION

This chapter recounts the first round of African political discourses addressing the challenge of European confrontation. Political discourses in this era shared what I called an "open historical horizon," that is, the assumption that various developmental options were open and total colonial subjugation could be avoided. I argued that three basic discourses can be identified, each shaped by a particular historical situation and a specific struggle: the optimistic Krio discourse, which operated in a situation where the establishment of independent African states seemed a possibility after the Select Committee proposal in 1865; Blyden's African regeneration discourse, which opposed colonial racism and paternalism in the last decades of the nineteenth century; and the African Rights Protection Society discourse, which struggled to preserve indigenous land rights and systems of rule in the Gold Coast in the 1890s.

The analysis of this first round has been a methodological adventure as well. I had set myself the task to avoid a simple history of ideas that ignores the actual political situations that shaped the meaning and *pointe* of political discourses. On the other hand, I wanted to avoid a description of political ideas as simply the ideological expression of class interests (see chapter 2). I reconstructed historically situated discourses as they addressed political issues perceived by contemporaries, and traced the heuristic that conditions the framework of ideas of the discourse concerned. As a tool for such a reconstruction, I attempted to identify the exemplars, that is those crucial stories or metaphors that articulate key real-life situations of collective concern.

In each of the three cases, such constitutive exemplars turned out to be operative. The image of the successful recaptive appeared to be the model for Horton's view of Africa's great leap toward universal modernity. The idea of the colorline became the model for Blyden's view of a uniquely African civilizatory mission. Similarly, Casely Hayford's image of Ethiopia Unbound models the ARPS conception of the political problem at hand, namely, breaking the colonial chains in order to reinstate self-rule and develop-from-our-own-roots. In each case also, the rise and fall of the discourse could be explained by the emergence and decline in social history of the collective experience that the key exemplar articulated.

In all three cases, finally, the highly local and temporal relevance of the discourse concerned did not preclude the emergence of a grand view of African development. The ideas of a "modern" Africa, of an "authentic" Africa, and of an Africa modernizing from indigenous roots have general relevance. Every revival during the next one hundred years of specific nineteenth-century variants of these ideas, however, will lack an essential precondition that the nineteenth-century discourses had, namely, the idea that the colonial experience could be avoided.[127] Around 1900 it was clear that this was not to be the case. Colonial subjugation was a reality, and politics would, for the time being, be politics within, even if about, the colonial system. These conditions shaped the second round of African political discourse to be discussed in the next chapter of this book.

NOTES

1. J.A.B. Horton, *West African Countries and Peoples, British, and Native. With the Requirements Necessary for Establishing that Self-government Recommended by the Committee of the House of Commons, 1865; and a Vindication of the Negro Race* (London: W. J. Johnson, 1868), 67.

2. See, e.g., E. A. Ayandele, "James Africanus Beale Horton, 1835–1883: Prophet of Modernisation in West Africa," *African Historical Studies* 4, no. 3 (1971): 691–707.

3. See, e.g., A. Okoth, *A History of Africa: 1855–1914* (Nairobi: Heinemann, 1979); J. D. Fage, *A History of Africa* (1978; reprint London: Routledge, 1995); R. Oliver & A. Atmore, *Africa since 1800* (1967; reprint Cambridge: Cambridge University Press, 1994). On African political systems, see M. Fortes & E. E. Evans-Pritchard, *African Political Systems* (Oxford University Press, 1940), and for concise

descriptions on Central African political systems, see J. Vansina, "A Past for the Future?" *Dalhousie Review*, 1992, and J. Vansina, "History of Central African Civilization" and "Kings in Tropical Africa," in E. Beumers & H-J. Koloss, *Kings of Africa* (Maastricht: Foundation Kings of Africa, 1992), 13–26.

4. These states needed to create an overall ideology for binding the enlarged kingdom into a nation. For the case of Asante, see T. C. McCaskie, "Inventing Asante," in P. F. de Moraes Farias & K. Barber, eds., *Self-Assertion and Brokerage: Early Cultural Nationalism in West Africa* (Birmingham: University of Birmingham Centre for West African Studies, 1990), 55–67.

5. The typical strategy would be to find local allies by using existing political divisions. A strategy also used by, for example, Cortez in challenging the mighty Aztec empire with his small army. See T. Todorov, *La conquête de l'Amérique; La question de l'autre* (Paris: Ed. du Seuil, 1982). A more basic cause of the decline of strong African states was the fact that the rapid development of armament in the nineteenth century took place outside Africa and thus constantly favored the Europeans and coastal African powers over inland states.

6. The Dutch followed only in 1863.

7. For the exceptional history of Sierra Leone, see Chr. Fyfe, *A History of Sierra Leone* (Oxford: Oxford University Press, 1962). See also P.E.H. Hair, "Africanism: The Freetown Contribution," *Journal of Modern African Studies* 5, no. 4 (1967): 521–539; R. W. July, *The Origins of Modern African Thought: Its Development in West Africa during the Nineteenth and Twentieth Centuries* (London: Faber & Faber, 1966), chapter 3; and A. Wyse, *The Krio of Sierra Leone: An Interpretative History* (London: C. Hurst & Co. 1989).

8. For more details see H. R. Lynch, *Edward Wilmot Blyden: Pan-Negro Patriot 1832–1912* (London: Oxford University Press, 1967), chapt. 1.

9. See Lynch, *Edward Wilmot Blyden*, chapt. 2 and 3.

10. Quote from Ayandele, "James Africanus Beale Horton," 692. Various definitions of "Creole" are used. Akintola Wyse, in *The Krio of Sierra Leone*, uses "born away from home." In Sierra Leone the term indicates the recaptives and their descendants. Elsewhere in West Africa they are known as Saros or Akus. See, for example, M. Dixon-Fyle, "The Saro in the Political Life of Early Port Harcourt, 1913–49," *Journal of African History* 30 (1989): 125–138.

11. Another example is the appointment of the first African bishop, Ajayi Crowther.

12. With the arrival of Edward Blyden in Sierra Leone the controversy between the Africans and the conservative church authorities was particularly heated. The controversy is beautifully described in H. R. Lynch, "The Native Pastorate Controversy and Cultural Ethno-centrism in Sierra Leone, 1871–1874," *Journal of African History* 5, no. 3 (1964): 395–413.

13. Richard Burton's *Wandering in West Africa* (1863) was very influential in propagating racism. One of the most impressive books on the development of the racist paradigm is P. D. Curtin, *The Image of Africa: British Ideas and Action, 1790–1850* (Madison: University of Wisconsin Press, 1964); see also P. D. Curtin, "'Scientific' Racism and the British Theory of Empire," *Journal of the Historical Society of Nigeria* 2, no. 1 (1960): 40–51.

14. Hair, "Africanism: The Freetown Contribution," 521, describes Africanism as "movements that seek the attainment of a government dominated by Africans and expressing in its institutions the characteristic spirit of Africa as interpreted by the modern African."

15. July, *The Origins of Modern African Thought* 229–302.

16. This curious event of a British parliamentary commission proposing self-government (and the government accepting the advice) resulted from conservatives (wanting to pull out of Africa) and humanitarians (sympathetic toward African self-rule) arriving at the same conclusion in this case. From a broader perspective, the event shows how completely different the political and intellectual situation was one decade later. Colonial occupation, in the way it actually happened, was hardly conceivable in the 1860s.

17. Horton, *West African Countries and Peoples* 74.

18. D. Kimble, *A Political History of Ghana: The Rise of Gold Coast Nationalism, 1850–1928* (Oxford: Clarendon Press, 1963), 159–160. Ironically, it was the humanitarian-oriented friend of the oppressed John Pope Hennesy who, as temporary British governor in West Africa, failed to support effectively the Fanti Federation and directed policies to suit the opposite agenda of making the coastal area into a colony. By 1872 the federation was already declining.

19. Race has not always been a major factor in British colonial relations. Sierra Leone has had an African West Indian governor, William Ferguson, and a chief justice, John Carr. The British historian Chr. Fyfe stated that the Sierra Leoneans: "did not feel themselves in a 'colonial situation' throughout most of the nineteenth century." Chr. Fyfe, *Africanus Horton, 1835–1883, West African Scientist and Patriot* (New York: Oxford University Press, 1972), 10. See also L. Mair, "New Elites in East and West Africa," in V. Turner, ed., *Colonialism in Africa, 1870–1960* (Cambridge: Cambridge University Press, 1971), 167–193, especially 183, on the changing relations between the educated elite and the chiefs.

20. See Fyfe, *Africanus Horton,* 52–55, and 115–118, on Horton's role in the Ashanti wars.

21. Samuel Lewis, African member of the Legislative Council, would be another good case. There is excellent historical work on Horton, D. Nicol, *Africanus Horton. The Dawn of Nationalism in Modern Africa* (London: Longman, 1969); Fyfe, *Africanus Horton*; R. W. July, "Africanus Horton and the Idea of Independence in West Africa," *Sierra Leone Studies,* new series, no. 18 (January 1966): 2–17; July, *The Origins of Modern African Thought,* chapt. 6; L. C. Gwam, "The Social and Political Ideas of Dr. James Africanus Beale Horton," *Ibadan* 19 (1964): 10–18.

22. Horton, *West African Countries and Peoples,* 60.

23. Quoted in Chr. Fyfe, *A History of Sierra Leone* (Oxford: Oxford University Press, 1962); idem, *Africanus Horton,* 9, from a Public Record Office from 1934.

24. E. A. Ayandele, "Introduction to the Second Edition," in Africanus B. Horton, *Letters on the Political Condition of the Gold Coast* (London: Frank Cass & Co., 1970), 6.

25. See Ayandele, "Introduction."

26. Horton, *West African Countries and Peoples,* 1.

27. Ibid., 67.

28. Ibid., 30.

29. Ibid., 30.

30. Ibid., 28.

31. Ibid., 274. Horton considered British Christian middle-class culture to be the most advanced for his time. But in different times others, for example, Africans, could supersede the British and set a new standard.

32. Horton, *West African Countries and Peoples*, vii.

33. Ibid., 6.

34. Ibid., iv.

35. Ibid., 29.

36. Horton even discussed such factors as the African way to carry children on the back: "the soft, yielding, underdeveloped tissues of the infant undergo various degrees of distortion, which ultimately form, after some generations, a permanent type." Horton, *West African Countries and Peoples*, vi. Horton held Lamarckian views on the formation of the genetic material by environmental factors (and thus even expected physical changes from the civilizational process). See July, *The Origins of Modern African Thought*, 5.

37. Horton, *West African Countries and Peoples*, 44–58.

38. Until the 1850s and Darwin's *Origin of Species*, the major dispute on race was between monogenesists and polygenesists. The former stressed that all humans are created in God's image, decendants of Adam and Eve and "of one blood"; the latter assumed natural distinctions between the races. The monogenesist argument was supported by enlightenment rationalism; also the Pope had spoken out clearly in the *Sublimus Dei* of 1637, after the expansion of the Spanish empire, that nonwhites were rational beings and potential Christians. Characteristically, monogenesism accepted the inferiority of African cultures and of most Africans, but denied this to be their natural or necessary state. Polygenesism received great impetus with nineteenth century scientific racism. See Curtin, *The Image of Africa*, and R. Hallett, "Theories of Race and Culture: 'The Negro's Place in Nature,'" in *Cambridge History of Africa V, 1790–1870* (Cambridge: Cambridge University Press, 1986), chpt. 13, 472–482.

39. Horton, *West African Countries and Peoples*, 20–57.

40. Ibid., 22–23.

41. J.A.B. Horton, *Letters on the Political Condition of the Gold Coast; Since the Exchange of Territory between the English and Dutch Governments, on January 1, 1868; together with a Short Account of the Ashanti War, 1862–4, and the Awoonah War, 1866* (London, 1870; reprint, London: Frank Cass, 1970), 152.

42. Horton, *West African Countries and Peoples*, 73.

43. Ibid., 99.

44. Unlike the common suggestion that Horton proposed a simple transplant of European institutions, he tailored his advice to the situation: "Constitutions are . . . productions that can neither be created nor transplanted; they are the growth of time." Horton, *West African Countries and Peoples*, 25.

45. In some cases, Horton even justified British violations of African sovereign rights: "It may produce displeasure amongst those who from 1842 had independent action, which has become a time-honoured custom to them . . . [but] it is only by these means that they can progress in their political history, and advance in civilization." Horton, *West African Countries and Peoples*, 32.

46. Shepperson's, Geiss's, and Davidson's reading of Horton lead to the conclusion that he basically represented imported ideas.

47. Ayandele, "James Africanus Beale Horton," 691.

48. Ayandele says of the West Africans: "[Their] ideas and hopes were determined essentially, quite exclusively, by the African milieu and the events on the continent. Hence the provincialism of Horton's *West African Countries and Peoples*." Ayandele, "James Africanus Beale Horton," 695.

49. For instance, in Horton, *Letters on the Political Condition of the Gold Coast*, 27; see also Ayandele, "Introduction," 26–27.

50. The political struggles expressed more than only educated elite concerns. The Fanti Federation, which Horton defended, is generally seen as a key event in African history.

51. See, for example, the interesting collection: P. F. de Moraes Farias & K. Barber, eds., *Self-Assertion and Brokerage: Early Cultural Nationalism in West Africa* (Birmingham: University of Birmingham Centre for West African Studies).

52. See chapter 2 on methodology.

53. Speaking in terms of the "social roots of ideas" may not be correct when it concerns the Krio. Horton's views are as much an expression of the collective experiences of that group as a contribution to the constitution of that group.

54. Horton, *West African Countries and Peoples*, 25–26.

55. As discussed in chapter 2, the methodological conjecture of this study is that an exemplar in political thought is a nodal point in two respects. First, it embodies, in a nutshell, the "disciplinary matrix" (Kuhn), the basic heuristic of a political conception. Second, it indicates the social roots, the key collective experiences that give political meaning to the ideas expressed (Skinner/Nauta). An exemplar, which is textual, thus refers to an exemplary situation or exemplary collective experience, a shared social drama.

56. Horton, *West African Countries and Peoples*, 25, 29, 59–60.

57. Ibid., 29, 59–61.

58. Ibid., 60.

59. Ayandele, "Introduction," 19.

60. It is interesting to note that Horton, the medical man, saw education mainly as instruction: infusing new elements into a receptive mind. Blyden, the man of letters who was also a great supporter of educational development, saw education basically as self-development: unfolding what is potentially already inside.

61. It cannot be excluded that had Horton lived longer he would, like his fellow Krios, have concluded that Africa had to do without the British help and that, consequently, he would have shown a more definite interest in African cultural traditions. In fact, very little is known about how Horton's views developed between 1873 and his death ten years later. The fact that the Ashantihene honored him with the "Title and Dignity of Prince" (letter of 1879, quoted in Fyfe, *Africanus Horton*, 133–134) indicates that he developed good contacts with Ashanti, which may have changed his views.

62. Fyfe, *Africanus Horton*, 156–159.

63. Horton, *West African Countries and Peoples*, 60.

64. Blyden, E. W., *Christianity, Islam and the Negro Race* (London: W. B. Whittingham & Co., 1887; reprint: Edinburgh University Press, 1967), 129.

65. See, for example, Lynch, *Edward Wilmot Blyden*, chapt. 2.

66. Compare, for example, Hargreaves, J. D. "Blyden of Liberia," *History Today* 19 (1969): 568–578, and I. Geiss, *Panafrikanismus. Zur Geschichte der Dekolonisation* (Frankfurt am Mein: Europeische Verlagsanstalt, 1968), to Ayandele, "James Africanus Beale Horton," in their comments on Blyden.

67. On Blyden, see H. R. Lynch, "E. W. Blyden: Pioneer West African Nationalist," *Journal of African History* 4, no. 3 (1963): 373–388; H. R. Lynch, *Edward Wilmot Blyden: Pan-Negro Patriot 1832-1912* (London: Oxford University Press, 1967); H. R. Lynch, ed., *Black Spokesman. Selected Published Writings of Edward Wilmot Blyden* (London: Frank Cass, 1971); H. R. Lynch, ed., *Selected Letters of Edward Wilmot Blyden* (New York: Kto Press, 1978); E. Holden, *Blyden of Liberia: An Account of the Life and Labours of Edward Wilmot Blyden, LL.D., as Recorded in Letters and in Print* (New York: Vantage Press, 1966); R. W. July, "Nineteenth Century Negritude: Edward Wilmot Blyden," *Journal of African History* 3, no. 1, (1964): 73–86; R. W. July, *The Origins of Modern African Thought*, chapt. 11; Hargreaves, "Blyden of Liberia"; P. O. Esedebe, "Edward Wilmot Blyden (1832–1912) as a Pan-African Theorist," *Sierra Leone Studies*, new series, no. 25 (July 1969): 14–23; V. Y. Mudimbe, *The Invention of Africa* (Bloomington: Indiana University Press, 1988), chapt. 4; M.J.C. Echeruo, "Edward W. Blyden, W.E.B. Du Bois, and the 'Color Complex,'" *The Journal of Modern African Studies* 30, no. 4 (1992): 669–684.

68. Lynch, *Edward Wilmot Blyden*, 29.

69. By then, African Americans had the new option of emigrating to the black republic of Haiti. Immigration to Liberia attained its height in the 1850s.

70. Lynch, "The Native Pastorate Controversy."

71. Lynch, *Edward Wilmot Blyden*, 128.

72. See Lynch, *Selected Letters of Edward Wilmot Blyden*, 9, and Geiss, *Panafrikanismus*, 127.

73. One of his key articles in this period is entitled "Ethiopia Stretching out Her Hands unto God." A magnificent piece, where Blyden argued that the Bible text "Ethiopia stretches out her hands" really should be read as "stretches out soon," thus announcing the new times for the black race. 'Negritia' is used in Blyden, *Christianity, Islam and the Negro Race*, 6.

74. Even the common notion of race is quite mistaken, see, for example, K. A. Appiah, *In My Fathers House, Africa in the Philosophy of Culture* (New York: Methuen, 1992), chapt. 2.

75. Blyden, "Africa and the Africans," quoted in G. A. Mosley, ed., *African Philosophy: Selected Readings* (Englewood Cliffs: Prentice Hall, 1995), 24.

76. The first quote is from a speech "Race and Study" given in Sierra Leone in 1895. Lynch, *Edward Wilmot Blyden*, chapt. 4. The second is from the opening speech for the Liberia College in 1881, "The Aims and Methods of Liberal Education for Africans." Blyden, *Christianity, Islam and the Negro Race*, 71–93.

77. Lynch, *Edward Wilmot Blyden*, 58–62 and chapt. 5.

78. Lynch, *Black Spokesman*, 207. Print of a letter to Booker T. Washington of November 28, 1894.

79. Blyden, *Christianity, Islam and the Negro Race*, 120.

80. Ibid., 504.

81. Lynch, *Edward Wilmot Blyden*, 71.

82. Mudimbe, *The Invention of Africa*, 127.

83. Blyden, *Christianity, Islam and the Negro Race*, 122.

84. Lynch, *Edward Wilmot Blyden*, chapt. 6. Blyden speaks of "genuine Negroes" and "half-casts."

85. An example of the biological interpretation of cultural matters is Blyden's severe critique of the Krio, or "Aku tribe," in a letter to the assistant undersecretary at the British Colonial Office in 1910. See Lynch, *Selected Letters of Edward Wilmot Blyden*, 498–502.

86. Blyden, *Christianity, Islam and the Negro Race*, 89, 90.

87. Lynch, *Edward Wilmot Blyden*, chapt. 4.

88. Ibid., chapt. 9.

89. Lynch argues that, especially after the Berlin Conference of 1885, Blyden stressed the need to preserve African culture and was supported by friends of Africa such as Mary Kingsley and the Africa Society. Lynch, *Edward Wilmot Blyden*, 200–210.

90. Especially Blyden's letters, published in collections by Lynch, *Selected Letters of Edward Wilmot Blyden*, show Blyden's views in his later life rather bluntly.

91. Langley, *Ideologies of Liberation*, 35, also stresses the importance of the book, quoting Lynch: "the greatest single effort at 'unfolding the African . . . through a study of the customs of his fathers.'"

92. Especially in the prominent *Fraser's Magazine*. See the list of Blyden's works at the end of Lynch, *Black Spokesman*.

93. Blyden, *Christianity, Islam and the Negro Race*, 121.

94. Ibid., 122, and Lynch, *Edward Wilmot Blyden*, 65.

95. J.E.C. Hayford, *Ethiopia Unbound. Studies in Race Emancipation* (1911; reprint, London: Frank Cass, 1969), 98.

96. The critique of the educated elite, whether justified by some anti-elitist political theory or by reference to cultural roots, is seldom convincing, if only because the critic himself is mostly very much part of this class.

97. Quoted in Kimble, *A Political History of Ghana*, 360.

98. An editorial of 22, March 1920 quoted by F. N. Ugonna, "Introduction to the Second Edition," in Hayford, *Ethiopia Unbound*, xv.

99. Kimble, *A Political History of Ghana*, 331. On the ARPS also see Kimble's chapter 9 and J. A. Langley, *Pan-Africanism and Nationalism in West Africa* (Oxford: Clarendon Press, 1973), chapts. 3 and 4

100. The Fanti Confederation was discussed in this chapter in the context of Horton. The ARPS emerged from the Mfantsi Amanbuhû Féku (the Fanti National Political Society).

101. Qquoted in Kimble, *A Political History of Ghana*, 348.

102. J. B. Danquah, "Introduction," 24–25, in M. J. Sampson, *Gold Coast Men of Affairs* (London, 1932; reprinted London: Dawson of Pall Mall).

103. Danquah adds a footnote here: "Hence the native name for foreign European Government is 'Aban,' i.e., Castle or fortification."

104. Danquah, "Introduction," 16–17.

105. July, *The Origins of Modern African Thought*, 435–436.

106. Modernization chaperoned by the "benevolent" British had proven to be mere subjugation.

107. The causes of this suppressed liberty were often not pursued using "deep" theories of imperialism or capitalism but were located in misplaced white superiority feeling and a failing colonial administration that contradicted "true imperialism." Practical political action, therefore, was directed at these apparent factors, rather than at the possible deeper causes.

108. J. E. Casely Hayford, quoted in Ugonna, "Introduction to the Second Edition," xxi.

109. J.E.C. Hayford, *Gold Coast Native Institutions. With thoughts upon a Healthy Imperial Policy for the Gold Coast and Ashanti* (1903; reprint, London: Frank Cass, 1970), 68.

110. J. W. de Graft Johnson, *Towards Nationhood in West Africa* (1928; reprint, London: Frank Cass, 1971), 107.

111. Hayford, *Ethiopia Unbound*, 8.

112. F. N. Ugonna, "Introduction to the Second Edition," xxii. Pages xxiii–xxvi give a very clear description of the idea of Ethiopianism; see also E. U. Essien-Udom, *Black Nationalism: The Search for Identity* (Chicago: University Press of Chicago, 1962).

113. Hayford, *Ethiopia Unbound*, 119.

114. The comparison with the Japanese case does not hold completely. In fact, Casely Hayford aimed at a status within the British empire, similar to that of Canada or Australia.

115. The renewed popularity of the word "Ethiopia" in Casely Hayford's time, which is in fact an archaic and mythical word for Africa, points directly to Ethiopia's historical victory over the Italians, which is often (probably incorrectly) seen as the first time a colonial army was beaten by an African army.

116. Danquah, "Introduction," 13–14. On the comparison with Japan, see also J. Mensah Sarbah, *Fanti National Institutions* (1906; reprint, London: Frank Cass, 1968), 237–256, and B. Davidson, *The Black Man's Burden: Africa and the Curse of the Nation-State* (New York: Times Books, 1992), 40.

117. Hayford, *Ethiopia Unbound*, 130–131. De Graft Johnson expressed his Pan-West-African vision thus: "With progress in Native institutions, Education and Wealth, the citizens of these territories, the land of radiant energy and sunshine, would be welded into one federal unit, each colony retaining its individual local autonomy but joining together in one unbroken chain of glory!" in his *Towards Nationhood*, 127.

118. Danquah, "Introduction," 17.

119. Ibid., 21, explains: "the 'historical school' (i.e. those who swear by none but 'the Bond of 1844')."

120. Ibid., 20.

121. Kimble, *A Political History of Ghana*, 358.

122. Atto Ahuma, *The Gold Coast Nation and National Consciousness* (Liverpool: Marples, 1911; reprint, London: Frank Cass, 1971), 1.

123. Ahuma in *The Gold Coast Chronicle*, January 4, 1892, quoted in Kimble, *A Political History of Ghana*, 331.

124. Ahuma, *The Gold Coast Nation*, 2.

125. De Graft Johnson, *Towards Nationhood*, especially chapt. 16.

126. Historical details of political movements and thinkers in this period are represented excellently in, for example, July, *The Origins of Modern African Thought*; Langley, *Pan-Africanism and Nationalism in West Africa*; Geiss, *Panafrikanismus*, G. Padmore, *The Gold Coast Revolution: The Struggle of an African People from Slavery to Freedom* (London: Dobson, 1953).

127. Of course similar options have been advanced in the twentieth century but only in an indirect way, as "an inspiration for" a new African society, never again with the realism and self-confidence derived from a situation where such options could still be part of a political program.

4

From "Unbound Africa" to "New Africa": African Political Discourses under Colonial Rule

> We must rid ourselves of the habit, now that we are in the thick of the fight, of minimizing the action of our fathers of feigning incomprehension when considering their silence and passivity. They fought as well as they could, with the arms that they possessed then; and if the echoes of their struggle have not resounded in the international arena, we must realize that the reason for this silence lies less in their lack of heroism than in the fundamentally different international situation of our time.[1]
>
> *Frantz Fanon*

The common view of African political thought perceives postwar developments, in particular the 1945 Pan-African Congress in Manchester, as signifying the beginning of modern nationalist opposition in Africa.[2] As a result of this conference, an effective partnership evolved between Nkrumah, Padmore, and a number of young nationalists in the West African Secretariat. Within a year, Jomo Kenyatta was back in Kenya as the leader of the Kikuyu Central Association. A year later, Nkrumah was back again in the Gold Coast (now Ghana), organizing the mass political action that led to Ghana's early independence in 1956. The African nationalist movement had taken off.

If the present book would follow this common view, it would omit nationalism's colonial prehistory and proceed from the year 1945. The idea of a prehistory of nationalism should be rejected, however. It betrays an anachronistic perspective that treats categories of a later period, which are assumed to embody the full idea of what nationalism "really" is, as a yardstick for assessing thought in an earlier period. In contrast, I attempt to understand political thought through its various specific historical discourses, deciphering their particular conceptions of liberation and reconstructing the options for political action within their particular historical context.

The task of reconstructing the major political discourses in the time of colonial rule is not an easy one. On the one hand, all intellectuals seem to share a basic concern for gaining self-government.[3] On the other hand, one finds large contrasts among the relevant political texts, which indicate important differences at the level of discourses as well.

My attempt at tracing a basic order in African political thought in the colonial era is assisted greatly by a striking preliminary observation. If one simply looks at the literary form of texts, typical resemblances and differences can be shown, suggesting that there are families of texts. Such typical differences can be illustrated by three influential books that appeared around the same time, 1937–1938: Kenyatta's *Facing Mount Kenya*, which is an academic ethnographic work; Azikiwe's literary *Renascent Africa*, which reads like a political manifesto; and, in contradistinction, Padmore's *Africa and World Peace*, which is an exercise in political analysis. I propose to begin my "mapping" of political thought in the colonial era through its main families of texts. In the next phase, I will use their specific role in political movements to identify key political discourses in the colonial period.

Before proceeding, however, let me first give a very general sketch of relevant historical events in the first half of this century.

THE HISTORICAL CONTEXT, 1900–1950

Actual colonial rule was well established in most of Africa around the turn of the century. African political opposition, in the form of trade unions and political movements, mounted after World War I. They were animated, among other factors, by the experiences of soldiers, especially those from Francophone Africa, and by U.S. president Wilson's declaration of the right to self-determination. In South Africa, the African National Congress and the I.C.U. (Industrial and Commercial Union) of Clements Kadalie were established, in Kenya the East African Association, in West Africa the National Congress for British West Africa (NCBWA), and in the United States Marcus Garvey's battle cry of "Africa for the Africans" was first heard.

In the first half of the 1930s, political assertiveness subsided to an all-time low before the proliferation of the nationalist agitation of youth movements and cultural associations in the 1940s began.[4] A number of these African movements will be discussed in more detail below.

Important developments took place outside Africa. Beginning in 1900, a number of Pan-African Congresses were organized by American and Caribbean black leaders, such as Silvester Williams and the prominent Pan-African organizer W.E.B. Du Bois.[5] Exerting greater influence in Africa, Marcus Aurelius Garvey was the flamboyant and inspired agitator from Jamaica, who brought together a massive but short-lived movement for African liberation based in New York. He rallied for a return to Africa and for the establishment of the "United States of Africa" of which he himself was elected provisional president. In 1914 he founded the Universal Negro Improvement Society (UNIA) with many branches, including some in African countries. Practical projects, such as an African church, a newspaper, armed forces, and a shipping company, the Black Star Line, were meant to be self-help enterprises for the black race, but they were short lived. Garvey's romantic and magnificent schemes, however, expressed many (Pan-)African ambitions and dreams, and give his name a mythical ring even today.[6]

Another American influence on African political thought materialized through the university studies in the United States of a number of later prominent Africans, such as Sol Plaatje and John Dube from South Africa, John Chilembwe from Nyasaland, and J.E.K Aggrey, Nnamdi Azikiwe, and Kwame Nkrumah from West Africa.[7] These studies contributed to a "commerce of ideas" across the ocean and some influx of Pan-African ideas into Africa.[8]

Radical ideas were also evolving among Africans in Paris and, to some degree, in London. African soldiers who fought for the French in World War I and experienced the limits of French assimilation politics established the Ligue Universelle pour la Défense de la Race Nègre and a number of other organizations and journals. In Paris, Pan-Negroist and communist influences were involved.[9] For instance, Tovalou Houénou cooperated with Garvey's UNIA, while Lamine Senghor and Tiémoho Garan Kouyaté were communist anti-imperialists. In Britain, the West African Students Union (WASU), hosting generations of Africans in its hostel, propagated its mission of "self-help, unity, and cooperation," whereas George Padmore's home, equally formative for the African intelligentsia, bred anti-imperialist radicalism.

The political ideas under study should be perceived in the light of this complicated historical background. In the first place, the situation was marked by a geographical separation: developments inside Africa and in the diaspora communities in the metropoles primarily evolved separately from each other. In the second place, there was a changing political cycle, with mounting political activity in two periods: after World War I and in the 1940s.

ETHNOGRAPHIC TEXTS AND THE DISCOURSES OF THE CULTURAL ASSOCIATIONS

I propose to map political thought via its main families of texts. A first example of such a family are works that are concerned with the description of indigenous African political and cultural systems. Examples of this ethnographic type of texts are some of the outstanding works of this century, such as Casely Hayford's *Gold Coast Native Institutions* (1903), John Mensah Sarbah's *Fanti National Constitution* (1906), Danquah's *Akan Laws and Customs* (1928), Kenyatta's *Facing Mount Kenya* (1938), A. K. Ajisafe's *Laws and Customs of the Yoruba People* (1924), and Busia's *The Position of the Chief in the Modern Political System of Ashanti* (1952).

The ethnographic type of texts resembles Blyden's *African Life and Customs* in striving to present a positive, sophisticated, and humanistic image of African traditions. Unlike Blyden's work, however, the ethnographic studies concern specific African cultures. They are detailed, empirical, and scholarly monographs, typically the products of the erudite members of the educated elite. Their authors remained closely related to the nobility of their people and aimed at countering colonial prejudice about African cultures.

Kenyatta's proud exposition of Gikuyu life, from cosmology to sexuality and political system, is an exemplary case. Although *Facing Mount Kenya* was written as a thesis during Kenyatta's anthropology studies in London under the famous anthropologist Malinowski, it also clearly served to boost the Kikuyu Central Association. The dedication of the book combines its cultural and political aims by stating: "To Moigoi and Wamboi and all the dispossessed youth of Africa: for perpetuation of communication with ancestral spirits through the fight for African Freedom, and in the firm faith that the dead, the living, and the unborn will unite to rebuild the destroyed shrines." In his introduction, Malinowski protested against occultism and superstition, but found the book "an excellent monograph on African life and custom."[10]

Following the format of this anthropological monograph genre, *Facing Mount Kenya* covers a range of aspects of Gikuyu life, such as kinship, land tenure, initiation, system of government, and religion, throughout its thirteen chapters. The description is detailed and very well informed, often impressing its readers with the civilized and sophisticated nature of Gikuyu culture and society. Despite its largely descriptive form of presentation, the text already signified a political statement, fundamentally contradicting colonial prejudice about African cultures. *Facing Mount Kenya* was simultaneously a vindication and a restatement of Gikuyu (African) identity, an academic anthropological monograph, and a political statement against colonial domination.

In order to reach an understanding of discourses, it is important to trace the specific political role of the texts. Two movements appear to be particularly relevant in the case of the ethnographic texts. The works of Sarbah and Casely Hayford had great political significance in the African Rights Protection Society (ARPS) during the early years of this century. The role of their works was, as explained in the previous chapter, to formulate a concrete indigenous alternative to the imposed colonial order. More than three decades later ethnographical accounts acquired a new relevance, this time in the context of the "tribal" cultural associations that were emerging as nationalist forces from the end of the 1920s onward. A wide array of African interest groups, professional groups, and associations that "were training grounds for the new nationalist elite" emerged in these decades.[11] The Kikuyu Central Association is a good example of such a movement.

The typical political role of the ethnographic texts was the reaffirmation of indigenous structures in struggles against the encroachment of colonial authority or of capitalist settler economies. This was the case with the works by the ARPS intellectuals in opposition to the Gold Coast land laws, with Danquah's support for the Akim Abuakwa authorities, as well as with Kenyatta's *Facing Mount Kenya* and the Gikuyu struggle against evictions by white settlers.

Apart from a political role, the ethnographic texts also shared a similar view on culture, history, and politics. According to this view of history, colonialism struck at the heart of African societies by creating a rupture within the indigenous cultural heritage. One of the results of this dramatic breach was a breakdown of indigenous institutions. In particular, the institutions relating to the distribution and use of land were considered central because the issue of land is strongly connected to the ensemble of indigenous institutions.[12] A political view suggests itself here, namely, that the rebuilding of African societies should proceed from a revival of indigenous political traditions and an involvement of traditional authorities, such as chiefs and tribal councils.[13]

The Discourses of the Cultural Associations

The ethnographic texts, thus, tend to embrace a body of ideas and to serve similar political movements. They indicate a particular type of political discourse, which can be called neotraditionalist. Let me examine this type of discourse.

Neotraditionalism harbors an interesting contradiction. It includes, on the one hand, the claim to represent what is truly "African" while, on the other hand, it formulates this representation in a universe of discourse derived from another, namely "Western,"' tradition. The ethnographic studies confirmed the identity of a people by redefining it in new concepts and oppositions. The dominant European discourse provided writers discussing Africa with a ground plan of basic oppositions, such as primitive versus modern, reason versus emotion, European versus African. It also provided the cornerstones of a vocabulary for African self-description with notions such as "chief," "tribe," and "nation" (with all the connotation that nineteenth-century European nationalism invested that term). It even provided an accepted format of social scientific description, namely, the format of the ethnographic monograph with its typical model of depicting a culture as a complete and unhistorical structure. Paraphrasing J. B. Danquah, one could say that the ethnographic literature fitted a situation where "for weal or woe, what they could best do to foster the national cause and liberty was to work from within the basic framework of the colonial universe of discourse itself."[14]

In order to understand the actual dilemmas of neotraditional discourse in the colonial period, one has to note that, after the early days of the African

Rights Protection Society, neotraditionalism did not indicate a clear political alternative. In most cases, it was not an argument to actually give back power to the chiefs or to actually institute a Pan-African state. Remarkably, the aim of ethnographic description in Kenyatta's *Facing Mount Kenya* was not to outline a concrete indigenous alternative to Western modernity. Kenyatta simply sketched a counterimage of the Western version, proving the high standards of civilization maintained by the indigenous tradition and thereby claiming the right of Africans to take their destiny into their own hands. This destiny itself, however, was not described explicitly as an indigenous alternative to the model of the nation-state such as the ARPS alternative had been described three decades earlier. Rather, it was an argument for African control of the nation-state.

The changed political agenda of the neotraditionalist argument indicates an inherent problem. On the one hand, neotraditionalism stressed the cultural, tradition-based nature of societies. It upheld the idea that society involves a substantial and not simply a formal or juridical bond between people, forging them into communities and binding the community and the state. On the other hand, the political units that were actually getting shaped in the colonial period were multi-ethnic and thus precisely not of that "substantial" nature. Between the level of the tribal community with a clear (or at least reinvented) identity and history, and the level of the black race as a whole (for which a shared identity was assumed), the political unit of the national state was materializing.[15] This state, being a multi-ethnic political unit, could not be conceptualized easily in a neotraditional mode of thought.

This inherent predicament for neotraditionalist discourses on applying a community-oriented idea of politics to a multicommunity national state resulted in a variety of views on the issue of the political order of the modern African state. In many cases the neotraditionalist expositions simply did not touch directly on the question of political order. The ethnographic works, then, only reaffirmed the existence of indigenous traditions that should inspire and guide Africans, but where it would guide them was not explicated. There were a few ways, however, in which the issue of the nation-state was in fact addressed: 1. by regarding the new nation as a kind of tribe; 2. by reinterpreting traditional political institutions as fit for the new state; 3. by introducing the idea of a federal state.[16]

1. In actual history many of the tribal cultural associations transformed themselves into national independence parties. The neotraditionalist argument returned in a generalized form after independence in the intellectual schemes of the "national ideological philosophies" of the new states. It gave the ruling party, or the African Socialist policy orientation, a quasi ethnographical justification. This position will be discussed in the next chapter.

2. De Graft Johnson's *Towards Nationhood in West Africa* (1928) advanced the interesting view that indigenous political institutions already

involved a kind of parliamentary system that could also fit the modern state. The key to De Graft Johnson's analysis is the so-called linguist in the traditional system. He suggested that in the African system the executive and the legislative branches were in fact separate. The chiefs were the executive, each with their own council and area of rule, with town councils at the local level. The highest authority was the Omanhin, with the title "His serene highness" or "Nana." His council, the House of Chiefs, De Graft Johnson maintained, was something equivalent to the British House of Lords but, unlike the British Lords, the chiefs were direct representatives of their people, elected by and accountable to them.

As De Graft Johnson explains, the legislators, the "Begwafu," were a separate category. The highest chiefs council, the Oman Council, would only choose their representative in the legislature. The Begwafu would each have a provincial legislative council as his constituency or be elected by proportional representation.[17]

In that system, the linguist would be the equivalent of a premier in a Western political system.[18] Appointed by the legislative council, he would be the practical head of the executive committee, which functions as cabinet or government. De Graft Johnson suggested that this system could be instituted step by step, reestablishing the indigenous system while simultaneously reinstating African self-rule.

3. In the case of Chief Obafemi Awolowo's neotraditionalism, ethnographic evidence served as an argument for a federal state. His *Path to Nigerian Freedom* gave detailed suggestions on how a democratic federal state in Nigeria should function. Nigeria, he maintained, consists of various nations, each with its own political tradition. Since "strictly speaking, the political structure of any particular national group is primarily their own domestic concern," each could have its own Regional House of Assembly, which altogether constitute the "United States of Nigeria."[19] The British influence had turned the chief system into an authoritarian one, therefore, "the Government must plan resolutely for the democratization of every Native authority" so that councilors and chiefs are elected and can be dispossessed.[20] The solution to ethnic diversity within one state should be local self-government intelligently integrated into a federal structure that takes care of a number of functions, such as the judiciary.

Awolowo also organized his views on African cultural traditions into an argument for democratic institutions: "The family unit . . . is the basic unit of our analysis. . . . But it must be borne in mind in this connection that the inherent, instinctive, and spontaneous love which members of the same family have towards each other, is non-existent among members of different families which constitute the state."[21] The social arrangements within the state must therefore be different from those in the family, while retaining the basic liberties. "When two or more families amalgamate, they will, under normal circumstances, want to retain as many of the rights and liberties which they enjoyed in their respective families."[22] This means that "as in the family then, so in the State . . . sovereignty belongs to the entire people." Such sovereignty at the state level, however, cannot build on "the spontaneous affection and transparent selflessness of a *pater familias vis-à-vis* his family."[23] Therefore, mechanisms for control and correction are necessary and, Awolowo argues, there need to be similar democratic institutions and liberties to those developed in the West. After all, there is nothing basically un-African about these mechanisms since they "automatically spring from the rights which a man enjoys in any given family."[24]

MANIFESTO TEXTS AND THE DISCOURSES OF THE YOUTH MOVEMENTS

The ethnographic texts, as I argued in the preceding section, indicated the way to a particular neotraditionalist type of discourse in colonial Africa. Apart from the ethnographic texts, African political endeavor in the colonial period produced a second family of texts, namely, peculiar literary political documents such as Casely Hayford's *Ethiopia Unbound* (1911), Azikiwe's *Renascent Africa* (1937), and Orizu's *Without Bitterness* (1944). These radical and personal expressions of the "angry young men" of the educated class, full of enchanting oratory, hymns, and summons, were probably the most influential political texts in the period.

This second family, which I will call the "manifesto-type" of texts, is characterized by a blend of literary styles, personal outpourings, and subtle argumentation, concurring to make a text that could only but inspire its reader. Casely Hayford's *Ethiopia Unbound, Studies in Race Emancipation*, already mentioned in the previous chapter, is probably the first example of this attractive form of political manifesto.[25] There is wit, serious reflection, and engaging oratory throughout the text, providing a subtle analysis of the colonial situation, a vision of the future, as well as an appeal to his contemporaries to remain self-confident and not to commit "national suicide." Through the main character, the bright and politically active hero Kwamankra, the reader gets an insight into Hayford's personal feelings and reflections as a young African in Britain around 1900. Hayford then recounts Kwamankra's experiences back in West Africa with paternalist and perverse colonial and missionary officials as well as with his Christianized and alienated former African friends. As a middle-aged man, Kwamankra appears, answering the questions of his young son, and providing reflections on the global political situation, racial oppositions, and colonialism.

Casely Hayford's text subtly but thoroughly undermined any justification for the existing colonial system. The message, skillfully conveyed in all parts of the narrative, inverted the colonial ideology by expounding that the now strangled and frustrated African social system and culture was in fact superior to what was imported: more humane, more civilized, and perfectly able to renovate itself in order to adjust to modern conditions. Most important, however, it represented the cherished African way that forestalls "national and racial death."

The most influential political manifesto after *Ethiopia Unbound* was Nnamdi Azikiwe's *Renascent Africa* published in 1937. This "gospel of the New Africa" embodies all the vigor and rhetorical sophistication that this type of political literature can achieve. The book radiates energy and inspiration. It alternates paragraphs of a more analytical nature, mostly polemical, with paragraphs that read like a modern sermon, being rhythmic and imaginative. *Renascent Africa* is full of tickling rhetorical inventions. The title of one paragraph reads "Blessed are the Strong" and another reads "ROME BURNS" with the subtitle "*And Nero Fiddles*"; the section then discusses the indolence of the Colonial Office. Nana Ofori Atta, the famous Omanhene (Paramount chief) of Akim Abuakwa state in the Gold Coast, is castigated in a section called "A Knighted African," and a paragraph discussing various contemporary justifications for imperialism is titled "The Ethics of Force." Here Rudyard Kipling's idea of "the white man's burden" is analyzed as a variant of "aggressive altruism" and "a vindication of the philosophy of force."[26]

The political role of the second family of texts, the political manifestos, has been quite different from the ethnographic texts. Historically, the manifesto literature attained great significance in two episodes. The first can be seen in the upswing toward activism after World War I, with President Wilson's affirmation of the right to self-determination. Here we have Casely Hayford's *Ethiopia Unbound*.[27] The second is apparent in the move toward the youth radicalism of the 1940s, mainly in Nigeria. Here we have Azikiwe's *Renascent Africa* and, later, Orizu's *Without Bitterness*. In all three cases the text actually preceded the movement. Old Blyden may have been right when he called *Ethiopia Unbound* "an inspiration" after reading the book a year before his death.

The manifesto played its most important role in the Nigerian youth movements. These were initiated by some "Nigerians" after returning from their studies in the United States, most prominently Nnamdi Azikiwe, H. O. Davies, and Eyo Ita.[28] Nnamdi Azikiwe (pronounced "Azikwe") became the leading figure: "To the outside world 'Zikism' and African nationalism appeared to be synonymous."[29] Azikiwe was the son of an Ibo clerk in the Nigerian Regiment, who had been stationed in various parts of the Nigerian territory, far away from his tribal community. Azikiwe went to the United States where he studied and taught at various segregated universities in the South, experiencing the atmosphere of discrimination and the upsurge of radical Negro resistance. On returning to West Africa, his primary concern was, therefore, not a territorial, nationalist struggle, but a universal, worldwide struggle for the black race. As editor of the *African Morning Post* in Accra, from 1935 to 1937, Azikiwe immediately established a reputation because of his direct American-style journalism and bold criticism of the colonial system—of colonial officials as well as local African leaders, whom he called "Uncle Toms" and "hat-in-hand-me-too-boss political scavengers." In castigating these leaders, he exclaimed: "is there any wonder then that in a country of twenty-one million souls less than six thousand non-Africans seem destined to guide and control them for ever?"[30]

Back in Lagos, Azikiwe started his daily newspaper *West African Pilot* where "his combative and provocative journalism was the principal source of his fame and power, and the most crucial single precipitant of Nigerian awakening."[31] With much energy and commercial acumen he took his newspaper into the first venture with a countrywide network of local agents and even provincial dailies. National dimensions were thereby not only organizationally but also imaginatively constituted. People, separated by boundaries of distance, ethnicity, history, and religion, were countrywide connected as readers, thus constituting, in Benedict Anderson's terms, a national "imagined community" as "Nigerians," perceiving issues as problems of a national community.[32]

Between 1938 and 1941, this new radicalism found expression immediately in the spectacular rise of the Nigerian Youth Movement (NYM) into a Nigeria-wide organization, mainly aiming at "the unification of the tribes of Nigeria (and raising of) national consciousness." The NYM successfully contested the Lagos Town Council and the Legislative Council elections against Herbert Macaulay and the National Democratic Party.[33] It had immediate national impact by campaigning against a monopoly of European cocoa firms and for "complete autonomy within the British Empire . . . a position of equal partnership with other member States of the British Commonwealth . . . and complete independence in the local management of our affairs."[34] Youth radicalism flared up again with the emergence of the Zikist Movement (1946–1950). This movement was guided by Nwafor Orizu's book *Without Bitterness*, published two years before, which outlined the principles of the new universal philosophy of Zikism for the redemption of Africa.

The primary channel for the expression of political ideas in these decades was the press, but other forms of writing also played a role. For instance, Azikiwe's *Political Blueprint of Nigeria* published in 1943, intended to establish the agenda for the postwar policies and for "self-government within 17 years." Another important book in that period was Awolowo's *Path to Nigerian Freedom* (1947), which, in a much more conservative tone than the youth movements, tried to design a strategy for converting indirect rule into self-rule based upon reorganized and democratized traditional political structures.

Political developments in Nigeria during the 1940s were very complicated.

The National Congress for Nigeria and the Cameroons (NCNC) under Azikiwe was the largest party. It was also a cross-tribal party, while Chief Obafemi Awolowo's Yoruba-oriented Action Group and the Northern Emirs represented other factors of power. Developments moved slowly into the direction of federalism. In Ghana, where a single party attained prominence, the anticolonial forces harnessed much more power so that, in the 1950s, Ghana became the pacemaker of decolonization.[35]

The Discourses of the Youth Movements

The manifesto type of texts played a prominent political role in the Nigerian youth movements. They formulated, what can be termed, "the discourses of the youth movements." Let me try to outline the basic characteristics of this type of discourse.

To begin with, the discourses of the youth movements indicated an important shift in the aims of liberation. The very image of the African future that the nationalist struggle entailed, the idea of Africa, changed completely between the ARPS discourse around the turn of the century (until *Ethiopia Unbound* in 1911) and the manifesto literature, especially *Renascent Africa* and *Without Bitterness* in 1937 and 1944 respectively. Initially, with the ARPS, the Africa that had to be "unchained" consisted of the concrete cultural and institutional heritages of different peoples. Unchaining this Africa involved the practical task of renovating these heritages to provide effective forms of social organization in the new, global, modern context. In 1919, with the NCBWA as a modern African political organization, the ties to the concrete African traditions became more distant, and, in practical politics, educated elites and chiefs became competitors.[36] With Azikiwe (1937), finally, the reference to concrete African traditions even became negative. Azikiwe affirmed that Africa had a glorious past, but he maintained that the concrete traditions represented stagnation and tribalism, that they were part of "Old Africa." Africa's future would involve a new start: "the disciple of the New Africa must hurdle over the barriers of race and tribe . . . so that truth may be allowed a chance to flourish on the earth."[37]

What then was Zik's long-term nationalist agenda? What had to be "reborn" according to *Renascent Africa* if not the concrete cultural and political arrangements of Africa? The answer was that the New Africa to be created was not defined by its roots but by its authors, the Young Africans. The connection between old age, wisdom, and position of rule was discarded. African identity should not be confused with a precept to turn toward tradition: "if the New Africa must be realized, then the Old Africa must be destroyed because it is at death-grips with New Africa."[38] Zik's conscious break with tradition corresponded to a break with the traditional, natural rulers as a political group. His Nigerian Youth Movement was the first multi-ethnic political mass movement in Nigeria. Azikiwe praised his own press company workshops as "laboratories of inter-tribal fellowship" since people of all tribes and backgrounds worked together.[39]

The shift in orientation from African heritages to a New Africa correlated with different political programs. In the first idea, modernization of tradition, the issue essentially was to rearrange indigenous political institutions, to value the autonomy of local communities, and to aim at a federal, rather than a centralized, state. The second idea, of a New Africa, was universalist.[40] Africa should acquire not only science and technology, as universal aspects of human progress, but also the universal systems of rights and liberties, including the necessary political and social institutions, such as the national state, elections, parliaments, and the *Trias Politica*.[41]

The discourses of the youth movements, as articulated by the manifesto literature, thus represented a transition toward a more standard political conception oriented to the nation-state. They were typically connected to the political practice of the nontribal organizations, such as the National Congress of British West Africa (NCBWA), the West African Student Union (WASU), the National Youth Movement (NYM), and the Zikist Movement in Nigeria. They also tended to involve conflicts with neotraditionalists and traditional rulers regarding who, the "natural rulers" or the politicians, could really represent the people and which kind of state should be erected, a federal or a unitary state. The famous debates between Chief Atta Ofori and Casely Hayford in the Gold Coast Legislative Council in the 1920s, between Azikiwe and Awolowo in the 1940s, as well as between Danquah and Nkrumah in the 1950s, are examples of such conflicts, which constituted a major front of political battle in the transition period to independence.

A second key aspect of the discourses of the youth movements was their topographical location—typically, it was radical nationalism in specifically African rather than in metropolitan situations. The totality of the colonial situation was a conditioning factor. The youth radicalism had to adjust to the restrictions in political activity imposed by the colonial government. The political activity involved struggles over particular policies of the local colonial administration and opposition against a specific governor or against representatives of the "lost generation" of colonial African elites.[42] The colonial system as such, at least in the prewar situation, was all-powerful and was not directly opposed from within the colonies.[43]

Political activity within Africa had to be politics within the system, thus conditioning its form. Opposition politics, even when rejecting the system as such, meant putting forward demands within its channels and institutions. Africans had to form "modern" political organizations and movements (NCBWA, ANC, NYM) to frame effective political action or participate in colonial representative institutions. Even where chiefs continued to rule, they operated within a new colonial framework, transforming and perverting the traditional system of chief councils. To the extent that some liberty of expression was allowed, journalism was an important avenue of political opposition: "in this century, there is no better means to arouse African peoples than that of the power of the pen and the tongue. . . . The Press is the avenue. Schools are also important, but the Press is a much wider and more potent avenue for this particular mission. And the pen is mightier than the sword . . . any direct attack, at the present, [is] suicidal."[44]

The confines of the colonial situation were also experienced in the language of the discourses.[45] Demands were formulated in terms of self-government (of nation-states), employing a vocabulary of rights, liberties, and political principles borrowed from European political thought.[46] Azikiwe's *Renascent Africa*, for example, was a direct attack on the justifications for colonialism but used the vocabulary of its British opponents. Moral obligations, natural rights, Christian values, democratic principles, and the Covenant of the League of Nations were harnessed. Azikiwe put forward a so-called immanent critique of the West, criticizing the system according to its own principles. This may be an important reason why the manifesto literature appears quite old-fashioned to the present-day reader.[47] The teachings of the "Gospel of the New Africa" to the "Renascent African" often read like Christian sermons with modified words. The "Beatitude of Youth," for instance, offers not less than twenty-three stanzas on "Blessed are the youth," such as "Blessed are the evangelists of the New Africa, who go from place to place, debating with the Scribes and Pharisees and Sadducees of the Old Africa, for they lay the foundations for a new social order which is intangible and immutable and inevitable."[48]

Old-fashioned as this may sound, within the situation of colonial opposition politics, it was probably the only effective language to use. Important tasks of the critics were to undermine colonial ideology, unmask the hypocrisy of rulers, appeal to the principles of European nations themselves, raise pride among Africans, and foster unity and hope within the younger generation. Azikiwe was aware of possible historical "causes" of colonialism and he referred to Marx and Engels, but that knowledge could not help him very much in colonial circumstances.[49] Paradoxically, one could conclude that the nationalists in the colonies shared a practical view of the forces governing the imperialist system as well as of their own position of weakness. Therefore they had to build their optimism mainly upon "softer" forces in history, such as their own self-consciousness and appeals to the moral, legal, and political principles of the colonizer. With the growing importance of international law, through the League of Nations declaration, the Atlantic Charter, and the UN declaration, appeal to principles became important resources for stating the African nationalist case.

The various aspects of the discourses of the youth movements discussed here can also shed light on the particular literary form of the manifesto literature. Physically situated in the colonized territories, politically oppositional, while relying on liberal democratic ideas, the manifesto texts emerged in a unique situation. Unlike the literature of ethnography and of political analysis, ready-made literary examples were not available, which meant that the vehicles of expression had to be invented. The literary form that appeared, the manifesto literature, was a new and rich amalgam that borrowed stylistic elements from oratory and poetic, and religious sources.

POLITICAL ANALYSES AND THE DISCOURSES OF THE LEAGUES

A third distinct type of political literature in the colonial period was the explicitly political treatise, exemplified by Sol Plaatje's *Native Life in South Africa* (1916), Padmore's works, from *Africa and World Peace* (1937) to *Pan-Africanism or Communism* (1956), and Nkrumah's *Towards Colonial Freedom* (1948).

I propose to call these works the "political analysis type" of texts.[50] As political in terms of inspiration as the manifestos, these texts are of a quite different kind. Here the colonial system as such is challenged. Padmore especially provided crystal clear analyses of Africa in world politics, the moving forces of imperialism, and the political and diplomatic opportunism and deceit in dealing with Africa. On entering into Padmore's universe of discourse, it is immediately clear that colonialism and the oppression of colored peoples everywhere is nothing but exploitation masked by an ideology in terms of "civilization" and "trustee-ship." From this point of view, there is hardly need to argue against colonial ideology since colonialism just needs to be explained scientifically and eliminated politically. Nkrumah, who collaborated closely with Padmore during the mid-1940s, wrote in his work *Towards Colonial Freedom* (1947):

The existence of the colonial peoples under imperialist rule means their economic and political exploitation. . . . In attempting to legitimize their presence they claim to be improving the welfare of the native population. Such claims are merely a camouflage for their real purpose of exploitation to which they are driven by economic necessity. . . . Colonial powers can not afford to expropriate themselves. And then to imagine that these colonial powers will hand freedom and independence to their colonies on a silver platter without compulsion is the height of folly.[51]

Probably because of its disengagement from colonial discourse, the political analysis texts read much like present-day works.[52]

The political analysis texts served a different set of political movements than to the ethnographic and manifesto texts. Their audiences were the anti-imperialist leagues and associations of Africans in the metropolitan centers.

In Paris, a radical anti-imperialist analysis of the colonial situation developed relatively early.[53] Radicalization occurred following the failed strategy of conservative African *délegués* in the French Parliament, primarily Blaise Diagne, to achieve full assimilation rights in France by promoting the massive participation of African soldiers in World War I.[54] The Ligue Universelle pour la Défense de la Race Nègre (after 1926 CDRN and from 1927 to 1937 LDRN) was founded in 1924 by Tovalou Houénou and was active in Paris, Senegal, and Dahomey.[55] Whereas Houénou was a Pan-Negroist who was involved in Marcus Garvey's UNIA and who promoted the establishment of a Negro African state, the later chief organizers, such as the Senegalese Lamine Senghor, and the Malinese Tiémoho Garang Kouyaté, were communists who had good contacts with the international League Against Imperialism and with Padmore in England as well as Du Bois in the United States.[56] Pan-Negroist and anti-imperialist ideas were combined. The LDRN stated:

The aim of our Ligue is the political, economic, moral and intellectual emancipation of the whole Negro race. It is a matter of winning back, by all honourable means, the national independence of the Negro peoples of the colonial territories . . . and setting up in Black Africa a great Negro State. . . . We think that the reason why our race suffers so much is that it is dominated, above all politically, by the other races.[57]

Anti-imperialism could thus serve racial liberation. Afrocentric ideas were also included:

The return to the customs, philosophy and social organization of our ancestors is a vital necessity. . . . We are the brotherhood standing against the fierce individualism of the westerners. We represent variety, as against white uniformity, which generates boredom. We have created artistic, peasant civilizations. . . . We demand a single Negro State.[58]

The Francophone metropolitan movements were supported by radical journals, such as *Les Continents* and *La Voix des Nègres* (later *La Race Nègre*). The major intellectual products of this period, however, concerned the field of culture not politics. It was the literary works of Négritude that left their imprints in the sediment of intellectual history, rather than the pamphlets of the activists. African oppositional activities in Paris were more radical than their London or African counterparts, yet their final result has been equally limited. The colonial powers were unwilling to discuss the colonial system as such and apparently could endure some metropolitan political opposition.[59]

In London, the main factor in activating African nationalism was the Italian fascist aggression against Ethiopia and the half-hearted reaction of the European powers. It proved that white European powers joined forces when the oppression of blacks was concerned and that the brute force of imperialism still ruled the world: "Force, the white man's god, is again supreme. Addis Ababa is occupied. . . . Poison gas, British oil, and the white man's duplicity all combined."[60] In 1934, the International African Friends of Abyssinia was formed. It became the International African Service Bureau in 1937 and the Pan-African Federation in 1944. Participants such as George Padmore, C.L.R. James, Sam Manning, Jomo Kenyatta, and the Sierra Leonian activist I.T.A. Wallace-Johnson were to play a prominent role in African and black politics in the following decades. This group combined a practical activist orientation with a serious study of the colonial-imperialist system and Western political ideologies, thus producing some of the best political texts. Their Pan-African-ism was meant to be "an independent political expression of Negro aspirations for complete national independence from white domination—Capitalist or Communist," which supported a "programme of dynamic nationalism."[61]

World War II changed the context of nationalist struggles significantly.[62] The proud Atlantic Charter, formulated by the Allied Forces in 1941, affirmed "the right of all peoples to choose the form of government under which they will live." Churchill, however, was quick to state that he would "not preside over the liquidation of the British Empire." Colonial territories, Churchill said, could develop "along the lines of their own national aptitude, their own culture, and their own tradition" but "educational and economic development should precede political responsibility.[63]

The war, in which many Africans served the Allied Forces, provided them with contacts with nationalist colored peoples from other parts of the world and had an enormous consciousness-raising effect. As Ndabaningi Sithole remarked:

The English streetgirls of London, the French streetgirls of Paris, and the Italian streetgirls of Naples did not help to preserve the white myth. Drinking and woman-raping white soldiers added their contribution to its annihilation. . . . After spending four years hunting the white enemy soldiers the African never regarded them again as gods.[64]

Criticism of the colonial system mounted, especially among Africans and Americans, but also within the Labour party and pro-Africa groups such as the Fabians.[65] Du Bois did whatever he could to put Africa on the agenda whenever the postwar future of the world was discussed. One such occasion was at the United Nations Conference in San Francisco in April 1945 where a manifesto was presented that argued that the Atlantic Charter should apply to the colonial question and resulted in a condemnation of colonialism.[66] For the organizations of colonized peoples, the Atlantic Charter stated the principle that should be acted upon. The West African Students Union (WASU), for instance, demanded "Internal Self-Government Now" and a guarantee for complete self-government soon, requesting from the governor of Nigeria "a United Nigeria with a Federal Constitution based on a Swiss or United States model with necessary modifications."[67]

In 1944, several organizations formed the Pan-African Federation, which took up the initiative to organize a major Pan-African Congress in Manchester in 1945. Kwame Nkrumah from the Gold Coast, who had just arrived from the United States, participated actively in the organization. As part of the congress, he wrote the "Declaration to the Colonial Peoples," which affirmed "the rights of all people to govern themselves" and formulated the famous call, "colonial and subject peoples of the world, Unite!"[68]

After the conference, the West African National Secretariat (WANS) was established as a coordinating body of nationalist movements because "power politics suggests that the world is indeed a jungle, but the Lion is no longer King." It stated that "West Africa is one country: Peoples of West Africa Unite!"[69] Nkrumah was secretary-general and Wallace-Johnson was chairman. WANS opted for mass actions, strikes, and boycotts, which was a style of politics that would unavoidably clash with what they considered to be the "bourgeois nationalists," who had determined local African politics for half a century or more. WANS called for the formation of an interterritorial mass party, an All–West African National Congress, whose ultimate aim was a United States of Africa.[70] Nkrumah formed the revolutionary cell, The Circle, but left for Ghana in 1947 so that the locus of political activity moved from Britain to Africa.[71]

The 1950s saw the process of decolonization begin. Nkrumah's very effective opposition, first as organizer of the established party United Gold Coast Convention (UGCC) and from 1949 onwards in his Convention Peoples Party (CPP), resulted in an African-dominated government in the Gold Coast as early as 1951 and independence in 1956. Most other African countries, except the Portuguese territories and the settler societies such as Rhodesia and South Africa, were independent by the early 1960s.[72] The new situation implied a drastic change in the political agenda and a new phase in African political thought. Instead of the rather simple issue of political independence, a multitude of problems related to the new order appeared on the agenda, such as nation building, national unity, the role of opposition parties, and neocolonial relations.

The Discourses of the Leagues

The totality of the colonial system conditioned both the limited scope of political activity and the vocabulary with which ideas were formulated, preventing the creation of a complete political as well as an intellectual counterposition.[73] Neither the discourse of the cultural associations nor that of the youth movements could challenge the colonial system effectively. Within the discourse of metropolitan radicalism, the spell of colonial discourse was finally broken.

The metropolitan noncolonial discourse, however, had at least two preconditions. First, it necessitated a certain physical distance from colonial realities: it was a discourse on Africa from a position outside of Africa. Second, it involved a different universe of discourse altogether, namely, Marxism: here the basic elements of colonial discourse were absent so that there were no "races," "civilizing missions," "empires," "higher religions," "tutoring," and "white man's burden." As soon as the colonial problem was analyzed using the Marxist vocabulary of concepts such as "capitalism," "imperialism," and "exploitation," a view of the colonial system could be presented without taking recourse to the colonial terminology.

These two preconditions for a noncolonial discourse were connected. The new universe of discourse made sense in metropolitan politics, where the colonial system as such could be put on the political agenda, where there was a large margin of freedom, and where this critical counterdiscourse had currency in broad leftist circles. In the colonies themselves, this outlook made no sense until after the overthrow of the colonial system actually became possible. Such an option appeared after World War II, and it was also only then that the radical anti-imperialist discourse could be transferred to Africa, thereby making the radical discourse of the metropolitan splinter groups around Kouyaté and Padmore the dominant nationalist factor.

The vocabulary of metropolitan discourse in its Marxist variants constituted both a break from the basics of colonial discourse and from neotraditionalism as well. The discourse was, like Azikiwe's, based on the tradition-modernity dichotomy. Liberation involved the struggle against imperialism, as well as against feudalism. True liberation would be the attainment of a new stage in human history rather than a return to the past. In this discourse, the withering away of traditional authority was both historically inevitable and a necessary element of democratization. This deeply rooted modernism shaped by Marxist-inspired radicalism, created the curious situation in which the most radically populist discourses in the midcentury were also the most fundamentally antitraditional ones.[74] Both radical nationalist discourses (liberal Zikist and socialist Nkrumahist) result in a similar negative position concerning indigenous political institutions and, consequently, in a positive orientation toward the nation-state.

CONCLUSION

The discussion in this chapter brought out the basic rifts in the ideological landscape during the colonial period. These ran between a neotraditionalist idea of "Africa of the tribes," a radical modernist idea of "Young Africa" and a Marxist-modernist idea of "anti-imperialist Africa." Each of these discourses had political relevance, mainly in particular contexts of action. With some generalization, one could say that neotraditionalism was most important before the 1940s, liberal nationalism after 1940, and Marxist-inspired anti-imperialism after World War II. There were basic differences between discourses developed within Africa (neotraditional and liberal nationalist) and those outside Africa (Marxist, Pan-African), as well as between modernist (liberal and Marxist) and neotraditionalist orientations.

During the colonial period, the territories became "solidified" so that the colonial administrative units grew into political realities. Their solidity became such that the territories emerged as objects for national liberation struggles. This placed the issue of the national state on the agenda of every tradition in political thought. It is this issue of the national state that conditioned a number of debates in the first decades after 1945. I will consider these debates in the following chapter.

NOTES

1. F. Fanon, *The Wretched of the Earth* (1961; reprint, Harmondsworth: Penguin, 1967), 166.

2. Y. Bénot, *Idéologies des Indépendences Africaines* (1969; reprint, Paris: Maspero, 1972), 58–60.

3. Between the early and late nationalists, the aim differed only in shades: "only 'external administration' by the British," "self-government" for the "next generation" J.E.C. Hayford, *Gold Coast Native Institutions* (1903; reprint, London: Frank Cass, 1970), 7, 127. Also, "self-determination," "Freedom and Independence" (Nkrumah 1947), "self-government in the shortest possible time" (United Gold Coast Convention [UGCC] 1947), and "self-government now" (Convention Peoples Party [CPP] 1949). This self-government was in most cases perceived as independence within the framework of empire or Commonwealth. Nkrumah used the more radical expression "complete independence" while in England in the immediate postwar years, but back in Ghana his political action ran under the slogan "self-government now."

4. In 1936 W. R. Crocker (an ex-civil servant) wrote of Nigeria that there was "no conflict between white capital and coloured labour, there are no political problems, internal or external, of any kind. Social problems . . . political problems like nationalism, as in India, are all non-existent." Quoted in J. S. Coleman, *Nigeria: Background to Nationalism* (Berkeley: University of California Press, 1958), 201.

5. Conferences were organized in London (1900), in Paris (1919), in London, Brussels, and Paris (1921), in London and Lisbon (1923), and in New York (1927), bringing black people of various continents, backgrounds, and views together to demand an end to racial discrimination and colonial exploitation, and to advocate self-rule. Apart from the 1921 conference, representation from Africa was quite limited at the conferences. The "ritual of Du Boisian congresses" J. Ayo Langley, *Pan-Africanism and Nationalism in West Africa* (Oxford: Clarendon Press, 1973), 286, has been highlighted in the literature (e.g., C. Legum, *Pan-Africanism. A Short Political Guide* [London: Pall Mall Press, 1962]), but their influence in Africa was limited before 1945. I. Geiss, *Panafrikanismus. Zur Geschichte der Dekolonisation* (Frankfurt am Mein: Europeische Verlagsanstalt, 1968); Langley, *Pan-Africanism and Nationalism in West Africa*.

6. Garvey's call for "Africa for the Africans" was more radical than the demands of the African elites in that time. Garvey was therefore one of the few black American radicals who was honored by the colonial administrations with prohibitions to travel to Africa. Garvey's wife edited a collection of his writings in Ami Jaques Garvey, ed., *Philosophy and Opinions of Marcus Garvey* (1932; reprint, New York: Universal Publishing House, 1967). See, for example, H. Campbell, *Rasta and Resistance: From Marcus Garvey to Walter Rodney* (Trenton: African World Press, 1987); R. Hill, ed., *Marcus Garvey: Life and Lessons, a Centennial Companion to the Marcus Garvey and UNIA Papers* (Berkeley: University of California Press, 1987). For Garvey's relevance to Africa see, for example, Langley, *Pan-Africanism and Nationalism in West Africa*; J. A. Langley, "Garveyism and African Nationalism," *Race* 11, no. 2 (1969): 157–172; R. L. Okonkwo, "The Garvey Movement in British West Africa," *Journal of African History* 21 (1980): 105–117; M. B. Akpan, "Liberia and the Universal Negro Improvement Association: The Background to the Abortion of Garvey's Scheme for African Colonization," *Journal of African History* 14, no. 1 (1973): 105–127; and relevant passages in Shepperson, "Notes on American Negro Influences"; and D. Kimble, *A Political History of Ghana: The Rise of Gold Coast Nationalism, 1850–1928* (Oxford: Clarendon Press, 1963).

7. The Tuskee Institute of the prominent activist Booker T. Washington was influential.

8. Shepperson, "Notes on American Negro Influences"; Geiss, *Panafrikanismus*. Langley's argument, like my own, is that political ideas were determined by local concerns of the local African political leaders rather than by "influences" from outside.

9. For a detailed and excellent analysis, see Philippe Dewitte, *Les Movements Negres en France, 1919–1939* (Paris: L'Harmattan, 1985): "l'évolution et aboutisse-ment d'un 'proto-nationalisme nègre' né au confluent de l'anti-impérialisme communis-te, du panafricanisme des Noirs américains et de la tradition humaniste et anti-raciste francaise" 387.

10. J. Kenyatta, *Facing Mount Kenya. The Traditional Life of the Gikuyu* (1938; reprint, London, Nairobi, and Ibadan: Heinemann, 1979), viii.

11. Coleman, *Nigeria: Background to Nationalism*, 211; see pp. 211–220 for the associations.

12. In practical politics, neotraditionalist discourse often focused on the issue of land rights. The ARPS was triggered by the issue of land laws, just like the Kikuyu Central Association. Also today, for instance in the South African PAC, neotraditiona-list views are popular and the land issue is given high priority.

13. Chief Obafemi Awolowo's proposals in his *Nigerian Path to Freedom* (London: Faber and Faber, 1947) does not belong to the ethnographic type of literature but represents the same political discourse. Remarkable in Awolowo's case is that he defended the traditional institutions not primarily against the British but against the radical nationalist line of Zik's party, the NCNC, which proposed a unitary state and the gradual abolition of traditional institutions. Awolowo even praised the idea of indirect rule.

14. See also the discussion of Hountondji, Mudimbe, and Appiah in chapter 7 of this book. Note that some of the greatest defenders of the "otherness" of African culture in the first decades of this century were romantic Europeans such as the British Mary Kingsley and the theosophists, who played a prominent role in supporting Indian

nationalism. See Carla Riseeuw, "Thinking Culture through Counter-Culture: The Case of the Theosophists in India and Ceylon and Their Ideas on Race and Hierarchy (1875–1947)," A. Copley & H. Rustau, eds., *New Religious Movements* (London: Oxford University Press, 1988). Also F. Hara's "The Secret Doctrine of Racial Development," *The Theosophist*, July 1904, 596–604, and August, pp 660–669.

15. As explained in the previous chapter, the national consciousness was largely evolving in the nationalist struggle itself.

16. The issues mentioned here were often not addressed in the form of ethnographic texts. Type of text and discourse are not related in a one-to-one way. One discourse can be sustained by different types of texts and one type of text can occur in different discourses.

17. In this category "lies the opportunity for the literate African to serve his countries cause," noted de Graft Johnson on page 107 of his *Towards Nationhood*, thus making it clear that, unlike the claims of the chiefs, true politics in the African system lies with the educated legislature not with the more ceremonial position of the chief.

18. On the linguist, see my discussion in the previous chapter of Casely Hayford's *Gold Coast Native Institutions*.

19. Awolowo, *Path to Nigerian Freedom*, 53.

20. Ibid., 81.

21. Awolowo, 1968, quoted in Langley, *Ideologies of Liberation*, 499.

22. Awolowo, 1968, quoted in Langley, *Ideologies of Liberation*, 496.

23. Both quotes from Awolowo, 1968, quoted in Langley, *Ideologies of Liberation*, 497.

24. Awolowo, 1968, quoted in Langley, *Ideologies of Liberation*, 498. Awolowo's example represents a type of argument also found in, for instance, Danquah and Busia.

25. *Ethiopia Unbound* is praised as "one of the most charming and suggestive books ever written about Africa," and a "wonderfully prescient book containing almost all the ideas and ideology of modern African thought." F. N. Ugonna, "Introduction to the Second Edition" in J.E.C. Hayford, *Ethiopia Unbound. Studies in Race Emancipation* (1911; reprint, London: Frank Cass, 1969), flap text and p. xx.

26. Hayford, *Ethiopia Unbound*, 55.

27. The National Congress of British West Africa (NCBWA) emerged as a modern-type political organization in this context. See also other texts, for example, Badele Omoniyi, *A Defence of the Ethiopian Movement* (Edinburgh, 1908).

28. I write "Nigerians" in quotes because it can be doubted if one can speak of a national identity at that point in time. See also Awolowo: "There are no 'Nigerians' in the same sense that there are 'English', 'Welsh', or 'French'." Awolowo, *Path to Nigerian Freedom*, 47–48.

29. Coleman, *Nigeria: Background to Nationalism*, 220.

30. N. Azikiwe, *Renascent Africa* (1937; reprint, London: Frank Cass, 1968), 165.

31. Coleman, *Nigeria: Background to Nationalism*, 223.

32. B. Anderson, *Imagined Communities. Reflections on the Origins of Nationalism* (London: Verso, 1983).

33. Herbert Macaulay was a colorful senior local figure. See, for example, R. W. July, *The Origins of Modern African Thought: Its Development in West Africa during the Nineteenth and Twentieth Centuries* (London: Faber & Faber, 1968), chapt. 18.

34. Quote from Coleman, *Nigeria: Background to Nationalism*, 225. In 1941 the NYM disintegrated after conflicts over the appointment of a Legislative Council representative (the Akinsanya crisis) and allegations of "tribal prejudice."

35. Langley, one of the most profound historians of African political thought, suggested that the "impatient young men" (Langley, *Pan-Africanism and Nationalism in West Africa*, 225) added new energy to the nationalist endeavor but remained essentially within the confines of "moderate and liberal nationalism," while the real change came with Nkrumah's effective mass politics (Langley, *Pan-Africanism and Nationalism in West Africa*, chapt. 5). My analysis is slightly different.

36. Between Casely Hayford and the chief spokesman of the Fanti chiefs, Nana Atta Ofori, the relation was often one of opposition.

37. Azikiwe, *Renascent Africa*, 17. Zik is back to "Hortonian" prejudices when it comes to indigenous traditions. Like Horton, he praised Africa's great past but rejected the "backward," "feudal," "tribal" concrete traditions.

38. Ibid., 18. On p. 91 Azikiwe states: "Whither are we bound? Towards a homogeneous and a united Africa for the regeneration of our race and individual countries? Or towards an heterogeneous and disunited Africa? Whatever we sow, we shall reap."

39. Ibid., 28.

40. It could be argued that Zik's universalist and liberal orientation ties him equally strongly to dominant European thought as I argued for the neotraditionalists: this time not to its romantic but to its Enlightenment tradition.

41. Moreover, the interpretation of the Pan-Africanist ideal was different. For de Graft Johnson this was "individual local autonomy . . . joining together in one unbroken chain of glory!" J. W. de Graft Johnson, *Towards Nationhood in West Africa* (1928; reprint, London: Frank Cass, 1971, 127). Within the universalist tradition (including Padmore-Nkrumah) Pan-Africanism was conceived of as a federation of states: "all the national units comprising the regional federations shall be autonomous in all matters regional, yet united in all matters of common interest to the African Union"(379). For the first variant, local autonomy and diversity are basic features. For the second, the constitution of a proud, viable, and free anti-imperialist block is a primary condition.

42. Azikiwe, *Renascent Africa*, 32.

43. At times the willingness to work and think within the system seems astonishing. Casely Hayford can discuss "healthy imperialism," de Graft Johnson "True Trusteeship," and even Azikiwe surprises the present-day reader when he writes in his discussion of imperialism: "historically speaking, imperialism is inevitable . . . the main problem for Africans is to adjust themselves to it, for what cannot be helped cannot be helped, especially if it be an obeisance to the law of nature." Azikiwe, *Renascent Africa,* 67.

44. Azikiwe, *Renascent Africa*, 17. The newspaper-nationalism of British West Africa did not even develop where colonial powers were more restrictive, as in German colonies. See A. A. Boahen, *African Perspecives on Colonialism* (Baltimore and London: John Hopkins University Press, 1987), for a discussion of the dilemmas of opposition under colonialism.

45. In addition to this hegemony of colonial vocabularies, the ideas of colonial racist ideology were so dominant that the simple task of countering racial stereotypes and the rhetoric about the so-called benevolent civilizing help of the colonizer already consumed much of the available intellectual critical energy.

46. When challenging European models, as we have seen in the case of neotraditionalist discourse, the vocabulary for describing what was typically African had been prepared by colonial discourse in the form of terms such as "tribes," "chiefs," or ready-made racial and cultural stereotypes.

47. For the same reason, Azikiwe's concrete "liberal" political ideas are rather familiar to us.

48. Azikiwe, *Renascent Africa*, 47. Or "Blessed are the youth of Renascent Africa, who are mentally emancipated, for they shall know who knows and knows that he knows, and he who knows not and knows not that he knows not, and he who knows and knows not that he knows, and he who knows not and knows that he knows not," 48; or preachings on "The black man is the black man's enemy" and "the black woman is the black woman's enemy" 205.

49. Reference to Marx on 51 of Azikiwe, *Renascent Africa*. Of course, if Azikiwe had believed in the Marxist theory of history, including Lenin's idea of colonialism as a "last stage," then he could have nursed other hopes. But he did not assume that history would replace the forces governing the world system with entirely new ones. Therefore, for him, liberation had to come from within the system. Like many other Africans who had contacted Marxist ideas in the metropoles, this Marxism could not change their political practice in the colonial situation.

50. Examples are Padmore, Nkrumah, Kouyate, L. Senghor, Plaatje, Danquah, and many less-known works, see, for example, *A Defence of the Ethiopian Movement* (1908) of the Nigerian Bandele Omoniyi in Langley, *Ideologies of Liberation*, 173–187.

51. Quoted in K. Nkrumah, *Ghana: The Autobiography of Kwame Nkrumah* (1957; reprint, London: Nelson; New York: International Publishers, 1971), 46–47; and in K. Nkrumah, *Towards Colonial Freedom* (1945; reprint, London: Heinemann, 1962).

52. A few similar analytical and empirical works appeared during the colonial period, especially in Francophone Marxist literature, but a similar conceptual detachment to colonial discourse was generally only achieved after the colonial period.

53. Phillip Dewitte, in his magnificent *Les Mouvements Nègres en France 1919–1939* (Paris: L'Harmattan, 1985), described the early 1920s as "Au tout début des années vingt, pour tous les militants et politiciens nègres l'indépendance est impensée, impensables, inimaginable même" 387.

54. Citizens of four places in Senegal even had full French citizenship.

55. Houénou was a Dahomeyan from a rich merchant family and of noble descent, a lawyer in Paris, at home in the high society, and a *bon vivant*. His war experience and an incident of racial discrimination made him into a radical critic of colonialism and discrimination. Houénou is described as a forerunner of the *Négritude* movement. E. Zinsou, quoted in Langley, *Pan-Africanism and Nationalism in West Africa*, 291. See also Dewitte, *Les Mouvements Nègres*, 217–223, for the highly interesting cross-fertilization with the Harlem Renaissance in New York.

56. Senghor was a war veteran who had been invalided by German war gas. He was arrested and died of tuberculosis in 1927.

57. Quoted in Langley, *Pan-Africanism and Nationalism in West Africa*, 312. Dewitte, *Les Mouvements Nègres*, 388, notes: "Les deux thèmes, pan-nègre et anti-impérialiste, prédominent à la tour de rôle en fonction de l'état des relations entre PCF et le mouvement nègre." Dewitte's final assessment of this issue is understanding: "En 1918 la civilisation nègre . . . n'existen pas. Avant même de parler du libération nationale ou sociale, les Nègres doivent reconquérir amour-propre et dignité" 390.

58. LDRN editorial in *La Race Nègre*, no. 1, 1935, quoted in Langley, *Pan-Africanism and Nationalism in West Africa*, 323.

59. Ironically, it was during the Popular Front Government in France (1936–1938), in which the Communists took part, that the LDRN and other nationalist and anticolonial movements had a hard time. Emile Faure, the LDRN secretary was exiled and the movement stopped.

60. *Gold Coast Spectator*, 9 May 1936, 814. Quoted in Langley, *Pan-Africanism and Nationalism in West Africa*, 334.

61. G. Padmore, *Pan-Africanism or Communism? The Coming Struggle for Africa* (London: Dobson, 1956), 148. The actions were generally directed at influencing Western (British) public opinion and politics. Their influence in Africa was limited, with some exceptions such as Wallace-Johnson who organized his West African Youth League and West African Civil Liberties League in Sierra Leone in 1938.

62. There had been moves toward a revision of colonial policies, including indirect rule (e.g., the report of Lord Hailey of 1939) from within the British government.

63. Coleman, *Nigeria: Background to Nationalism*, 238.

64. From the essay "The Cracked Myth" in N. Sithole, *African Nationalism* (Cape Town and New York: Oxford University Press, 1959), 162–163. Rev. N. Sithole was a former president of the Zimbabwean ZANU party.

65. American government officials condemned colonialism and within the American black community there was a new interest in Africa. For several years the journal *New Africa* was published in New York and disseminated nationalist ideas, also to Africa.

66. The text of the manifesto for the United Nations, as well as a number of other important African manifestos, can be found in appendix G in Langley, *Ideologies of Liberation*, 762–764.

67. Coleman, *Nigeria: Background to Nationalism*, 239.

68. Langley, *Ideologies of Liberation*, 758–760. The appendix also includes the other declarations of the Manchester Pan-African Congress.

69. Quoted in Langley, *Pan-Africanism and Nationalism in West Africa*, 360, 358.

70. Nkrumah traveled to Paris to discuss West African unity and radicalized nationalist action with the African deputies in the Assemblé National: Apithy, Gueye, Houphouet-Boigny, and Senghor.

71. The document known as "The Circle" is reprinted, as Appendix B, in *Ghana: The Autobiography of Kwame Nkrumah*. It includes such dictates as to obey the orders of the Circle, help brother members, avoid the use of violence, fast and meditate the twenty-first day of each month, and accept the leadership of Kwame Nkrumah. The final aim of the Circle was defined as a "Union of African Socialist Republics."

72. The sudden breakdown of the colonial system after 1945 is often explained by: 1. the weakening of the European powers in the war and the rise of the new superpowers; 2. the new generation of radical African nationalists, and their new mass-

mobilization strategies; 3. the general conscientization of the younger generation of Africans.

73. The situation concerning civil liberties was even much worse in the German colonies and settler societies in East and Southern Africa. See, for example, the grim colonial reality in what is now called Malawi, where Chilembwe staged a rebellion in 1915. (R. I. Rotberg, *Strike a Blow and Die* [1967; reprint, London: Heinemann, 1970]).

74. I will return to this issue in the next chapter in discussing Padmore's and Nkrumah's views in the 1950s.

5

Post-Colonial African Political Discourses

The dominant political ideal during the colonial period was self-government. In the 1950s this ideal finally appeared within reach in the form of an Africa made up of independent nation-states. The possibility of independence created a completely new political horizon in which the actual construction of the nation-state became the focal issue. A number of new problems appeared on the agenda. What political system should be chosen for the national state? What is the "African" substance of this state? How can Pan-African ambitions be framed in an Africa consisting of national states? How can true independence, beyond "flag independence," be achieved?

The boisterous ideological struggles over these issues went through major shifts at intervals of about a decade in the following forty years. The radical nationalism of the Manchester Pan-African Congress of 1945 and the West African National Secretariat (WANS) was followed, in the 1950s, by a dominant liberal democratic orientation exemplified by Nkrumah's "tactical action." The 1960s brought the golden age of African Socialist ideologies. Important events in this period were the Dakar Colloquium (1962), the launching of *Ujamaa* (1962) and the Arusha Declaration (1967) by Tanzanian president Nyerere, Nkrumah's Consciencism (1964), and the Kenyan government paper on African Socialism (1965). In the 1970s Marxism became prominent in a context of stagnating development, the rise of dependency and underdevelopment theories, and the successful liberation wars in the Portuguese colonies. In the 1980s all projects for building an alternative society seemed to have halted. The Ethiopian famine, the unprecedented destruction of the Mozambiquan experiment, and the deepening economic crisis of the 1980s left little hope for a better future. Although outrageous events such as famines, wars, and genocide continued in the 1990s, inspiring prospects came to life

again with the widespread call for democratization. Even where democratization actually did not proceed very far, as was the case in most countries, the
thorough delegitimation of authoritarian politics created a new political
environment.

My analysis in this chapter does not concern the various types of political
regimes and their proclaimed ideology, such as Marxism-Leninism, Authenticity, Humanism, or Nayoism. These have been studied thoroughly by political
scientists.[1] My concern is with discourses that developed intellectually to such
a level that they survived the system or leader proposing them, thus becoming
part of intellectual history. These discourses constitute "the history of the
present," and produced "a range of vocabulary . . . which becomes
foundational" for present-day political thought.[2]

Table 5.1
Successive Discourses in Nkrumah's Thought

1945–1952	N	the discourse of revolutionary anti-imperialism	par. IV.4
	K		
1952–1961	R	the discourse of democratic modernization	par. V. 2
	U		
1961–1965	M	the discourse of African Socialism	par. V. 3
	A		
1965–1972	H	the discourse of revolutionary anti-imperialism	par. V. 4

The central landmark from which I will map this intellectual history is
modern Africa's figurehead, Kwame Nkrumah. The discourses that Nkrumah
presented at different stages in his career provide the sign-boards to the
various ideological orientations in post-colonial Africa (Table 5.1). Taking
bearings on this landmark provides a convenient way of locating the ideological positions of various post-colonial African theorists. After discussing
Nkrumah, I will follow each of the discursive paths indicated by his career,
thus covering the entire terrain.

KWAME NKRUMAH

From Revolutionary Anti-Imperialism to Democratic Modernism

In the previous chapter I discussed the anti-imperialist radicalism of
Nkrumah's London days. This radicalism also inspired Nkrumah's stormy
entry into the Ghanaian political scene and the successful nationalist agitation

of "positive action" by his Convention Peoples Party (CPP) during 1950–1951. When he was released from prison after a massive electoral victory in 1951, Nkrumah landed directly in the seat of prime minister of an all-African government under British supervision. "Positive action" was then exchanged for "tactical action," which involved conventional democratic and statist policy orientations.

Ideologically Nkrumah moved away from the radicalism of the West African National Secretariat, such as expressed in his London works *Towards Colonial Freedom* (1945/1962) and the document of *The Circle* (1947).[3] These texts strongly rejected colonial boundaries (the Balkanization of Africa). They stated the ideal of a Union of Socialist Republics in Africa and underlined the need for a political vanguard. The radical model of thought was, furthermore, designed around an intrinsic connection between decoloniz-ation and ending economic exploitation through a social and economic revolution. All this was not heard of much in the 1950s. The book *I Speak of Freedom*, presenting Nkrumah's speeches during the 1950s, expressed a framework of thought focusing on the political realm within a national (not a Pan-African) context.

This remarkable shift toward the ideal of a democratic, unitary, and national state along with a humanitarian vocabulary of political, civil, and human rights also occurred in George Padmore's work. His *Pan-Africanism or Communism* is the work of a social-democrat not a "non-Stalinist Marxist."[4] Padmore wrote: "Pan-Africanism means politically government of, by and for Africans; economically it means democratic socialism, liberty of the subject and human rights guaranteed by the law. . . . Pan-Africanism sets out to fulfil the socio-economic mission of Communism under a libertarian political system."[5] Nkrumah not only avoided identification with socialism, in 1954 he even introduced legislation prohibiting the diffusion of communist literature and barring communists from a number of posts, including teaching-posi-tions.[6]

One could account for the "liberal turn" of the radicals by pointing to the quite limited political margins of that period in Ghana or to the political situation in the 1950s, where anticommunism was a prerequisite for political survival in the West.[7] To all appearances, however, Nkrumah and Padmore actually thought along liberal democratic lines during the 1950s. The intellec-tual monsoon was blowing from the West. Structural functionalist social theory, belief in modernization of underdeveloped nations, and liberal democratic political discourse were dominant. Nkrumah's and Padmore's sails were probably not secure enough to maneuver against these prevailing ideological winds. They moved with the dominant discourse rather than against it.

Nkrumaism: The Discourse of African Socialism

In 1961 Nkrumah changed his orientation once more, aiming at a "second revolution" based on a socialist strategy of economic and political reforms. A presidential system and one-party rule were introduced in Ghana, the official glorification of his person as the *Osagyefo* ("victorious leader" or "redeemer") was stepped up and a number of important persons were evicted from the party. The ideological counterparts of these political changes were the launching of Nkrumaism, the establishment of the Ideological Institute at Winnaba, and the launching of the political group and journal *The Spark* (named after Lenin's *Iskra*).[8] These changes were effected in the context of increasing stagnation both within the party and the political system and within the economy and society at large. Nkrumah had estranged practically all progressive forces from the party and continued to do so, for instance, by his violent repression of the 1961 Takoradi railway strike.[9]

The renewed radicalism of the Second Revolution was sustained by a new discourse that expressed the need to confront underdevelopment and capitalist neocolonialism by way of an alternative, "African" socialism. This alternative would build on the African heritage of communal and socialist ways of life. It would end the "exploitation of man by man" by promoting social property and a mixed (private-public) economy under the control of the state, by constructing a Pan-African and Third World force in world politics, and by belief in God.

The new discourse was enunciated in Nkrumah's book *Consciencism, Philosophy and Ideology of Decolonization and Development, with Particular Reference to the African Revolution* (the 1964 subtitle). This is an extraordinary text. It is a political statement that is not made up of political, economic or ethnological facts and theories, but of deliberations on the philosophical doctrines of idealism and materialism, reflections on God, Spirit, and the African personality, and even a set theoretical proof of the proposed metaphysics. *Consciencism* was an attempt to design a complete worldview or "philosophical ideology." It has been described by one of its adherents, Kofi Baako, as "applied religion" and "a socialist nondoctrinary philosophy.[10] In Nkrumah states:

A new harmony needs to be forged, a harmony that will allow the combined presence of traditional Africa, Islamic Africa and Euro-Christian Africa, so that this presence is in tune with the original humanist principles underlying African society. Our society is not the old society, but a new society enlarged by Islamic and Euro-Christian influences. A new emergent ideology is therefore required, an ideology which can solidify in a philosophical statement, but at the same time an ideology which will not abandon the original humanist principles of Africa.

Such a philosophical statement will be born out of the crisis of the African conscience confronted with the three strands of present African society. Such a philosophical statement I propose to name *philosophical consciencism*.[11]

In order to analyze Nkrumah's discourse in his African Socialist period, the time between his turn to socialism in 1961 and his book *Neo-colonialism* of 1965, several sources are available apart from *Consciencism*.[12] I will use what is probably Nkrumah's most impressive book, namely, *Africa Must Unite*, published in 1963.

Africa Must Unite presents a very clear discussion of precolonial and colonial heritages, the nationalist struggle, and the development of independence in Ghana. It subsequently discusses dilemmas in Ghanaian politics that involved the Convention Peoples Party, the opposition, the economy, the constitution, and the various Pan-African initiatives. The reader is invited to sit next to Nkrumah in the cockpit of society and is given a view backward through history and forward to the challenges ahead, hearing Nkrumah's instructions on how exactly to use the societal steering wheel to proceed in the direction of progress and socialism. The discourse located itself at the center of political power. From this position, "stability and resolute leadership in the building of our country" are perceived as being of foremost importance. Nkrumah compared his assignment with that of Sisyphus's task "to roll a whole people uphill," which requires a "managing director."[13]

This idea of "a people" with its "managing director" involves particular views about the national state and about politics within that state. First of all, Nkrumah's idea of the advancement of a people implied a strong rejection of regionalism. One could have expected his Pan-Africanism to bring about a weakening of the national idea, and his intention to build on African heritages to lead to a recognition of communal and regional structures, but actually Nkrumah had a strong focus on the national state and national integration. Pan-Africa integration was to proceed from national integration and thus national integration should not be frustrated by regionalism.[14] Nkrumah argued that obeying the call for federalism of the UGCC opposition and of traditional rulers such as the Ashantihene would leave only "token sovereignty" for the national government.[15] The fate of Nigeria, where Azikiwe's national party (the NCNC) could not preclude the rise of regionalism and thus could not construct a strong central state, was abhorred by Nkrumah. In addition, Nkrumah considered traditional leadership, which was proposed as the key to a regional system of government, to be something to overcome. The people had to be released "from the bondage of foreign colonial rule and the tyranny of local feudalism."[16]

The second supposition of Nkrumaism was that political monism was the best system within the Ghanaian national state. Society's "great leap ahead" required a massive synchronization of the energies and the minds of the population. The government, party, and the people should coincide: "the aspiration of the people and . . . the government are synonymous" and there should be "direct consultation" between them.[17] Similarly, the trade unions should toe the line. Under socialism, they were considered to have "a new role" in "carrying out the government's program."[18]

The drive for synchronization also concerned human character and consciousness: "Africa needs a new type of citizen, a dedicated, modest, honest and informed man. A man who submerges self in service to the nation and mankind."[19] *Consciencism*'s important chapter, "Society and Ideology," expresses the total nature of the proposed collective commitment in quite an outspoken way. The ideology is proposed here as the main solution for the problem of order in society: "seeking to establish common attitudes and purposes for the society." "The ideology of a society is total. It embraces the whole life of a people, and manifests itself in their class-structure, history, literature, art, religion." "It is this community, this identity in the range of principles and values, in the range of interests, attitudes and so of reactions, which lies at the bottom of social order."[20] Nkrumah's subsequent discussion was concerned with the "social sanction" and "the subtle methods of 'coercion' and cohesion" that organize a society outside the scope of direct central control.[21] The resulting "new harmony," Nkrumah stated, "may be described as restatements in contemporary idiom of the principles underlying communalism."[22]

In order to create this communalism for rapid development, certain liberties may have to move to the background. Nkrumah confirmed that he found the idea of censorship repugnant, running "counter to everything for which I had struggled in my life," yet "we had embarked upon a course that aimed to push forward the clock of progress. Were others to be given the freedom to push it back?"[23] The extensive use of the 1958 Prevention of Terrorism Act, which caused the death of the leader of the opposition J.A.B. Danquah in detention, was not, as far as principles are concerned, ruled out by the discourse of Nkrumaism.

The Discourse of Revolutionary Anti-Imperialism

In the mid-1960s, Nkrumah moved to a philosophical position that its adherents called "scientific socialism." Of course, the February 1966 *coup d'état*, which ended CCP rule in Ghana and forced Nkrumah to spend the last six years of his life exiled in Conakry contributed to his change of ideas. Nkrumah moved from a position of power to a position of an outsider so that a discourse situating itself in the central control room of society was replaced by one situating itself in the margins, among the "masses of workers and peasants": in theoretical terms it was the guerrilla camp and in practical terms it was Nkrumah's home in Conakry.

The new discourse had already developed before Nkrumah's overthrow. The book *Neo-colonialism, the Last Stage of Imperialism* was published in 1965, and in the introduction to *Handbook of Revolutionary Warfare: A Guide to the Armed Phase of the African Revolution* (1968), Nkrumah mentioned that he was already preparing a manual on guerrilla warfare while still in Accra. In a way, Nkrumah's revolutionary anti-imperialism revived many of his positions expressed while he was in London. In content, as well as in style, the similarities between the *Handbook* (1968) and the document *The Circle* (1947) are striking.[24]

Nkrumah's ideological change after 1965 can be substantiated by the fact that the logic of "tactical action" in the 1950s as well as Nkrumaism, *Africa Must Unite,* and *Consciencism* cannot be justified from the scientific socialist point of view presented from 1965 onward. Nkrumah himself, never confirming that he had changed his position on certain topics, endowed the change with an objective basis by stating that now the "armed phase on the African Revolution" had started.

Athough it was not long ago, it is hard to recapture the context and meaning of radical anti-imperialist thought throughout the 1960s and 1970s. Rethinking socialism as an unquestioned political ideal and as a certain gift of history, as it was often perceived before the collapse of socialist systems in the world, requires considerable historical empathy today.[25] First of all, let me present the basics of Nkrumah's scientific socialist account. After World War II, workers' protests within the capitalist states along with the threat of both communism and fascism forced governments to grant concessions that led to the creation of welfare states. This expensive system meant that external colonial exploitation had to be intensified: "therefore, it became necessary for international finance capital to carry out reforms in order to eliminate the deadly threat to its supremacy of the liberation movements."[26] This necessity led to a policy of replacing old-fashioned "direct colonialism" with its rationalized form, namely, "collective imperialism" under the leadership of the United States. The new system involved granting "sham independence" and thus creating the system of neocolonialism: "A state can be said to be a neocolonialist or client state if it is independent de jure and dependent de facto. It is a state where political power lies in the conservative forces of the former colony and where economic power remains under control of international finance capital."[27]

The seminal image that captures Nkrumah's idea of neocolonialism as a mechanism of domination appears in Nkrumah's discussion of the question, "Who really rules such places as Great Britain, West Germany, Japan?":

Lurking behind such questions are the extended tentacles of the Wall Street octopus. And its suction cups and muscular strength are provided by a phenomenon dubbed "The Invisible Government," arising from Wall Street's connection with the Pentagon and various intelligence services.[28]

Typically, the octopus metaphor does not depict a person or a simple conspiracy of persons nor a mechanistic or cybernetic system such as is embodied in center-periphery or world systems theories. The Wall Street octopus is an animated entity, sinister, sucking, and strangling, in which the center masters the periphery.

From a Marxist point of view, Nkrumah's analysis leaves many questions unanswered. The modes of production in Africa and related classes were not discussed, nor was the possibility of introducing socialism in Third World societies that had been incorporated into the capitalist system without fully becoming capitalist formations. Nkrumah's political message, however, was communicated with great clarity, embodied in such statements as: "the African Revolution is an integral part of the world socialist revolution."[29] Thereby Nkrumah stated a position that remained dominant within the Left until well into the 1980s.

Nkrumah's position implied a fierce critique of the nonradical African leaders and governments (more specifically of the Monrovia and Brazzaville groups of states, which objected to the militant stand of the Casablanca Group in which Ghana participated). They were declared to be merely the "puppet governments" of "client states" and the product of tactics devised by the imperialists who "decided to play their own version of nationalism."[30] In the struggle for liberation no role would exist for the leaders of most independent African states. Liberation would be the work of the workers and peasants: the "broad masses of the African people who are determined once and for all to end all forms of foreign exploitation, to manage their own affairs, and to determine their own future."[31] Their struggle required an All-African People's Liberation Army with a strong Pan-African coordination.

While revolutionary warfare held the key to African freedom, socialism provided the specific content of the new social order. Nkrumah now criticized the "muddled thinking" about African Socialism: "there is only one true socialism and that is scientific socialism, the principles of which are abiding and universal." He summarized this socialism as: 1. common ownership of means of production; 2. planned methods of production by the state, based on modern industry and agriculture; 3. political power in the hands of the people "in keeping with the humanistic and egalitarian spirit which characterised traditional African society"; 4. application of scientific methods in all spheres of thought and production.[32]

Despite all the ardor and spirit in the three main books of the Marxist-Leninist phase in Nkrumah's intellectual life, they leave behind a tragic resonance. For the reader, the need for resistance emerges more clearly than the possibility of resistance. The octopus is strong and enveloping. Optimism can only be located in the Marxist theory of history, which predicts an end to capitalism and a future state of total freedom. Nkrumah possessed the ability to design comprehensive and noncontradictory analyses in order to outline what should be done. The reader, however, is left with doubts about the degree to which these analyses can be translated back to real-life situations.

The Four Nkrumahs

Nkrumah's intellectual career, as I have argued above, represented different political orientations at different times: socialist anti-imperialism at the end of the 1940s, liberalism or democratic socialism in the 1950s, African Socialism in the first half of the 1960s, and Marxism-Leninism in the second half of the 1960s. The diverse political orientations coincide with different struggles, namely, "positive action" for national independence (until 1951), followed by "tactical action" and obstruction of a "disruptive" opposition. From 1961 on, the struggle for a socialist nation was on the agenda, while after the 1966 coup, the Pan-African armed struggle against neocolonialism occupied center stage.

Table 5.2
The Four Nkrumahs

Period	Organization	Role	Policy	Location	Concern	Key Text	Discourse
1945–1951	WANS Circle	activist	exile politics/ "positive action"	margin	economic exploitation	pamphlet e.g., *Towards Colonial Freedom*	Revolutionary Anti-Imperialism
1951–1961	CPP	party leader	"tactical action"	center	political freedom	speech e.g., *I Speak for Freedom*	Democratic Modernism
1961–1965	state party	national leader	nation building	center	socialist nation-state	philosophical book e.g., *Consciencism*	African Socialism
1965–1972	African Liberation Army	revolutionary	armed struggle	margin	African revolution	manual/ pamphlet e.g., *Handbook*	Revolutionary Anti-Imperialism

The different political orientations also coincide with different political roles. Nkrumah changed from an activist to a party leader then to national leader and finally to an exiled revolutionary (Table 5.2). Likewise, the various genres of Nkrumah's writings correspond with these roles. *Towards Colonial Freedom* (1945/1962) is an anticolonial pamphlet by a nationalist militant whereas his *Autobiography* (1957) and *I Speak of Freedom* (1961) contain the speeches and statements of a political leader who is dedicated to freedom, democracy, and progress. *Consciencism* (1964) is the philosophical tract of a national leader. In his "Philosophy and Ideology for Decolonization," Nkrumah is the nation-builder who lays deep and solid foundations for a state while speaking on behalf of the nation and continent.[33] In his last years, exiled in Conakry, Nkrumah returned to the political pamphlet, publishing works such as the *Handbook of Revolutionary Warfare* (1968). At various points in time, more analytical texts appeared, like *Africa Must Unite* (1963), *Neo-colonialism: the Last Stage of Colonialism* (1965) and *Class Struggle in Africa* (1970).

There is also continuity in Nkrumah's development, especially in political style. His autobiography recounts the pathetic moment when he sailed out of New York to return to Africa in 1945. Nkrumah said farewell to the Statue of Liberty: "You have opened my eyes to the true meaning of liberty. . . . I shall never rest until I have carried your message to Africa."[34] In many ways Nkrumah remained inspired by a drive for liberty, embodying it in different ideological schemes. His role was always that of the spokesman of the struggle and the designer of grand schemes that evolve fully fledged from the mind of the theoretician. The roles of others were thus defined as followers, namely, as executors of the projects designed by the leader. In such a scenario, the political process concerns mobilization and execution rather than deliberation; unanimity is required while differences of view are an anomaly.

The Beninese philosopher Paulin Hountondji brilliantly analyzed the deeper logic of "unanimism" or antipluralism in the discourse of *Consciencism*. His analysis questions the whole project of designing a "Philosophy and Ideology for Development, with Particular Reference to the African Revolution" (subtitle of the 1964 edition of *Consciencism)*. Hountondji connected this critique with an attempt to pinpoint the mistaken premises of the CCP political project in the first half of the 1960s under Nkrumaism.[35]

Hountondji noted a contrast between the original 1964 edition and the revised 1970 edition of *Consciencism*. The 1964 edition had maintained that African societies are basically classless and that their communal worldview could provide a basis for African socialism. In the 1970 edition of *Consciencism*, Nkrumah abandoned the original idea of classlessness but maintained the idea that a progressive politics in Africa requires a collective philosophy or an ideological synthesis.

Hountondji argued that by abandoning the idea of classlessness the search for a collective philosophy becomes an illusory project since a plurality of classes implies a plurality of ideological orientations in politics. The idea of "restoring the lost unity of African consciousness . . . a unified system of thought" is a classical example of the philosophy of consciousness that tries to reconcile real social differences at the level of consciousness.[36]

Hountondji maintained that the project of Consciencism should be rejected from a political point of view as well. In the first place, it attempted to translate "theoretical unanimity into a value to be struggled for."[37] Instead, we should reaffirm the value of pluralism. In the second place, consciencism tried to provide metaphysical foundations for issues that are essentially political and that, therefore, require the public deliberation of all those concerned in an open political process rather than an exercise of ideological reflection by a single leader. According to Hountondji, we should "assert the autonomy of the political as a level of discourse."[38]

A similar criticism of antipluralism can be directed at the idea of politics in Nkrumah's later writings. There is a remarkable schematism here since the single dichotomy between oppressor and oppressed is said to determine the world. Whether we talk of Jehovah's Witnesses, the Peace Corps, development aid, the BBC World Service, or "the literature spread by so-called liberal publishers," they all function as agents of imperialism. Even Nkrumah's quite sophisticated book *Class Struggle in Africa* (1970) was designed according to this basic scheme. It assumes that the logic of the ideological order can be reduced to the political order which is in turn defined by the economic order. There is only the Wall Street octopus and its victim, "our enemy and ourselves," so that not a single fact or circumstance is allowed to escape the dichotomy.[39]

Such a reductionism creates an argument for unanimism that Hountondji's discussion of consciencism does not include. If the world is essentially divided into the "enemy and ourselves" and if ideological differences can be reduced to these fundamental camps, then there are only two ideological options: that of the oppressor or that of the oppressed. In this situation, there can be no legitimate plurality of opinions among the oppressed. The oppressed are only to be united in "an ideologically monolithic party of cadres."[40] Whereas the unanimism in consciencism is derived from the "nature" of a group or nation, the unanimism of Class Struggle is derived from the historically required ideological choice of the oppressed. In both cases political pluralism is considered faulty.

The present chapter will use Nkrumah's intellectual career as a guide to post-colonial African political thought. My interpretations of key authors will show that the three discourses that Nkrumah embodied at different stages of his life—democratic modernization, African Socialism, and radical anti-imperialism—are also the major historical discourses in the post–World War II period.

MODERNIZATION DISCOURSES

At first glance, postwar African political discourse until the move toward African Socialism in the 1960s was characterized by an astonishing degree of consensus. The nationalist struggle was fought under the flag of democratic rights, and when independence was visible on the political horizon most intellectuals favored a liberal democratic orientation. When taking a closer look at the major points of conflict in this period, however, it emerges that beneath the level of shared convictions very different models of thought were operative.

Two major points of contention arose in the first decades after World War II: federalism, and (African) socialism and the single-party state. These often led to bitter struggles. The issue of federalism, for instance, divided the major players in Nigerian, Zik and Awolowo, as well as the central figures in Gold Coast politics, Nkrumah and Danquah. Both Zik and Nkrumah, building on their earlier "New African" position (as discussed in the previous chapter), were protagonists of a central state that would overcome tribal differences between peoples within the national borders and which would be able to implement a process of rapid modernization.[41] Awolowo and Danquah, on the other hand, resisted the substitution of indigenous linguistic, cultural, and ethnic communities, including their inherited forms of leadership, with a totally new, centralized nation-state.

In the early 1960s, another issue of contention arose, namely, socialism and the single-party state. There was a strongly felt need for the central state to have an assertive role in the development process. Protagonists of an African Socialist orientation suggested that the developmental state would be handcuffed by adhering to standard democratic institutions such as the separation of executive, legislative, and judicial powers, political pluralism, and civil liberties. Accordingly, a socialist single-party system would be more appropriate. The opponents of African Socialism were, in most cases, inspired both by a commitment to democratic values and institutions and by the conviction that socialist development strategies would not work. The issue of political pluralism and the role of the state raised debates throughout the 1960s that were largely the same as those at the end of the 1980s when single-party rule was abolished in many African countries.

Political confrontations over federalism and socialism were bitter and in the case of Danquah even led to his death while he was imprisoned under the Prevention of Terrorism Act. In the domain of ideas, however, the confrontations produced some of the best political arguments. These arguments are discussed here in order to map the basic dimensions of the ideological landscape in the 1950s and 1960s.

The Liberal Modernization Discourse

For many nationalists, the basic argument against European colonialism had been an inherent criticism, namely, that colonialism contradicted the very ideas and ideals of freedom and democracy proclaimed by the West itself. These nationalists subscribed to the ideals of freedom and democracy, considering them to be universal human values that should apply to Africa as much as to any other part of the world.

Probably the best example of a liberal modernizer is the Nigerian Nnamdi Azikiwe ("Zik"). Azikiwe's thought (which was discussed more extensively in the previous chapter) is archetypal for a thoroughly universalist belief in the possibility of transcending racial, ethnic, as well as social cleavages. By adhering to the universal values of freedom, democracy, and human welfare,

Azikiwe argued, individuals and groups could "move to the higher plane" of identification with the national and human community.

Azikiwe believed liberal democratic institutions were the expression of these universal values. Moreover, he considered them to be indispensable for any modern society, since no other system is capable of avoiding authoritarianism and the misuse of power. Similarly, Azikiwe argued that nation building requires a parliamentary democracy. People will not shed tribal identities unless they have their individual liberties firmly guaranteed and are protected against poverty: "By adapting the best elements so far experienced by human beings all over the world, in the practices of capitalism or socialism or welfarism . . . a Nigerian ideology based on the eclecticism now universally appreciated as the welfare state, is the right incentive."[42] Pragmatic reasoning also dictates the choice for democracy, as Obafemi Awolowo argued: "A nation groping more or less in the dark, and striving for bare subsistence, cannot afford to depart from laws and principles which are sufficiently verified, and from routes which are well charted, to embark on experiments which the verdicts of history declare to be utterly ruinous."[43]

The Social-Democratic Modernization Discourse

In the 1960s the liberal democratic state lost credit because a growing number of people believed that only a strong and intervening developmental state could enforce the desired "great leap ahead" for African societies. Democratic ideals as such were not abandoned; yet, for the sake of development, the state as the most powerful institution in society would have to take the lead in the development process. The resulting discourse situated itself in the steering cabin of society. It indicated the key problems that a newly independent society faces and it outlined what should be done, in which order, and what the expected results would be.

Dunduzu Kaluli Chisiza from Malawi is an interesting example of this developmentally assertive variant of democratic discourse. He was secretary-general of the Malawi Congress and an influential politician when he died in a car accident in the early 1960s. Chisiza proposed a "Pragmatic Pattern of Development," which was concerned with democratic values but even more so with a coordinated program of modernization. His highly pragmatic orientation is exemplary for the type of discourse that has dominated much of developmentalist policy design in the last forty years.[44]

Chisiza exemplifies the energetic social-democratic modernizer. His clear and direct style and practical turn of mind, without losing sight of emancipatory objectives, is reminiscent of Africanus Horton nearly a hundred years earlier. For instance, he proposed strategies for ultimately "completing the annihilation of tribalism," a four-step program for the "political regrouping of neighbouring countries" as an alternative to Pan-Africanism as an "operation roof-top" and an argument for effective but limited political pluralism including all the necessary institutional mechanisms to guarantee effective control of state power.[45] Typically, he worked in close cooperation with the West, particularly by using foreign investment and development aid. For Chisiza even nonalignment was a matter of opportunism: "Paradoxical as it may sound, the safest way of aligning with the West is not to align with the West."[46]

The Neotraditional Modernization Discourse

A liberal orientation in matters of political arrangements does not have to ignore African cultural heritages, as was the case with the liberal and social-democratic modernizers. The combination of liberal universalism with a strong link to local traditions has a long history in the Gold Coast, from the Aboriginal Rights Protection Society in the 1890s, to the United Gold Coast Convention, and to the Ghanaian opposition under J. B. Danquah. In the 1950s and 1960s it constituted one of the main ideological positions countering both African Socialism and Marxism.

In politics, style, and class as well as in the model of political thought, Danquah himself personified this tradition. When he died in prison in 1965, Danquah's political and intellectual work was continued by Kofi Busia who was a Brong (Ashanti) nobleman, an Oxford sociologist, an opposition leader, and a prime minister. The main texts in this Ghanaian tradition are erudite and sophisticated, and their positions are moderate, pragmatic, and open-ended. This moderation does not mean, however, that they suggested westernization as a solution to Africa's problems. If we examine the example of Kofi Busia, his books typically begin with elaborations on African culture and analyses of the contemporary African situation in terms of "challenges" to be tackled on the basis of the "heritages" of Africa itself.[47] Busia can therefore be called a neotraditionalist as well as a liberal modernizer. There is, one could say, a neotraditional "Akan" and a liberal "Oxford" Busia.[48]

The discourse was not an eclectic mixture, however. The key aspect of the discourse was a specific interpretation of the conceptual pair "tradition" and "modernity." Tradition here referred to the concrete heritage of the Akan people rather than to the generalized African tradition of the African Socialists or the general sociological stereotype of a traditional society. Studies in history, culture, and society were considered to be necessary to know the traditions that were relevant for development. Again, "modernity" was conceived of as a general feature of world historical development that Western societies expressed in specific ways and African societies could express in different ways.

The remarkable thing about this tradition-modernity vocabulary is that it does not define two opposites. The idea of modernity indicates a range of challenges that a particular tradition is facing. Depending on its specific resources, traditions need to develop new solutions in order to shape their own modernity. In the words of Busia: "These are the challenges Africans face. Their cultures must change and grow but they must retain that identification with the past which gives every people its sense of uniqueness and pride." The fact that "Africans belong to the stream of human history" does not have to lead to a loss of cultural identity since "there is always room for conscious choices. Cultural change is a selective process."[49]

Busia's discourse involved a quite unresentful assessment of colonialism.[50] Rather than regarding colonialism primarily as political domination or economic exploitation, Busia asserted that "colonialism is, above all, a social fact." Africans came into contact with other peoples and ways of life, which resulted in a change of culture. It is characteristic of Busia's position that he considerd the confrontation with superior technology—arms, bulldozers, motorcars, and all of the attendant social and cultural changes—as the most prominent experience of colonialism.[51] Consequently, Busia believed the essence of decolonization to be the synthesizing of African culture with modern science and technology rather than simply the act of attaining political independence.

In the field of politics, such a synthesis involves building a modern state on African heritages. Busia noted that "Africans cherish democratic values."[52] The Ashanti political system had its own resources in this regard, involving its own system of checks and balances to prevent arbitrary authoritarianism. Busia described, for instance, the political institution of the commoners or young men holding meetings that had a decisive voice in the rejection of candidate chiefs through their spokesman, the Nkwankwaahene.[53]

The modern territorial state, however, involves the crucial new aspect that it is multicultural and multi-ethnic in composition. According to Busia:

In traditional societies, all members held the same religious beliefs, shared the same rituals, held the same views about the universe. The highly valued solidarity of traditional society was based on conformity; but it is old-fashioned to hope to achieve solidarity on the basis of conformity in the circumstances of today. In the contemporary situation, a State consists of people holding different religious beliefs . . . ; they may hold different views . . . in science or philosophy, or politics, and in other ideologies or subjects. It is assumed that they can all nevertheless agree on the validity of the ideals of democracy and be equally loyal to them.[54]

The fact of pluralism of the political community is the major challenge to traditional African political systems and requires a "new institutional expression of cherished values."[55] The proponents of a single-party system misread the signs of the times. Their idea that "the state replaces the tribe" and that the family can be a model for the state ignores the actual pluralism of modern African societies.[56] Under modern circumstances, the equivalence of tribal unity can only be achieved with considerable coercion. This, Busia argued, is shown by the fate of Ghana under Nkrumah as well as that of Tanzania under Nyerere.

The idea of a single party cannot even claim to exemplify the African political tradition at the level of the tribe, as Busia maintained. Traditional systems involved mechanisms for hearing minority voices and for preventing authoritarianism. Such mechanisms, however, are absent from the single-party system.[57] Opposition does not divide society, rather it promotes social cohesion because "the opposition helps to make all citizens, including those who disagree with the party in power, a part of the democratic system." Effective "methods and institutions for the preservation of liberty" are necessary. If closely analyzed, this means that Africa cannot dispense with any of the key ingredients of the idea of democracy: "a democratic society provides methods and institutions for the preservation of liberty. These include organs as newspapers, trade unions and other voluntary associations, political parties." African democracy will thus differ in form from the European example, but it should comply with "the common standards by which it (should) be judged."[58]

One of the key differences with Europe, Busia insisted, is the nation-state: "Africa should break loose from this alluring European model. It does not fit in with the social realities of the continent." "We should . . . accept the fact of pluralism rather than fly in the face of the facts and attempt to achieve monolithic state structures through coercion."[59] In fact, Busia argued, tribal solidarities can provide structures for people to manage their own affairs locally and provide indigenous traditions of checking the encroachment of dictatorship at the national level.

Busia's arguments on single-party rule remained largely unrefuted. After the early 1960s, however, the issue of democracy became secondary to what was considered a much more fundamental issue, namely, socialism. Political visions of a totally new societal alternative dominated African political thought.[60]

THE DISCOURSES OF AFRICAN SOCIALISM

In the early 1960s a remarkable new style and message emerged in African political thought. The often sophisticated political texts by liberals and Marxists, meant for a politically educated audience, were drowned out by speeches, memoranda, and party programs on "African Socialism," which targeted the new broad national public.[61] The topics could be "exploitation of man by man," "the humanist society beyond capitalism and communism," or "the national family." In most cases, the authors of this new style of African political thought had a background in the teaching profession, were dedicated members of one of the world religions, and belonged to the top echelons of the newly independent states.

Two approaches have to be avoided in the interpretation of African Socialist discourse. On the one hand, the great majority of texts should not be mistaken for a primarily academic attempt at theorizing about society, history, or humanity nor for an attempt at philosophy in the sense of a tightly argued intellectual exercise with academic pretensions. On the other hand, the opposite tendency should be avoided. This approach claims that it suffices to simply "explain" African Socialism in the light of the interests of the new leaders or the new dominant class.[62] African Socialism deserves to be studied as a political discourse in its own right, which means that it is part of the political project of specific groups in society, while constituting an ordered set of ideas and concepts that shape people's interpretations of vital political issues and thus their actions.

African Socialism was a peculiar event in intellectual history. At one time, it seemed to represent African political thought as such, the golden age of African political thought as well as the impulse that was finally expounding the African vision of society to the whole world. After this glory, it is even more astonishing to observe the speed with which African Socialism evaporated both as a policy orientation and as a theoretical position. None of the variants of African Socialism appears to have survived the eclipse of the political leader who proclaimed it.[63]

The discourse of African Socialism emerged around 1960 in a new political situation that formed independent states and turned nationalist movements into national governments. A completely new horizon for political action appeared. For independence to be real, societal change would be needed beyond the available models of the West and the East: "trying to create something which is uniquely ours" and "to grow, as a society, out of our own roots."[64] African cultural heritages could render this alternative by suggesting two consecutive choices, first rejecting capitalism for socialism, and then rejecting Marxist socialism for African socialism.

At issue here were not simply the principles of political democracy (the main concern of the liberals) or the details of political economics (the main concern of the Marxists) but the whole moral, cultural, social, and economic order of society. This broad agenda suggested wide-ranging, "philosophical" reflections on humanity, God, history, and society. In actual politics, these theoretical teachings had practical aims such as nation building (fostering national unity in the new nation-states), designing a developmental alternative to break neocolonial dependency (the "second phase of the freedom struggle"), and justifying the new political leadership and its party.[65] Each of the branches of African Socialist discourse discussed below had its specific political roles. I will not examine these roles as such but will instead focus on the key intellectual characteristics of each branch.

The Developmental Discourse of African Socialism

For authors such as Mamadou Dia, Tom Mboya, and Kwame Nkrumah, African Socialism was basically an issue of development policy. Nkrumah's conscienciscm, for instance, was presented as a synthesis of indigenous, Christian, and Muslim heritages, but the main function of the synthesis was to unite society in a crash program of industrialization and nation building.[66] Similarly, the principal Kenyan document on African Socialism, the *Kenya Government Sessional Paper Number 10* entitled "African Socialism and Its Application to Planning in Kenya" (1965), made reference to "African tradition," but it was basically an exercise of adjusting practical policy options to the needs of the African situation.

Most of the standard elements of African Socialist policy are discussed in the Kenyan sessional paper.[67] It argued for a mixed economy with a state sector, a cooperative sector, a limited private sector, and joint ventures with foreign investors. Productive resources should be under social control, which meant that the "commanding heights" of the economy and key sectors, such as banking, the import and export trade, and distribution of land, should be controlled by the state. Actually, in the case of land, African Socialist policy contradicted African tradition, which considered the distribution of land to fall within the jurisdiction of the relevant traditional authorities.[68]

Within the developmental discourse of African Socialism, the core issue was "a transformation of structures, particularly economic ones" which could end neocolonial dependence.[69] Such a national strategy would be viable only if political units larger than national states were created. Developmental African Socialism was thus connected to the idea of Pan-Africanism.

For Mamadou Dia, who acted as an energetic Senegalese leader of government until his fall in 1962, African Socialist structures would be built on quite different premises from those of the West: "Born to affirm a system of values unrelated to the value of money, the non-Western civilizations of Asia and Africa could only produce relations in which monetary considerations always remain secondary."[70]

The Cultural Discourse of African Socialism

Different arguments for African Socialism can be found in Senghor and in Nyerere. They put forward elaborate arguments defending the African character of the African Socialist alternative. This is especially the case for Léopold Sédar Senghor. A wide range of arguments for an African variant of socialism based on African communalism could be reported, however, I will limit my discussion here to Senghor.[71] As a poet, a theoretician of Négritude, and former president of Senegal, Senghor was probably the most well known African intellectual of this century. In his sophisticated arguments, Senghor was not content with rebuking the common stereotypes of "capitalism" and "communism." He seriously discussed contending ideologies and concluded:

We stand for a middle course, for a democratic socialism, which goes so far as to integrate spiritual values, a socialism which ties it in with the old ethical current of the French socialists. Historically and culturally we belong to this current. Besides, the French socialists—from Saint-Simon to the Léon Blum of *For All Mankind*—are not so utopian as they are reputed to be. In so far as they are idealistic, they fulfil the requirements of the Negro-African soul, the requirements of all men of all races and all countries.[72]

Interestingly, Senghor's discourse did not involve the usual championing of the nation-state, so common among African Socialists. Senghor distinguished between fatherland and nation:

The fatherland is the heritage handed down to us by our ancestors: a land, a blood, a language or at least a dialect, mores, customs, folklore, art—in a word, a culture rooted in a native soil and expressed by a race. . . . The nation groups such fatherlands together in order to transcend them. Unlike them, it is . . . a conscious will to construct and reconstruct.[73]

The choice is, therefore, for a pluralist federalism: "far from rejecting the realities of the fatherland, the nation will lean on them." The nation-state should resist the temptation of "the uniformization of people across father-lands."[74] Diversity should be maintained and the tyranny of the state warded off through the decentralization and the deconcentration of its economic and political institutions. Democracy, citizens' rights, and the rights of the opposition should be respected, although the government should "take all necessary steps to curb demagogic opposition."[75] Senghor's position on democracy parallels Azikiwe's or Busia's position rather than the African Socialist stance of Nkrumah or Nyerere.

Because African cultural roots are plural, the specificity of what is "African" cannot be conditioned by a shared African cultural heritage. *Africanité* is anchored, one could say, at a "deeper" human level, namely, in the Negro-African soul. This Négritude defines not only a different social order but also an epistemology, an imagination in short, a way of being human.[76] Senghor was here clearly the heir of Edward Blyden's Negroist orientation, while proposing a more open and dynamic conception of this Négritude than his famous predecessor.[77]

Senghor suggested a dynamic symbiosis of races and cultures in which cultures strive "not to be assimilated, but to assimilate." Senghor disputed the fact that Europe presents itself as the universal culture: "Just as much as black Africa, Europe and its North American offspring live by means of archetypal images. For what are free enterprise, democracy, and Communism but *myths*, around which hundreds of millions of men and women organize their lives?

Négritude is itself a myth." Senghor proclaimed a polycentrism of cultural difference that, however, still allows criticism in terms of humanism. "The neohumanism of the twentieth century stands at the point where the paths of all nations, races, and continents cross, 'where the four winds of the spirit blow.'"[78]

The Political Discourse of African Socialism

With his famous idea that *Ujamaa* (familyhood) is the basis of African Socialism and his ardent defense of one-party rule, Julius Nyerere provides an exemplary case of African Socialism as basically a political idea. The works of Nyerere, the former *Tanganyika African National Union* (TANU) party leader and president of Tanzania, are mostly collected speeches.[79] They lack the erudition and sophistication of Senghor's texts but have an enormous clarity and directness. By casting some well-chosen stereotypes of the positions that he discarded and providing catchy formulations of his own stance, Nyerere always managed to provide a clear-cut and influential definition of the problem at hand. Two of his formulations follow: "We, in Africa, have no more need of being 'converted' to socialism than we have of being 'taught' democracy. Both are rooted in our own past—in the traditional society which produced us." And "The European socialist cannot think of his socialism without its father—capitalism!"[80]

Nyerere's discourse is based on a few simple oppositions expressed in well-known incantations such as "exploitation of man by man" (to characterize capitalism or the system of the West) versus the philosophy of "inevitable conflict between man and man" (to characterize communism or the system of the East). The fundamental unattractiveness of both systems prepares the ground for Nyerere's alternative, which is derived from the humanist African tradition. Nyerere used African tradition primarily as a counterimage to the West and the East, clearing the space for an alternative rather than defining the shape of that alternative. Detailed analyses of social and political institutions in African societies are absent. Nyerere's papers on democracy and one-party rule, for instance, are considerably more lengthy in analyzing the British system than the African one.[81]

African tradition taught Nyerere a set of humanistic values as well as giving him a basic idea of the political community as a kind of family. Essential for a democratic political community, Nyerere concluded, is the attitude of mind of those concerned and not the specific institutions. The form of democratic government should be adapted to the historical realities in which it is applied. In Britain, under capitalism, where there are fundamental divisions between rich and poor, and capital and labor, a two-party system may be appropriate. This, however, can hardly be called an ideal situation: "each party fights with the hope of winning as many seats as possible. They fail to win them all. And then, having failed, they quite blandly make a virtue of necessity and produce the most high-sounding arguments in praise of their failure."[82] The Tanzanian situation is one where the common struggle against a foreign enemy has created a party that represents "the interests and aspirations of the whole nation."[83] In a situation where rapid development is the general aim, the only relevant thing to quarrel about is who can do the job best. The choice of leadership in a single-party system should therefore be made strictly by using the ballot box and internal party democracy should be guaranteed. "For the task of imposing party discipline, of limiting freedom of expression in Parliament, with no rival party to help would sooner or later involve us in something far worse than the factionalism of which I accused the two-party enthusiasts."[84] In the Tanzanian situation opposition parties are not necessary: "where the differences between the parties are not fundamental, . . . you immediately reduce politics to the level of a football match. . . . This, in fact, is not unlike what happens in many of the so-called democratic countries today.[85] If, however, differences are in fact fundamental, then:

there can [therefore] be no question of national unity until the differences have been removed by change. And "change" in this context is a euphemism, because any change in fundamentals is properly termed "revolution." What is more, the reason why the word "revolution" is generally associated with armed insurrection is that the existence of really fundamental differences within any society poses a "civil war" situation and has often led to bloody revolution.[86]

Nyerere's message was clear, opposition in a good society where the "party is identical with the nation as a whole" (such as in Tanzania) is either useless or insurrectional. According to Nyerere political pluralism does not even serve freedom:

It is the responsibility of the government in a democratic country to lead the fight against all these enemies of freedom. . . . It is therefore also the duty of the government to safeguard the unity of the government from irresponsible or vicious attempts to divide and weaken it—for without unity, the fight against the enemies of freedom can not be won. . . . *There can be no room for difference or division.*[87]

The various aspects of Nyerere's *Ujamaa* discourse are already contained in its basic metaphor of the family. If, in essence, the state is an expanded family community, then the basis of the state is a fundamental solidarity, a state of mind disposing people to cooperate, share, seek compromise, and avoid formalizing interhuman relations. Fundamental differences of opinion or interest are not expected and leadership will be "natural." There is no need for a separate political sphere, let alone for formal political institutions and checks and balances. The exemplar of the family also implies the idea of the political leader as a *pater familias* who can naturally speak on behalf of his family. The problem of political representation, therefore, will not arise. The leader guides his people as their *Mwalimo* (teacher) rather than holding a political office.

The exemplar of the family suggests how the political process should be organized. Beyond that, it also states a substantial ideal of the good life and the good society. Tanzanians do not have to debate about their society any more since their national ideology already articulates their ideal. The true state of the country is already defined by the leader.

This true state is, however, not yet realized. As in all idealists' strategies for social change, ideals have to become embodied in stubborn reality, particularly in human minds and institutions. People have to be made "ripe" for it and made to turn their backs on temptations such as money and individualism. The process of implementation of the ideal needs protection against subversion and manipulation. Who can do this? Automatically the enormous weight of this responsibility rests upon the shoulders of the trusted leaders who have insight and moral stamina. In this discourse, politics contracts to become a matter of moral backbone instead of an organized political process. The famous Arusha Declaration, for instance, does not say a word about how the people can control the political process but includes a whole section on leadership.[88]

It is interesting, at this point, to contrast Nyerere's argument for African Socialism with Nkrumah's perspective. For both of them the pluralism of ideas and communities had to be overcome, finally, by unification. However, they constructed completely different arguments to defend this option. *Conscienscism* provided a philosophical exposition on the communal nature of human life and on the universal necessity for discouraging deviance and promoting consensus. The conclusion of Nkrumah's "deep level" argument was the need for a coherent collective worldview, a collective ideology that directs the evolution of society on a wide range of issues. In contrast, Nyerere did not design a worldview. Nyerere advanced a very sketchy image of a communal Africa and a number of pragmatic rather than philosophical arguments related to developmental needs and the political process. Arguing against Nkrumah would require a general argument on man, on communities, and on the possibility of shared identities and ideologies. Arguing against Nyerere would require empirical expositions on actual forms of African solidarity and on the possibility of avoiding stagnation and authoritarianism under single-party rule.[89]

The fate of African Socialism was not sealed, finally, in academic or political debates but in its dramatic failure as a development strategy. African Socialist governments were initially sustained by the exceptional historical situation of newly established "young" nations with the goodwill of their populations, as well as by some potent donors. However, in the course of the 1960s failure became apparent already. African Socialism was a peculiar discourse that was tailored to the ideological needs of the new African elites in the 1960s. It harnessed many of the sentiments of self-assertion as well as many stereotypes of African cultures that are affirmed throughout African political thought. Ultimately, however, it neither addressed key issues in political theory nor issues concerning development policy in a new and constructive way. With hindsight, African Socialism has been rather a peculiar episode in the history of African politics rather than a substantial and lasting contribution to African political thought.

THE DISCOURSES OF REVOLUTIONARY STRUGGLE

Throughout the previous section I have discussed democratic modernization and African Socialist discourses in their various forms. In African thought before the mid-1990s, one also finds clearly Marxist-inspired discourses. Radical intellectuals such as Lamine Senghor, Guaran Kouyaté, and George Padmore were discussed in the previous chapter, and I mentioned Wallace Johnson and the Ghanaian Spark group. Before 1965, Marxism held a minor position in African political thought. Most African countries followed a liberal modernizationist orientation after attaining their independence in a relatively peaceful manner.

A discourse on revolution developed primarily in those situations where an anticolonial war was fought, such as in Algeria, in the Portuguese colonies, and, in a different way, in South Africa. In a global context, Marxism became current during the 1960s with Dependency Theory as the inspiring innovation in development theory. Various types of radical and Marxist-inspired discourses thus developed in Africa, whereas the rival option of African Socialism lost its appeal. Marxist-inspired radicalism became the hegemonic paradigm, at least intellectually, for two decades or more and accounted for practically all important political writings in Africa between the mid-1960s and the mid-1980s.

Most commentators have interpreted these discourses as variants of Marxism. My discussion in this section can benefit hermeneutically from the current post-Marxist era and provide new interpretations of radical African thought as well as underline the diversity of its orientations.

Overcoming Colonial Alienation: Frantz Fanon

The need for a revolutionary struggle to liberate Africa was most forcefully argued by Frantz Fanon, the Algerian psychiatrist, freedom fighter, and intellectual of West Indian origin. The compact, penetrating, and perceptive presentations of his book *The Wretched of the Earth* (*Les Damnés de la Terre*) (1961) can hardly be matched by twentieth-century political literature. Much of the impact of Fanon's texts, especially of the sections "Spontaneity: Its Strengths and Weaknesses" and "Pitfalls of National Consciousness," derives from avoiding the usual textbook wisdom and armchair theorizing on revolution. Instead, these sections have the compelling authority of Fanon's own practical revolutionary experience. Fanon's texts seem visionary in their message.[90] In 1961, in the middle of the decolonization process, Fanon was able to give an analysis of the pitfalls of postindependence national leadership that, more than three decades later, remains as striking as any critique could be.

Frantz Fanon is mostly discussed with reference to his views on the question of violence in colonial liberation. There are also good descriptions of his political ideas.[91] The task of the present analysis is to capture a specific model of thought in Fanon's discourse, a model that, as I will show, shapes a discourse on Africa in its own right.

The starting point of Fanon's analysis was the colonial condition, a situation characterized by oppression, racial segregation, and a chasm between the elite and the masses as well as between city and countryside. It was an essentially racist condition, involving more than racial segregation but also the internalization of racism and thus the deformation of all human beings involved.[92] The colonial condition created both settler and "native" in their dialectical relation as master and slave: "For it is the settler who has brought the native into existence."[93] The native has to interiorize the colonial system that, once it has entered "under his skin," leads to profound alienation. Fanon claimed that he had to deal with many syndromes related to this alienation in his psychiatric practice.

Colonial alienation is not only a psychological affair but also a socially produced condition. Its abolition, therefore, involves the actual elimination of the colonial situation. The personal, psychological level and the collective, political level are two sides of the same coin.

If colonialism "produced" the native, the "decolonization is the veritable creation of new men . . . the 'thing' which has been colonized becomes man during the same process by which it frees itself."[94] Liberation can, therefore, never be a gradual process or a matter of "replacing the foreigner," namely, the white man. The mutually constitutive master-slave relation is not overcome when the slave becomes master but only when the whole setup and the related identities are eliminated. Fanon, therefore, rejected African évolué culture and African independence that was based on a compromise with colonialism. Violent struggle is the only way to become free.

Fanon thus valued violence for practical reasons and as medication against colonial alienation—as a destroyer of the old identity. In Hegel's master-bondsman relation, it is through labor that emancipation is possible. In Fanon's colonial master-slave relation, it is the "work" of violence that makes emancipation possible. "The militant is also a man who works . . . to work means to work for the death of the settler."[95]

The main revolutionary force in the work of liberation would be the unalienated peasants, the "mettlesome masses of peoples" who are "rebels by instinct." Contrary to Marxist expectations, the salaried workers in the cities who are pampered by the colonial power cannot be identified with the mass of the people according to Fanon. The political and trade union cadres of the nationalist movements shared with the political elites a disdain for the rural masses, and were poorly prepared for radical de-alienation and armed struggle. They tended to concentrate their politics in the cities, they refused to support anticolonial peasant uprisings, such as the Mau Mau in Kenya, and even persecuted those few radicals who really identified with the people.

The radicals have to flee to the countryside and will "discover that the country people never cease to think of the problem of liberation except in terms of violence . . . of armed insurrection." The armed struggle then moves from countryside to town: "It is with this mass of humanity, this people of the shanty towns, at the core of the *lumpenproletariat*, that the rebellion will find its urban spearhead."[96] The key agents in the struggle are the militants and the people, not the middle class: "it is absolutely necessary to oppose vigorously and definitely the birth of a national bourgeoisie and a privileged caste." These "Blacks who are whiter than the Whites" in fact follow a racial and chauvinist program of substitution: "replacing the foreigner" without changing society.[97] "We observe a falling back toward old tribal attitudes, and, furious and sick at heart, we perceive that race feeling in its most exacerbated form is triumphing." "If the national bourgeoisie goes into competition with the Europeans, the artisans and craftsmen start a fight against the non-national African," demanding that "the Foulbis and the Peuhls return to their jungle or their mountains."[98]

This bitter attack on the African bourgeoisie was matched by Fanon's famous prediction of the role of the national leader: "In spite of his frequently honest conduct and sincere declarations" (or exactly because of these), he "constitutes a screen between the people and the rapacious bourgeoisie since he stands surety for the ventures of that caste and closes his eyes to their insolence. . . . He acts as a breaking-power on the awakening of the consciousness of the people.[99]

Fanon's work easily uncovers the particular model upon which his idea of colonial liberation was designed, namely, that of overcoming psychological alienation. The personality is the exemplar for the political; political liberation is a therapeutic process, a process of reestablishing collective self-identity.

This exemplar can be used here to reconstruct the architecture of Fanon's discourse. Let me, for that purpose, first analyze what was assumed and implied by the model of psychological alienation and then trace its consequences for Fanon's political conception. The three basic assumptions of the alienation model are: 1. there is a definite unit or entity that is alienated, based on the idea of the person; 2. there is a healthy, natural, or good state of the person, and healing is conceived as a return to this state; and 3. healing is not automatic or natural, it requires an act of will, a *prise de conscience.*

Each of these assumptions can be shown to determine Fanon's political conception.

1. In the first place, the whole idea of political alienation assumes that there was already something such as a nation that was subsequently alienated, just like a personality had to exist for it to become alienated. According to Fanon colonialism involved more than a range of instances of oppression and resistance among diverse African communities. The colonized were "a coherent people who keep their moral standards and their devotion to the nation intact." Fanon speaks of the "old granite block upon which the nation rests."[100] This suggests that in fact the nation precedes colonialism. Fanon does not consider here precolonial African states or "tribes," in fact he strongly opposed "primitive tribalism;"[101] nor does he assume that urban militants implanted the idea of a nation. In Fanon's account the exiled militants find a peasant nation already present.

Quite apart from the historical error that may be involved in assuming a pregiven "nation," there is a theoretical reduction. The rich and diverse heritages of peoples, life forms, religions, and cultures are reduced to a single entity. The empirical variety remains undiscussed and can, therefore, neither complicate nor enrich the revolutionary alternative that is sketched.[102] The concept of "the nation" ("the people" or "the oppressed") remained a non-empirical, mythical category in Fanon's thought. Such a "subject of revolution" was the artifact of his psychological model of alienation and liberation.[103]

2. Fanon's discourse is indebted to the psychological model in a second way, namely, by its conception of the liberation struggle. Healing psychological alienation involves exorcizing the interiorized alienating influences in order to reestablish self-identity. It is a process of returning to the true foundations. Fanon's conception of the political struggle is strikingly similar. It is a process that involves mobilizing the true, original national forces in the majority of the poor and the peasants who are "the solidly massed presence of the new nation" and have kept "their moral values and their devotion to the nation intact."[104] Their main task is to effect the complete exorcization of the colonialists as well as the African bourgeoisie. In that act they construct a truly independent nation as the reestablishment of collective self-identity.

The model of alienation can be retraced at specific points in Fanon's conception of the liberation struggle. First, "the people," as the true source of nationhood, indicates the unalienated healthy kernel. The description of the people results in some of the few, but typical, romantic exaltations in Fanon's texts. For instance, Fanon describes the radicals fleeing to the countryside: "The peasant's cloak will wrap him around with a gentleness and firmness that he never expected. These men . . . wander through their country and get to know it. . . . Their ears hear the true voice of the country, and their eyes take in the great and infinite poverty of the people."[105] Second, the demonlike enemy is perceived as the alienating intrusion. Fanon's description of the alienated elite, on the other hand, is unforgiving: "In under-developed countries, we have seen that no bourgeoisie exists; there is only a little greedy caste, avid and voracious, with the mind of a huckster, only too glad to accept the dividends that the former colonial power hands out to it. . . . [N]ot even a replica of Europe, but its caricature.[106] Third, Fanon's idea of liberation involves healing by exorcism: a return to purity. Fanon's description of the new nation, finally, totally inverts the present sick state of the nation: "Then the flag and the palace where sits the government cease to be the symbols of the nation. The nation deserts these brightly lit, empty shells and takes shelter in the country where it is given life and dynamic power. . . . The capital of under-developed countries is a commercial notion inherited from the colonial period.[107] A real national policy, a policy of the rural masses, could even move the government as a whole toward the countryside. In this way, the nation returns to its source and is truly liberated and healed.[108]

3. The third way in which Fanon's political conception is shaped by the model of overcoming alienation concerns the driving force of change. For interpreters who treat Fanon as a Marxist, his relative unconcern with the standard Marxist theory of history and society must be astonishing. He provided no theoretical discussion on the possibility of avoiding a capitalist stage in the sequence of modes of production. Fanon was not a Marxist here. He simply proposed to discuss the matter at the practical level, stating, for instance, that "the bourgeois phase in the history of underdeveloped countries is a completely useless phase."[109] The question for Fanon was not what history has in store but what ought to be done. As in the case of psychotherapy, it is, finally, a matter of deliberate action and a *prise de conscience* of the oppressed. Fanon could, therefore, freely suggest lines of action that derive from his own practical experience in the struggle. For instance, he stated that "the combined effort of the masses led by a party and of intellectuals who are highly conscious and armed with revolutionary principles ought to bar the way to this useless and harmful middle class."[110] Fanon's prescriptions also included inhibiting the development of the intermediary sector (traders), shielding the youth from "disintegrating influences" and educating the masses (while "avoiding sweeping, dogmatic formulae").[111]

The revolutionary process, thus, depended on highly conscious revolutionaries and on political education. This leads to Marx's question: "Who educates the educators [the revolutionaries]?" Fanon's account of the struggle suggested a circular process where the people teach the militants and the militants teach the people. This mechanism itself again reveals a psychological model, namely, that of counseling, where the therapist triggers and directs the process of self-discovery and of awakening what is already predisposed in the patient.

My interpretation of Fanon displays a peculiar discourse on national liberation the basic structure of which is conditioned by the exemplar of psychological alienation. At the end of this chapter, I will contrast this discourse with the radicalism of Nkrumah and Cabral. Several critiques of Fanon, although well argued, seem to escape Fanon's basic concern. If one identifies Fanon's idea of the liberation struggle with Marx's idea of the struggle for socialism, as Zahar does, then Fanon fails to discuss most of the basic questions regarding class, history, and economic structure. But Fanon, as I tried to argue, developed a different type of discourse with a different concern. In fact, he certainly did not want to identify his alternative with the socialism of the socialist bloc: "The Third World ought not to be content to define itself in the terms of values which have preceded it. On the contrary, the under-developed countries ought to do their utmost to find their own particular values and methods and a style particular to them."[112]

Mastering Our National Historicity: Amilcar Cabral

Although primarily a man of action, as the leader of the Guinean and Cape Verdian liberation movement PAIGC, Amilcar Cabral is often considered to be one of the foremost African political theorists of the twentieth century. His impressiveness derives from the "forthrightness and candour" of his writings as well as from his willingness to discuss critically the limits of revolutionary theory when applied to African situations.[113] He virtually refused to discuss the theory of revolution in general and disconnected from his experiences in the Guinean liberation war. Paradoxically, it is precisely this thoroughly concrete and situational character of his thought that makes it of general value.

Compared to Fanon's vigorous prose, Cabral's texts are sober but they are equally condensed. The difference with Nkrumah is much greater. Where Nkrumah seems satisfied only when a theoretical scheme is complete and everything fits in, Cabral suspects theoretical perfection: "In reality phenomena don't always develop in practice according to the established schemes."[114] When invited to speak at the Tricontinental Conference of revolutionary movements in Havana in 1966, Cabral subtly suggested discussing a struggle that the organizers did not put on the agenda explicitly, namely, "the struggle against our own weaknesses."[115]

Cabral's major concern was the struggle leading to national liberation. At first sight, Cabral's thought on that issue was in line with contemporary Marxism, and he explicitly compared the Guinean struggle with those of Cuba, Vietnam, and China. In that interpretation, Cabral is considered special because of his analysis of specific issues in the liberation struggle, such as the role of culture and the role of the petty bourgeoisie. Let me follow the main lines of his reasoning in order to asses this reading of Cabral.

The situation in Guinea led Cabral to his famous discussion of the petty bourgeoisie in the struggle for national revolution: "the colonial situation neither allows nor invites the meaningful existence of vanguard classes (an industrial working class and rural proletariat)."[116] In this situation one could look at the *lumpenproletariat* or the peasantry as the agent of the revolution. However, the *lumpenproletariat* did not prove to be a progressive factor in the struggle, and in Guinea "it must be said at once that the peasantry is not a revolutionary force . . . we know from experience what trouble we had to convince the peasantry to fight."[117] "Even extreme suffering does not necessarily produce the *prise de conscience* required for the national liberation struggle."[118] This brings in the petty bourgeoisie: "events have shown that the only social stratum capable both of having consciousness in the first place of the reality of imperialist domination and of handling the State apparatus inherited from that domination is the native petty bourgeoisie."[119]

Thus analyzed, the situation is a curious one since the petty bourgeoisie itself is an unreliable factor, a "service class" and a product of the colonial system. Its "natural tendency is to become 'bourgeois' to allow the development of a bourgeoisie of bureaucrats and intermediaries in the trading system, to transform itself into a national pseudo-bourgeoisie."[120] The class analysis of the revolution threatens to conclude here with a contradiction, namely, the class leading the revolution has the natural tendency to betray its own objectives. Cabral's famous solution for this dilemma was that: "in order to play completely the part that falls to it in the national liberation struggle, the revolutionary petty bourgeoisie must be capable of committing *suicide* as a class, to be restored to life in the condition of a revolutionary worker completely identified with the deepest aspirations of the people to which he belongs."[121] Cabral thus analyzed the theoretical dilemma to its logical conclusion and formulated an unexpected and practical solution.

If Cabral's solution is assessed according to his basically Marxist vocabulary, then it is not unproblematic. It implies, for instance, that the revolution is not an objective necessity but rather relies on the conscious choice of a revolutionary intelligentsia and a class commitment that counters its (assumed) "natural" tendencies.[122] It also implies that the leadership should "remain faithful to the principles and the fundamental cause of the struggle." In short, the conditions for national liberation "stamp on it certain characteristics that belong to the sphere of morals."[123]

This interpretation of Cabral's theory of the Guinean liberation struggle leads to the odd conclusion that Cabral, heralded as one of the greatest African political thinkers of this century, in fact constructed a rather shaky and contradictory theory of revolution. Rather than accepting this conclusion, I intend to follow Thomas Kuhn's advice to avoid ignoring inconsistencies and to press such points even harder. As Kuhn's "bright sunny day" experience proved, this can result in uncovering deeper principles of order that suddenly make us understand the rationale of the paradigm.[124]

Let me first look at the vocabulary that Cabral uses. Here one finds some of the standard Marxist notions, such as class, productive forces, and revolution. It should be noted, however, that there were also a wide range of notions that do not conform to the Marxist paradigm. Cabral describes societies as integrated wholes that produce their own history and are "following the upwards paths of their own culture."[125] The metaphors that Cabral uses are also insightful. He frequently speaks of culture as "the flower of a plant," and that which "plunges its roots into the humus of the material reality." He states that "the capacity . . . for forming and fertilizing the germ which ensures the continuity of history lies in culture." Cabral also speaks of the "cultural personality" of a people and "the life of a society."[126]

Society is thus conceived in organic terms and we are far removed from the mechanical metaphors derived from the building trade, such as infrastructure-superstructure, the "iron laws" of history, or the "steeled cadres."[127] The organic view of society is matched by a similarly idiosyncratic conception of development: "the unfolding behaviour (development) of a phenomenon-in-motion, whatever the external conditioning, depends mainly on its internal characteristics."[128] The internal process of a society is then the living and interconnected development of its productive forces, its related social structure and culture. This development embodies the historicity of that society.

In light of this new understanding of Cabral's discourse as devised from the exemplar of organic "unfolding . . . of internal characteristics," the rest of his thought on revolution follows as a matter of course. Apparent odd contradictions even become logical consequences.

The essence of colonialism, the discourse suggests, is to frustrate the original development of society: "the denial of the historical process of the dominated people by means of violent usurpation of the freedom of the process of development of the productive forces."[129] Colonialism captures the history of a people: "There is a preconception held by many people, even on the left, that imperialism made us enter history at the moment when it began its adventure in our countries. . . . Our opinion is exactly the contrary. We consider that when imperialism arrived in Guinea it made us leave history—our history."[130]

The next step in Cabral's compelling argument for a revolutionary nationalism simply derives from this characteristic of colonialism. Revolutionary national liberation is an act by which a people recapture their own development, it is "the regaining of the historical personality of that people, it is their return to history through the destruction of the imperialist domination to which they were subjected."[131] This is also the reason why Cabral located the basis for resistance against colonialism in the people's culture. The culture represents the roots from which the indigenous history can reclaim the initiative.

In the last instance, liberation involves an act of a political, economic, and cultural nature. More than simply achieving political independence, liberation is regaining mastery over one's collective future and also involves control over the "national productive forces" (which have to undergo a "mutation" in the direction of socialism for that purpose). In Cabral's seminal expression it constitutes a people's "mastering of its own historicity."

From this fundamental position, Cabral derived a range of interesting views on culture: "the armed liberation struggle is not only a product of culture but also a *factor of culture*."[132] On the one hand, culture is one of the main forces of liberation. On the other hand, there will be "harmonizing" and "unification" of the various cultural heritages in the course of the struggle: "The national liberation movement . . . must be able to conserve the positive cultural values of every of the well-defined social group, of every category, and to achieve the *confluence* of these values into the stream of the struggle, giving them a new dimension—the *national dimension*."[133]

Like Fanon's exemplar of psychological healing, Cabral's exemplar of organic unfolding suggests a preexisting subject of the struggle in the form of a nation. Cabral is tempted, therefore, to speak in the case of Guinea of "the people," "our" history, "national culture," as if these entities made sense before the struggle started. At the same time, Cabral seems to have been quite aware of the role of this idea of the nation as a necessary fiction, essential to unite and inspire the people but actualized only in the struggle itself. Therefore, he refrained from trying to define a national culture or a national philosophy and could thus avoid the pitfalls of African Socialism, with its self-appointed spokespersons for the nation who were designing essentialistically conceived national cultures.

In the specific conditions of our country—and we should say of Africa—the horizontal and vertical distribution of levels of culture is somewhat complex. In fact, from the villages to the towns, from one ethnic group to another, from the peasant to the artisan or to the more or less assimilated indigenous intellectual, from one social class to another, and even, as we have said, from individual to individual within the same social category, there are significant variations in the quantitative and qualitative level of culture. It is a question of prime importance for the liberation movement to take these facts into consideration.[134]

This pluralism in matters of culture implies the impossibility of continental or racial cultures since "from the economic and political point of view one can note the existence of various Africas, so there are also various African cultures."[135]

The new understanding of Cabral's discourse as founded on the exemplar of the organic "unfolding of internal characteristics" also resolves what initially appeared as the main anomaly in Cabral's thought, namely, the idea that the petty bourgeoisie should "commit class suicide." Yet there is no contradiction here. The step that the petty bourgeoisie should take is simply part of the process of a society reestablishing the connection with its history. The "subjective" factor in history is part and parcel of Cabral's idea of society and culture. The appearance of a contradiction only arises if Cabral's revolutionary nationalism is interpreted according to the framework of Marxist theory.[136]

At the end of his famous presentation "National Liberation and Culture" Cabral formulated the aims of national independence and the new social order.[137] They included:

Development of a *people's culture* and of all the aboriginal positive cultural values
Development of a *national culture* on the basis of history and the conquests of the struggle itself
Constant raising of the *political and moral awareness* of the people (of all social categories) and of *patriotism*, spirit of sacrifice and devotion to the cause of independence, justice and progress
Development of the technical and technological *scientific culture*, compatible with the demands of progress
Development, on the basis of a critical assimilation of mankind's conquest in the domains of art, science, literature, etc., of a *universal culture*, aiming at perfect integration in the contemporary world and its prospects for evolution
Constant and generalized raising of feelings of humanism, solidarity, respect and disinterested devotion to the human being.[138]

We see here that the whole idea of liberation in Cabral's view is a collective *prise de conscience* of a people in a struggle to regain creativity and self-mastery. Cabral's is thus a classical example of a theory of emancipation. It can benefit from the Marxist theory of society but it is a discourse in its own right.

Class Struggle and Delinking from the Global Capitalist System: The Academic Marxists

The works of Abdoulaye Ly and Majhemout Diop from Senegal, in the late 1950s, provide early examples of the tradition of sophisticated Marxist analysis that has been prominent in African political thought in the second half of the twentieth century. Their works primarily concerned the class analysis of the late colonial system. According to Diop the primary subject of the revolutionary struggle would be the proletariat ("an alliance with the peasantry under the direction of the working class").[139] Abdoulaye Ly, following a Maoist line, stressed the revolutionary potential of the peasantry and the

great floating mass of the "less educated" . . . the manual workers—wage earners—directly emerging from the peasantry and remaining in close contact with them, who sell their raw labour to the towns (warehouses), to the large plantations (cocoa, coffee, pineapples), in the large seasonal crop areas (*navetanes*), or in the forest zones ("swimmers" for the floating of timber).[140]

Ly's and Diop's texts, although heavily loaded with theory, have a good eye for detail, representing a type of political analysis that is empirically well informed and closely related to political action.

In the following decades, political discourse on the struggle against neocolonialism increasingly adopted the form of academic analyses, especially in studies of political economy. Such discourses were primarily located in the new African universities where, as places of relative freedom, the new African intelligentsia could be found.[141] With the radical anti-imperialists eliminated from political influence in most countries during the 1960s, the universities constituted rare places to reflect on the failures of African Socialist and capitalist development policies.

The major intellectual event in African political theory in the 1970s was the emergence of neo-Marxist theories of dependent capitalism and underdevelopment. Academically, the underdevelopment theories were the counterattack against dominant development theory; politically, they were inspired by the revolutionary socialist successes of Mao Ze Dong and Ho Chi Minh.[142] Colin Leys's *Underdevelopment in Kenya: the Political Economy of Neo-Colonialism* (1975) has been particularly influential in African radical discourse. This book provided an application of underdevelopment theory to a specific African country and at the same time attempted to avoid a purely economic interpretation of underdevelopment. Leys gave an account of the complexities of the emerging class structure, the changing role of international capital, and the nature of the political process, in particular the role of the national leader and his margin of operation and manipulation.[143]

The outlines of the conception of underdevelopment theory can be sketched as follows. The history of the last centuries is essentially that of the worldwide expansion of capitalism. Whether through trade, plunder, or exploitation, the surpluses generated in the periphery are exteriorated to the center which prevents the development of capitalist accumulation in the periphery. Instead, dependent relations of production and dependent classes develop in the periphery. Such a situation allows political independence, that is to say "flag independence," thus firmly locking such societies in their subordinate position within the international capitalist system. In this situation there are basically two alternatives for Third World development. The first is the Japanese path of breaking into the international market of manufactured products. It is very doubtful if this option still exists for the great majority of underdeveloped countries. The other is to opt for a much simpler "homemade" technology, manufacturing for the domestic market or markets of like-minded states. This strategy, however, requires "a very different class structure and a very different political leadership. In other words it implies radical social changes in the periphery."[144]

The real alternative for an underdeveloped country may indeed be either to play a very subordinate role in an international capitalist system, with little benefit to the majority of its people, or to seek an independent role in an alternative system of poorer but noncapitalist countries, a role which promises less, but might be more capable of fulfilling its promise.[145]

Dependency theory is designed on a spatial model of center and periphery linked by relations of subjugation and exploitation. The political content of this model derives from the historical case of the Chinese revolution, symbolized by the Long March. The periphery, that is, the countryside, struggled against the all-powerful center, the cities. The communists organized the periphery, the "victims" of the system, and they cut the exploitative relations between the center and the periphery, thus eliminating the source that sustained the center. As a result, the center was dismantled. This story depicts in a condensed form the political logic of underdevelopment theory, namely, that the essence of the system is extraction from the periphery, while the elimination of the system involves cutting the links of extraction (delinking). The exemplar suggests analysis and strategy as well as remedy.

The introduction of dependency and underdevelopment theory into African political discourse had an enormous impact. It provided a firm foundation for the idea of neocolonial domination that shaped the intellectual framework of a whole generation of outstanding African intellectuals. Leys' book *Underdevelopment in Kenya: the Political Economy of Neo-Colonialism* (1975) and his subsequent change of position in 1978 triggered, for instance, what has become known as the "Kenya debate."[146] The intensity of such debates, mainly limited to academic partisans, derived from the fact that the theory implied a program of political action. The theory suggested that the real struggle belongs to the masses united against imperialism as well as against its local agents who are in control of the neocolonial states.

In the second half of the 1970s the major assumptions of underdevelopment theory were undermined by empirical studies. First, the masses, if analyzed more closely, turned out to be actually a plurality of groups and classes. Rather than being the victims of the imperialist system, they constituted societies with their own dynamics that engaged in complicated interrelations with national and transnational actors. Second, the assumption of imperialism as an entity "acting" in a more or less coordinated manner to subvert the periphery constituted a rather radical simplification. Finally, the national elite turned out to be actually much less externally directed than previously assumed and more complicated and contradictory in itself. These complications led to a variety of positions, which Gavin Kitching, in an interesting account of the debates, compared to those of the Narodniki, Bolsheviks, and Mensheviks in the Russian discussions in the early twentieth century.[147]

The failures of African Socialism were interpreted by Marxists as requiring a return to a more straightforward scientific socialist orientation. This orientation received new inspiration in the mid-1970s when the ex-Portuguese colonies (Guinea Bissau, Angola, and Mozambique) chose a Marxist orientation after liberation. In political thought, this scientific socialist stance can be exemplified by the concise book by A. M. Babu *African Socialism or Socialist Africa?* (written in prison in Tanzania and published in 1981). Babu built his merciless critique of African Socialism on a standard Marxist understanding of the historical process as a movement from capitalism to proletarian socialism. This universal logic toward developing "the productive capacity to the maximum" does not circumvent Africa.[148] If African leaders proclaim an "African way" or a "third way" and deny the fact of class struggle, they only confuse the African revolution since "that is where imperialism wants us to be."[149] In fact, Babu argues, an indigenous road to capitalism is blocked. In this "age of proletarian revolution" there is only the socialist alternative, involving an alliance between the proletariat, the peasantry, and the intellectuals.

Babu's eloquent and comprehensive argument is far removed from the sophisticated academic exchanges in the Kenya debate.[150] Instead of relying on empirical detail, Babu builds his analysis on theoretical premises. The empirical evidence that made Colin Leys and others change their views toward the end of the 1970s (see above) could not affect Babu's type of argument, although historical experience did. The lack of success of Marxist-Leninist governments after 1975 and especially the famine in "Marxist-Leninist" Ethiopia in 1984 marked the end of this scientific socialist or African Marxist alternative even before the socialist world crumbled in 1989.[151]

My account of the tradition of academic Marxist thought does little justice to the bulk of elaborate and sophisticated works in political economy that were produced in the decades between 1970 and 1990 by such eminent scholars as Claude Ake, Dani W. Nabudere, Samir Amin, Mahmood Mamdani, Issa G. Shivji, Julius O. Ihonvbere, and many others. The net result for political thought of all this impressive work, however, is not different from what my sketchy analysis has shown. By the end of the 1980s practically all Marxist options had been discredited. The agenda of political thought shifted to issues such as democratization and human rights, so long disparaged as "bourgeois concerns," and to the new issue of civil society. The perspective of radical social change turned, more modestly, to the issues of social movements and popular struggles for democracy. This will be dealt with in chapter 7 which discusses contemporary intellectual developments.

Three Discourses of Revolutionary Struggle: Nkrumah, Fanon, and Cabral

The key message of my discussion of revolutionary discourses is a double one. On the one hand, the differences are relevant. The discourses of Fanon and Cabral have their own architecture and do not just represent applied versions of Marxism. On the other hand, one should acknowledge the similarities. Most political economists and radicals, from Nkrumah to Amin, shared a basic Marxist vocabulary. Although the great number of sophisticated theoretical and empirical Marxist studies in the 1970s and 1980s have done much to refine, decorate, furnish, and color the Marxist edifice, its basic architecture remained the same.[152]

In order to map the most important contrasts, I want to return for a moment to the three key theorists discussed before, Nkrumah, Fanon, and Cabral. The key exemplar in each of their discourses can guide the way.

Nkrumah's image of the Wall Street octopus provides an essentially global view of imperialism. Africa is perceived as a victim and African history as a process of subjection. Since the enemy is presented as global and enveloping, the struggle must also be global or at least include the whole African continent. Local circumstances, cultural contradictions, and intrahuman aspects remain either outside the range of vision or are analyzed strictly in terms of the global dualism of imperialist versus anti-imperialist forces. This is true for Nkrumah's schematic Marxism as well as for sophisticated Marxist analyses because both assume that ethnic, cultural, social, and political phenomena are ultimately conditioned by the political-economic order (or are politically irrelevant).

If the global capitalist system is the source of all distortion, then liberation is the end of trouble. There is no reason to design partial solutions or to speculate about an alternative system. The heuristics of the discourse direct all attention to understanding the cause: the capitalist system. While Cabral called for a discussion of "our own weaknesses" and of the complications of motivating and organizing the people, Nkrumah focused on "know the enemy": the system and the malicious operations of imperialism.

Fanon's revolutionary thought is designed quite differently. His model is not a global monster, a global political-economic system, but rather an interhuman or even intrahuman drama, namely, alienation. At the individual level, the resolution of this drama involves regaining self-identity, and at the collective level it involves complete national liberation and the creation of a society that differs totally from the imperial example. Where Nkrumah studied the system of the enemy, in Fanon's analysis the enemy is hardly more than the background of his discussion that centers on the militants' own actions. The key to liberation lies in the person and in the people, while the aim is defined in terms of these actors, namely, as regained self-identity.

Fanon's psychological model of liberation also accounts for his lack of attention to the historical and cultural diversity of the peoples who are struggling. After all, human beings share a basic psychological makeup. Whatever their specific backgrounds and cultural orientations may be, persons and nations undergo a similar alienation and have to go through a similar process of a reestablishment of self-identity. Of course, the outcome, the free society, will be different according to different contexts, but this does not need special attention. Like the therapist, who is primarily concerned with a specific illness and not with the individuality of the patient, the revolution is primarily concerned with liberation and not the cultural specifics of a people.

Between the universality at the macro level of the global system and the universality of the human psyche and its possible disorders, there is an infinite variety of communities, societies, and cultures, each with their specific histories. Conceptualizing the struggle at the middle level, as Cabral did, conditions a different discourse on liberation, one that cannot ignore situational specifics.

Cabral was neither a professional politician nor a professional psychiatrist but rather an agricultural engineer. In essence, for him, liberation meant the practical creation of a community that could freely develop its specific productive capacities. The key expression "mastering your own historicity" refers to mastering a development that is specific to a nation.

Conceptualizing development at the middle level of concrete communities also suggests that there are no laws of evolution to guarantee that liberation will succeed. The theorists of the global capitalist system could pretend to know the laws of that system, which told them that capitalism and imperialism

Table 5.3
Three Discourses of Revolutionary Struggle

	EXEMPLAR	TYPE OF EXEMPLAR	IDEA OF LIBER-ATION
Nkrumah	octopus Chinese revolution	economic	delinking
Fanon	the alienated person	psycho-analytical	reestablishment of self-identity
Cabral	organic nature	biological	"unfolding" development / "mastering historicity"

would eventually give way to a new type of social formation: socialism. Even Fanon's psychological model suggested that alienation is not the natural state and will be redressed. Cabral's discourse, however, has to do without such theories that make implicit promises. He has to refer to the rights and good intentions of historical actors rather than to "facts of theory."[153] Liberation involves a *prise de conscience* of the whole nation, especially of the petty bourgeoisie. Cabral's "organic" model involves an objectivistic promise for a better world but only in a weak version. He suggests, for instance, that the "unfolding behaviour (development) of a phenomenon-in-motion" is its natural behaviour.[154]

My argument has been that the three discourses conceptualize the problem of liberation by choosing an exemplar from a different level: the global, the personal, and the communal (Table 5.3). Although, finally, Nkrumah, Fanon, and Cabral were comrades in the anti-imperialist struggle and would probably agree on most specific issues, nonetheless they present different liberation discourses.[155]

NOTES

1. For example, C. Young, *Ideology and Development in Africa* (New Haven and London: Yale University Press, 1982); D. Ottaway & M. Ottaway, *Afrocommunism* (New York and London: Africana Publishing, 1981).

2. Quotes from J. Tully, ed., *Meaning & Context. Quentin Skinner and his Critics* (Cambridge: Polity Press, 1988), 16–17. Tully explains here how Quentin Skinner's historical hermeneutics can still be guided by a concern that is contemporary to us.

3. See K. Nkrumah, *Ghana: The Autobiography of Kwame Nkrumah* (1957; reprint, London: Nelson; New York: International Publishers, 1971), 303–304.

4. G. Padmore, *Africa and World Peace* (1937; reprint, London: Frank Cass, 1972), x.

5. Padmore, *Pan-Africanism or Communism? The coming struggle for Africa* (London: Dobson, 1956), 21–22. The book remained silent on the societal system that should fulfill the Pan-Africanist ideal of "universal brotherhood, social security and peace for all peoples everywhere" 18. It would definitely not be communism. Padmore argued that African independence was a necessity to prevent Africans from turning to communism.

6. In his excellent book *Idéologies des Indépendences Africaines*, 105, Yves Bénot resented that Nkrumah "n'a jugé utile de mentioner cette période de maccarthysme larvé" in any of his publications. Bénot's denunciation of Padmore as a mix of "l'obsession anti-communiste et l'empirisme britanique" (p. 195) is inappropriate, however. After working for decades in the communist movement and for African nationalism, Padmore knew perfectly well what he left behind when discarding Bénot's "idéologie socialiste véritable" 194.

7. See Basil Davidson, *Black Star. A View of the Life and Times of Kwame Nkrumah* (1975; reprint, Boulder: Westview Press, 1989) for this argument. My argument is that the framework of thought expressed in Padmore's *Panafricanism or Communism*, or Nkrumah's *I Speak of Freedom*, is quite different from the radical thought expressed after the Manchester Conference in 1945.

8. Several interpreters want to mark consciencism and African Socialism off from Nkrumahism, which they considered to be the malicious invention of the conservatives around Nkrumah, such as Kofi Baako. See P. J. Hountondji, *African Philosophy. Myth and Reality* (1976; reprint, Bloomington: Indiana University Press, 1983), chapt. 6, or Bénot, *Idéologies*, 201. Nkrumah did not distance himself from this Nkrumahism, however.

9. Even Basil Davidson, the sympathetic observer and staunch supporter of Nkrumah, states that Nkrumah tried to make "a revolution without revolutionaries." B. Davidson, *Black Star. A View of the Life and Times of Kwame Nkrumah*, 178. On the evictions, see pp. 126–132 in the same book.

10. K. Baako, "Nkrumaism—Its Theory and Practice," *The Party* (CPP Journal, Accra, 1961), 4–7. Quoted from reprint in P. Sigmund, ed., *The Ideologies of Developing Nations* (New York: Praeger, 1963), 188, 189.

11. K. Nkrumah, *Consciencism. Philosophy and Ideology for Decolonization* (1964; reprint, New York: Monthly Review Press, 1970), 70.

12. For example, Baako, "Nkrumaism."

13. Both quotes from K. Nkrumah, *Africa Must Unite* (1963; reprint, New York: International Publishers, 1970), 83.

14. Even Pan-Africanism was basically justified in terms of progress. "The obvious solution is unity, so that development can be properly and cohesively planned." Nkrumah, *Africa Must Unite*, 53.

15. Nkrumah, *Africa Must Unite*, 62. Basil Davidson comments that Nkrumah, "so much more constructive than his regionalistic opponents, called for a constitution in which the central government held all the ultimate power." Davidson, *Black Star. A View of the Life and Times of Kwame Nkrumah*, 150. Note how much the valuation of exactly this idea of a centralized state has changed, even with Davidson himself. Davidson, *The Black Man's Burden*.

16. K. Nkrumah, *I Speak of Freedom. A Statement of African Ideology* (London: Mercury Books, 1961), 44; see also chapter 5 in that book. Padmore stated: "tribalism is undoubtedly the biggest obstacle in creating a modern democratic state and an integrated nation out of small regional units inhabited by backward people still under the influence of traditional authority." Padmore, *Pan-Africanism or Communism?*, 288. In his *Africa Must Unite*, 84, Nkrumah is pragmatic: "If, in the interregnum, chieftancy can be used to encourage popular effort, there would seem to be little sense in arousing the antagonism which the legal abolition would stimulate."

17. Quotes from Nkrumah, *Africa Must Unite*, 126, 129. The hegemony of Nkrumah's CCP was confirmed in several national elections where the opposition was defeated even in its own strongholds. The democracy within the CCP itself, however, was much more of a problem. Julius Sago (alias Ikoku), the radical supporter of Nkrumah and editor of *The Spark*, blamed the degeneration of the CCP on the absense of democratic structures and influence "from below." S. G. Ikoku, (Julius Sago), *Le Ghana de Nkrumah: autopsie de la 1re Republique (1957–1966)*, trans. Y. Bénot (Paris: Maspero, 1961). Original: *Mission to Ghana* (Benin City: Ethiope Ed.).

18. Nkrumah, *Africa Must Unite*, 126–127. Typically, imperialist conspiracies not discontent may destroy the unity: "African workers, as the likeliest victims of these infiltrations, must be on their guard" 127.

19. Ibid., 130.

20. Quotes on Nkrumah, *Consciencism*, 57, 59, and 61 respectively.

21. Ibid., 65.

22. Ibid., 74.

23. Nkrumah, *Africa Must Unite*, 77.

24. A similar congruence in style can be observed between Nkrumah's *Africa Must Unite* and *Class Struggle in Africa*. Nkrumah presents himself to the reader in completely different roles: as practical pamphleteer (*The Circle* and *Handbook*), fact-gatherer (*Neo-colonialism*), metaphysician (*Consciencism*), and political-economic analyst (*Africa Must Unite* and *Class Struggle*).

25. Not only the inspiration of radical thought thirty years ago is not easily grasped today, but also the concrete fears behind its politics are easily overlooked. Radicals linked imperialist acts of destabilization with the orchestration of world affairs and not without reason, since a number of radical African leaders were murdered primarily at the orders of Western powers (Lumumba, Mondlane, Cabral, Machel). See the astonishing facts about CIA murder plans brought together in Madeleine Kalb's *The Congo Cables. Cold War in Africa. From Eisenhower to Kennedy* (New York: MacMillan, 1982).

26. K. Nkrumah, *Handbook of Revolutionary Warfare* (London: Panaf, 1969), 5.

27. Nkrumah, *Handbook*, 8.

28. K. Nkrumah, *Neo-Colonialism: The Last Stage of Imperialism* (London: Nelson, 1965), p. 240 (emphasis is mine).

29. K. Nkrumah, *Class Struggle in Africa* (London: Panaf, 1970), 10.

30. Nkrumah, *Handbook*, 32; see also Nkrumah, *Class Struggle,* chapt. 3.

31. Nkrumah, *Handbook*, 23.

32. Ibid., 29, 28.

33. This is the subtitle of the 1970 edition of *Consciencism*.

34. Nkrumah, *Ghana*, 48.

35. Note that Hountondji is not at all in the anti-Nkrumah camp. As for the factual analysis of the Nkrumah period, he used Julius Sago's (Ikoku's) interpretation in *Le Ghana de Nkrumah*. In fact, apart from its analytical sophistication, Hountondji's discussion (like Ikoku's) is one of the few examples of a critical analysis of Nkrumah that is still basically sympathetic to his venture. Many sympathizers run the risk of shouting down Nkrumah's words with their own songs of praise.

36. P. J. Hountondji, *African Philosophy. Myth and Reality* (1976; reprint, Bloomington: Indiana University Press, 1983), 149.

37. Hountondji, *African Philosophy*, 154. Hountondji also criticized the doctrine of consciencism itself, for example, its claim to put forth a coherent doctrine, while in fact providing an arbitrary connection between elements such as materialism, the possible existence of God, egalitarianism, humanistic ethics, self-determination, and socialism.

38. Ibid., 154. "A plurality of beliefs and theoretical choices does not preclude committment to the same political ideal. The only necessary basis for committment is that common interests are at stake: national interests in the case of anti-colonial struggle, class interests in the case of the struggle for socialism" 154. See also Hountondji's article "What Philosophy can do," *Quest* 1, no. 2 (1987): 3–30, on delimiting politics from philosophy.

39. Nkrumah, *Neo-Colonialism*, 43.

40. Nkrumah, *Handbook*, 44; see also idem, *Class Struggle*, chapts. 3 and 6.

41. However, Zik acquiesced to the federal structuring of Nigeria at the 1953 constitutional conference.

42. Quoted in Langley, *Ideologies of Liberation*, 471.

43. Ibid., 494.

44. D. K. Chisiza *Africa—What Lies Ahead* (Indian Council for Africa, 1961) is in fact one of the few elaborate African expressions of this discourse, which normally remains taken for granted. C. Young, *Ideology and Development in Africa* (Newhaven and London: Yale University Press, 1982), 183. "Developmentalism" was, after all, so firmly entrenched in ongoing aid programming that it could do well without explicit ideological statements.

45. Quotes on Chisiza, *Africa*, 5.

46. Chisiza, *Africa*, 11.

47. K. A. Busia, *The Challenge of Africa* (New York: Praeger, 1962) begins with two chapters on Akan funeral rites and Akan values and African culture. His *Africa in Search of Democracy* (London: Routledge, 1967) begins with a chapter on the "religious heritage" followed by one on the "political heritage." The contrast with great contemporaries of Busia is interesting: whereas Nkrumah seemed to write from an imaginary position of the capital of the whole continent, and Azikiwe from a relatively detribalized position in the metropolis Lagos, Busia's orientation point was basically an African cultural and societal tradition, namely the Akan tradition.

48. The two elements neatly correspond to the two main forces Busia relied on in politics, namely, the liberal West and the traditional rulers. Compare, for example, Kwame Ninsin's analysis of the anti-CCP opposition in his "The Nkrumah Government and the Opposition on the Nation State: Unity versus Fragmentation," contribution to a symposium on the life and work of Kwame Nkrumah. (Legon: Institute of African Studies, 1985).

49. K. A. Busia, *The Challenge of Africa* (New York: Praeger, 1962), 46–47, 47, 137. Busia contrasts his views with the racial particularism of the early Négritude movement. It can be charged, however, that Busia, just like Horton one century earlier, so identified with modern European society that he actually had a strong tendency to identify modernity with the West.

50. See chapter 3 of K. A. Busia, *Africa in Search of Democracy*; also see A. A. Boahen, *African Perspecives on Colonialism* (Baltimore and London: John Hopkins University Press, 1987).

51. See especially Busia, *The Challenge of Africa*, ch. 4.

52. Busia, *Africa in Search of Democracy*, 108.

53. K. A. Busia, *The Position of the Chief in the Political System of Ashanti* (1951; reprint, London: Frank Cass, 1968), 9.

54. Busia, *Africa in Search of Democracy*, 97.

55. Ibid., 87.

56. Ibid., 33.

57. Busia added more specific criticism of single-party rule. Even if we hear "the cry 'one man, one vote' . . . it should be noted that this is valueless without freedom of speech and association or public discussion." Busia, *Africa in Search of Democracy*, 99. If the party demands loyalty to its policies and leadership, how can differences of opinion be maintained within the single party? Similarly, the fact that voters can eliminate candidates in elections (such as happened in Tanzanian elections) only proves that voters can eliminate personnel, not policies. Even the choice of personnel is incomplete since it is a choice among the leadership, not a choice of the leadership.

58. Quotes in Busia, *Africa in Search of Democracy*, 101, 98, 98, and 110 respectively.

59. Quotes in Busia, *Africa in Search of Democracy*, 116, 119.

60. Although Busia's sophisticated arguments could have received new enthusiasm in the democratization discourse in the 1990s, he seemed to be practically forgotten.

61. Besides an orientation toward the general public, the African Socialist authors kept a keen eye on the opinions of the well-wishers in the West who were subsidizing their programs, as well as on the contending superpowers.

62. Ch. Clapham, "The Context of African Political Thought," *The Journal of Modern African Studies* 8, no. 1 (1970): 1–13.

63. For example, Nyerere, Kaunda, and Senghor.

64. J. Nyerere, *Freedom and Socialism: A Selection from Writings and Speeches, 1965–1967* (Dar es Salam: Oxford University Press, 1968), 2.

65. Quote from Nyerere, *Freedom and Socialism*, Introduction. The term "second independence" is used by a variety of authors.

66. See also Padmore's discussion of Pan-African Socialism in W. H. Friedland & C. G. Rosberg, *African Socialism* (Stanford: Stanford University Press, 1964), 223–237.

67. It is clear that actual Kenyan policies were rather capitalist in orientation. The launching of the document was itself an important maneuver in the Kenyan political scene at that time. See C. Leys, *Underdevelopment in Kenya: The Political Economics of Neo-Colonialism* (London: Heinemann, 1975).

68. Such authority could be different from that of the chief. See, for example, E.A.B. van Rouveroy van Nieuwaal & D. I. Ray, *The New Relevance of Traditional Authorities to Africa's Future*, special issue of *Journal of Legal Pluralism* 37, no. 38 (1996).

69. Mamadou Dia, "Independence and Neocolonialism," P. Sigmund, ed., *The Ideologies of Developing Nations* (New York: Praeger, 1963), 232–238; a translated section of Dia, *Nations Africaines et Solidarité Mondiale* (Paris, 1960), 236.

70. Mamadou Dia, "Independence and Neocolonialism," 238.

71. The African communalistic culture as a 'We' culture has been a frequented subject for decades, especially among philosophers. For example, T. Ntumba, "Afrikanische Weisheit. Das dialectische Primat des *Wir* vor dem *Ich-Du*," in W. Oelmüller, *Philosophie und Weisheit* (Baderhorn: F. Schöningh, 1988); K. C. Anyanwu, "African Political Doctrine," in O.E.A. Ruch & K. C. Anyanwu, *African Philosophy. An Introduction to the Main Trends in Contemporary Africa* (Rome: Catholic Book Agency, 1984), 369–383; Ch. B. Okolo, *African Social & Political Philosophy: Selected Essays* (Nsukka: Fulladu Publishing Company, 1993).

72. L. S. Senghor, *On African Socialism* (1961; reprint, New York: Praeger, 1964), 46; see pp. 26–48 for the general discussion of ideologies. Senghor's discussion of Marx is characteristic of a common view of Marx in the 1960s: essential mistakes in Marxism are recognized, while Marx is still respected as a humanist, the philosopher of the *Economical and Philosophical Manuscripts*.

73. Senghor, *On African Socialism*, 11. On p. 12 he quoted Hegel, "It is not the natural limits of the nation that form its character, but rather its national spirit." The nation is an essential aspect of humanization. Note that Senghor's view of the nation-state resembles that of Busia.

74. Ibid., 11, 13.

75. Ibid., 53.

76. According to present-day scientific understanding, Senghor mixed biological and cultural categories in an unacceptable way. Négritude is presented as both a matter of "blood" and "culture." He suggested that certain biologists support that "the psychological mutations brought about by education are incorporated in our genes and are then transmitted by heredity." Sigmund, *The Ideologies of Developing Nations*, 249. This is definitely incorrect according to most biologists.

77. Senghor's Foreword to H. R. Lynch, ed., *Selected Letters of Edward Wilmot Blyden* (New York: Kto Press, 1978).

78. All three quotes in Sigmund, *The Ideologies of Developing Nations*, 250.

79. A selection of Nyerere's many speeches and short texts were brought together in three books: *Freedom and Unity*, *Freedom and Socialism*, and *Freedom and Development*.

80. "Ujamaa: The Basis of African Socialism" is reprinted in W. H. Friedland & C. G. Rosberg, *African Socialism* (Stanford: Stanford University Press, 1964); quotes on pp. 246 and 245. The question of the practice of *Ujamaa* policies and also of the political role of the ideology in Tanzanian politics has been frequently discussed. The fact is that the idea of *Ujamaa* was hardly known among Tanzanians and was not even actively spread by distributing Nyerere's "Ujamaa: The Basis of African Socialism." F. G. Burke, "Tanganyika: The Search for Ujamaa," in Friedland & Rosberg, *African Socialism*", 203. This indicates that it should not be mistaken for a national philosophy shared by all.

81. "Dr. Nyerere's writings are more a protest against the colonial past than a systematic philosophy of the future." Burke, "Tanganyika," 205.

82. Ibid., 199.

83. J. Nyerere, *Freedom and Unity: A Selection From Writings and Speeches, 1952–1965* (Dar es Salam: Oxford University Press, 1968), 199.

84. Ibid., 200.

85. "Democracy and the Party System" (1963) is reprinted in Nyerere, *Freedom and Unity*, 195–203. On another occasion Nyerere suggested, "Given such responsible opposition I would be the first to defend its rights. But where is it? Too often, the only voices to be heard in 'oppostion' are those of a few irresponsible individuals." Sigmund, *The Ideologies of Developing Nations*, 201.

86. Nyerere, *Freedom and Unity*, 195–197.

87. Sigmund, *The Ideologies of Developing Nations*, 199. This view of politics deviates from the idea that the executive, legislative, and judiciary should be separate powers. The large powers of the executive under Nyerere could partly explain why Nyerere's humanist speech did not hinder the extensive use of the Prevention of Terrorism Act against opponents in Tanzania.

88. See, for example, the Arusha Declaration, part 5 and part 2-d.

89. Both types of refutations have been advanced, for example, by Busia.

90. At least grasping a deeper logic of the liberation struggle.

91. On violence, see, for example, R. Zahar, *Colonialism and Alienation: Concerning Frantz Fanon's Political Theory* (New York: Monthly Review Press, 1974). Originally published in German *Befreiung und Entfremdung* (Frankfurt am Mein, 1969); K. Wiredu, "The Question of Violence in Contemporary African Political Thought," *Praxis International* 6, no. 3 (1986): 373–381; S. Federici, "Journey to the Native Land. Violence and the Concept of the Self in Fanon and Gandhi," *Quest:*

Philosophical Discussions 7, no. 2 (1994): 47–70; on political ideas, see E. Hanson, *Frantz Fanon: Social and Political Thought* (Columbus: Ohio State University Press, 1977).

92. Fanon considered the colonial situation to be typified by the issue of race predominating over the issue of property; the superstructure dominates the infrastructure.

93. F. Fanon, *The Wretched of the Earth* (1961; reprint, Harmondsworth: Penguin, 1967), 28.

94. Ibid., 28.

95. Ibid., 67. The famous discussion of R. Zahar on Fanon (Zahar, *Colonialism and Alienation*) gives a convincing analysis of Fanon's views in this respect, and discusses the difference between work and violence. Her interpretation stresses the psychological basis of Fanon's views, referring mostly to Fanon's book *Black Skin, White Masks*.

96. Quotes on Fanon, *The Wretched of the Earth*, 101, 103.

97. Quotes on Fanon in ibid., 161, 115.

98. Peul and Fulbe are peoples in West Africa. Last three quotes in ibid., 127, 125, 127 respectively.

99. Quotes on Fanon, *The Wretched of the Earth*, 133, 135.

100. Quotes on ibid., 101, 88.

101. Ibid., 164.

102. Fanon's tendency to conflate African peoples under broad categories like "blacks" or "the oppressed" might be one of the reasons why he appears to have had particular impact outside Africa (e.g., among African-American radicals; see Hanson, *Frantz Fanon*, 4–10). Although probably all African intellectuals have read his work and his greatness is recognized, it is relatively rare to find him cited or discussed by African authors. Wiredu, "The Question of Violence."

103. Marxist theory may be another source of Fanon's abstract category of the "nation" and the "masses." Here one finds a similar reduction of a multitude of social and cultural differences under one category that is proposed by the theory as "the" subject of "the" revolution; Fanon's "oppressed" taking the place of Marx's "proletariat."

104. Quotes on Fanon, *The Wretched of the Earth*, 104, 101.

105. Ibid., 100. Fanon's subsequent detailed discussion of the various ways in which the rebellion gets frustrated, perverted, and, finally, reorganized is far from romantic. It should also be noted that his discussion of violence in this second stage of the struggle is much more practical than his ideas concerning spontaneuos anticolonial violence (e.g., pp. 106–107).

106. Fanon, *The Wretched of the Earth*, 141.

107. Quotes on ibid., 165, 150.

108. It should be stressed that Fanon's discourse does not include the standard Marxist-Leninist idea of mobilizing the rural majority of the people to capture state power. That state itself is rejected.

109. Fanon, *The Wretched of the Earth*, 142.

110. Ibid., 140.

111. "The young people of an under-developed country are above all idle: occupations must be found for them." Ibid., 158.

112. Ibid., 78.

113. P. Chabal, *Amilcar Cabral: Revolutionary Leadership and People's War* (London: Cambridge University Press, 1983), 167.

114. H. Bienen, "State and Revolution: The Work of Amílcar Cabral," *The Journal of Modern African Studies* 15, no. 4 (1977): 568.

115. A. Cabral, *Unity and Struggle: Speeches and Writings* (London: Heinemann, 1980), 121. Cabral's modesty seems to reflect also on his commentators. Visionary writers such as Kwame Nkrumah and Cheik Anta Diop are often practically silenced by the glorifications of their admirers whereas discussions on Cabral tend to be down to earth.

116. Ibid., 132.

117. A. Cabral, *Revolution in Guinea: An African Peoples' Struggle. Selected Texts by Amilcar Cabral* (London: Stage 1, 1969), 50.

118. Quoted in Chabal, *Amilcar Cabral*, 174.

119. Cabral, *Unity and Struggle*, 134.

120. Ibid., 136.

121. Ibid., 136.

122. Like all "vanguard theories" within the Marxist traditions, this conscious element, which the vanguard introduces, is according to the Marxist theory a "subjective" factor that contradicts the theory itself. See Rosa Luxemburg's critique of Lenin's contention that the revolutionaries have to introduce the right consciousness to the proletariat because by itself it just develops a "trade union cosciousness." L. Kolakowski, *Main Currents of Marxism*: Vol. 2, *The Golden Age* (Oxford: Oxford University Press, 1981), 82–88.

123. Cabral, *Unity and Struggle*, 136.

124. See chapter 2 above.

125. Cabral, *Unity and Struggle*, 143.

126. Quotes on ibid., 142, 140–141.

127. An organic mode of thought was less foreign to Marx himself than to the mechanicism of the Second International and Marxism-Leninism. (L. W. Nauta, "Heuristischer Wert und Unwert der Dialektik," in A. Honneth & A. Wellmer (Hrsg.), *Die Frankfurter Schule und die Folgen* (Berlin and New York: de Gruyter, 1986), 299–312.

128. Cabral, *Unity and Struggle*, 122.

129. Ibid., 141.

130. Cabral, *Revolution in Guinea*, 56.

131. Cabral, *Unity and Struggle*, 130.

132. Ibid., 153.

133. Ibid., 147.

134. Ibid., 144.

135. Ibid., 149.

136. On "revolutionary nationalism" or "developmental nationalism," see R. H. Chilote, "The Political Thought of Amilcar Cabral," *The Journal of Modern African Studies* 6 no. 3 (1968): 387.

137. Presented as the Eduard Mondlane Memorial Lecture at the Syracuse University, New York, on February 20, 1970.

138. Cabral, *Unity and Struggle*, 153.

139. Quoted from Langley, *Ideologies of Liberation*, 653.

140. Quoted from Langley, *Ideologies of Liberation*, 645–646.

141. Also journals such as the *Review of African Political Economy* (ROAPE).

142. The theoretical debates are represented in most contemporary textbooks on development theory. I limit my discussions to the implications of neo-Marxist theories for political conceptions.

143. Leys, *Underdevelopment in Kenya*, 211.

144. Ibid., 16.

145. Ibid., 24.

146. See, for example, G. Kitching, "Politics, Method, and Evidence in the 'Kenya Debate.'" In H. Berstein & B. K. Campbell, eds., *Contradictions of Accumulation in Africa: Studies in Economy and State* (Beverley Hills: Sage, 1985); and Y. Tandon, ed., *The Debate. Debate on Class, State & Imperialism* (Dar es Salam: Tanzanian Publishing House, 1982). On the impact of Leys's analysis, see, for example, J. Gugler, "How Ngugi wa Thiong'o Shifted from a Class Analysis to a Neo-Colonialist Perspective," *Journal of Modern African Studies* 32, no. 2 (1994): 329–339.

147. Especially G. Kitching, *Development and Underdevelopment in Historical Perspective: Populism, Nationalism and Industrialization* (London: Oxford University Press, 1982). One position was to play down the differences within the people, another suggested that a process of "proletarization" was already well under way (thus claiming the possibility of a proletarian socialist revolution), while a third contended that the complicated dynamics would result in a nonsocialist line of development, at least for the time being.

148. A. M. Babu, *African Socialism or Socialist Africa?* (London: ZED Press, 1981), xii.

149. Ibid., 60.

150. Including, for instance, a discussion of differences between the bourgeois and proletarian worldview.

151. On Afro-Marxism see D. Ottaway & M. Ottaway, *Afrocommunism* (New York and London: Africana Publishing, 1981). The failure of actual attempts at alternative development strategies had a significant, albeit indirect, influence on leftist political discourse: "Tanzania played a role for many Kenyan radicals rather like that played by the Soviet Union in the political struggles of Communists in western Europe in the inter-war period. [Its failure] had rather the same effect in Kenya as the 1956 revelations about Stalinism had on western Communism in the post-war period." Kitching, "The 'Kenya Debate,'" 145.

152. The case of Samir Amin is exemplary here. It is scholarly and engaged, absorbing any new issue that emerges: from economic dependence, to social history, to fundamentalism, and to democracy. His theoretical framework has remained largely unaffected (see chapter 7 of the present book).

153. "For us the basis of national liberation . . . is the inalienable right of every people to have their own history." Cabral, *Unity and Struggle*, 130.

154. Cabral, *Unity and Struggle*, 122.

155. At two crucial points, Fanon's and Cabral's own exemplars produce myths similar to Marxism. The first is the idea of coming socialism: although in less objectivistic terms than Marxism, their discourse suggests that capitalism will be replaced by a socialist society. The second one is the idea of a "subject" of revolution.

I argued that Fanon and Cabral import the idea of "the nation" as a kind of historical subject; the nation is a theoretically, rather than an empirically, substantiated notion.

6

Three Basic Types of Discourse

The previous chapters constitute a "long and winding road" through African political discourses. They have proved at least one point, namely, that these discourses, rather than reproducing European examples, as is often alleged, constitute a diverse and rich heritage intimately connected to the political history of Africa itself.[1] I want to proceed now with a systematic inventory of this heritage.

In the opening chapter, I stated that the tasks of this study involve hermeneutics, analytics, and criticism. In the three historical chapters, I have asumed the role of the hermeneutic, attempting as Thomas Kuhn said; "to learn to think like" the historical authors.[2] In the present chapter, I will adopt the more detached view of the analyst, and I will assume the role of the critic in the final chapter. From the analytical point of view, the intellectual structure rather than the historical context or the political role of discourses is of interest. A philosopher's analysis should uncover assumptions, oppositions, and the heuristics that shape the ground plan of a tradition—it is much like making an X-ray that passes through the surface tissue of ideas, while exposing the intellectual bone structure.

At first glance, the historical material exhibited in the previous chapters already indicates that the search for a single ground plan of modern African political thought is misguided. The political conceptions of, for instance, Blyden, Horton, and Babu are as incompatible as the physics of Aristotle, Newton, and Einstein.[3] This fact of basic paradigmatic diversity compels me to formulate the philosopher's task in terms of a plural form, namely, uncovering different ground plans of African thought.

The diversity of African political thought is clearly not a matter of historical periodization. In fact, authors that may be a century apart in time can appear to be very close in ideas. Kanduza Chisiza in the 1960s, for instance, reads like an echo of Africanus Horton in the 1860s, while George Ayittey in the 1990s revives the spirit of John Mensah Sarbah around 1900, and Leopold Senghor himself recognizes his proximity to Edward Blyden's thought.[4]

The intellectual currents run parallel to the flow of time. Depending on the theoretical starting point, philosophers appear to be compelled to follow similar approaches, thus reproducing similar models of thought. Although discourses are contextually conditioned, as I argued in the historical chapters, they unfold models of thought that reappear in different contexts.

Examples can be elucidating at this juncture. When the theoretical starting point is the idea of modernization or development, then the stage is literally set for a particular line of exposition. It creates a "topology," one could say, that locates every factor within the framework of a developmental process (involving lower and higher stages, a basically linear transformation process, and a positive valuation of this "development"). A common image representing this topology is that of a statistical curve indicating growth. Once the setting of the stage is taken for granted, it will give its particular cast to every issue under discussion.

The intellectual stage can also be set differently: the central image being, for instance, that of a circle marking off a domain, separating "inside" and "outside," and thus defining purity and pollution, or authenticity and alienation. Within this particular stage setting, the issue of development is not simply that of growth but involves vital choices, such as those between indigenous and alien forms of modernization. Within the modernization framework such a choice does not even emerge.[5]

The analysis of such basic models of thought is the necessary philosophical complement to historical analysis. In its absence one can claim to be a competent historian, but not an interesting commentator, let alone an efficient critic of political thought. The philosopher's investigation needs to go deeper than that of the historian. Neither the greatest historical detail nor the widest empirical scope can uncover basic paradigms. The philosophical exercise is reconstructive, which means that, based upon the historical material (but not identical to it) a discursive order or a model of thought is presented. The claim of such a reconstruction is that various historical discourses can be said to have an intellectual bone structure that is the same as or similar to the reconstructed model of thought.[6]

The agenda of the present chapter is to actually reconstruct such models of thought. For that purpose, I will follow a bottom-up strategy. First of all, I will take a retrospective view of the historical discourses, then I will reconstruct the basic models of thought. The result of this analytic and reconstructive labor forms the condensation of my historical study. In the final chapters, I will use the reconstructed models as an analytical tool for my inventory of African political thought at the end of the twentieth century.

AUTHENTIC AFRICA

"Black Consciousness," Steve Biko stated: "is based on the self-examination which has ultimately led them [the blacks] to believe that by seeking to run away from themselves and emulate the white man, they are insulting the intelligence of whoever created them black. Black Consciousness therefore expresses group pride and the determination of the black to rise and attain the envisaged self."[7] The Nigerian philosopher K. C. Anyanwu, formulating his "African political doctrine" within a rather different "unpolitical" philosopher's discourse, stated: "the spirit of this work is to identify and remove all the beliefs, ideas and thoughts that impede the manifestation of the African spirit. If it is allowed that the African spirit is dead and that this work is merely a post-mortem then the African people too are all dead. How can a people be alive when its God and spirit are dead?"[8] Both appeals for authenticity echo Blyden's ardent summon: "Be yourselves . . . if you surrender your personality, you have nothing left to give the world."[9]

The arguments of Biko, Anyanwu, and Blyden are not part of the same struggle and do not represent the same positions within the political spectrum. Neither did Biko and Anyanwu derive their ideas from Blyden's works. Their historical (and political) distance, however, does not preclude intellectual proximity. The settings in which their acts of argumentation take place are basically similar. They share an intellectual world or, phrased differently, they belong to the same intellectual family, which I will call the "family of identity discourses."[10]

At issue now is to define, so to say, the "genetic code" of this family, that is, the intellectual ground plan underlying their type of discourse. For that purpose, let me first take a comprehensive look at relevant forms of identity discourse.

Edward Blyden as Classical Example

After Blyden, identity discourse returned in a number of variants in the twentieth century. First of all, identity discourse appeared in the discourse of Négritude, which defended the beauty and unity of the African mode of being and underlined its clear difference from the Western mode.[11] Négritude was mainly concerned with characterizing *Africanité* at the phenomenological level. Unlike Blyden, it did not give much attention to the theoretical underpinnings of these characteristics with reference to natural evolution or God's creation.[12] Ethnophilosophy is another example of identity discourse. It shares the Blydenite thrust toward defining what is essentially African. Here, however, the essence is sought in African cultural traditions (or "the" African cultural tradition), rather than in race or African personality. A similar strand of thought, in this case inspired not by philosophy and ethnography but by historiography and linguistics, was developed by the Senegalese scholar Cheik

Anta Diop.[13] Other orientations, such as African-American Afrocentrism and South African black consciousness, combine racial, psychological, cultural, and historical grounds to argue for a deeply rooted African identity.

The classical example of identity discourse remains Blyden's work. His philosophy is a rather complete and ideal-typical formulation covering a whole range of questions from the genesis and order of the world to its phenomenology and normative implications. First of all, however, Blyden is exemplary in capturing the sentiments, worries, and drives that are characteristic of identity discourse. Blyden experienced being thrown into a world that was burdened with the world-historical drama that started with the appearance of the white man in Africa. For Blyden, this drama entailed more than the handicap of exploitation and injustice, it was a threat to the very existence of the African as an African. In the light of the magnitude of this drama, the basic affirmation of identity discourse, namely, that there is something like "the African," instantly became more than a factual statement. It was a performative statement as well, expressing commitment and pride and defining a mission. It dissected the world into grand (racial) units (black and white), separating friend from enemy.

Blyden's more strictly theoretical arguments (presented in more detail in chapter 3 of this book) can be summarized as follows:

1. The various aspects of "Negro" identity fit together into one complete mode of being, including a mode of social life (African communalism), of religious life, and of psychological makeup (the African personality). It makes sense, therefore, to speak of "the" African, "the" African culture, and "the" African mode of being beyond observable individual Africans, African cultures, and African peoples. The major cultures in the world define their specific mode of being.

2. This African mode has deep roots. Blyden not only traced African cultural traditions back to classical Egyptian times but he also considered the African race to be the evolutionary human adaptation to the continent's physical conditions. Africa belongs in a historical and biological sense to the "Negro" race (Blyden's term for African). The African mode is, therefore, fundamentally distinct from other modes of being, and Western influence is fundamentally alien to Africa.

3. Finally, Blyden's identity discourse provides a normative framework. Blyden considered the "Negro" and "his" history to be the expression of the benevolent plan of God. Creation involved different races, each with its particular qualities and own world-historical mission. This divine sanction makes it not only natural but also obligatory for Negroes to guard their identity. In Blyden's terms, the Negro should follow his "racial instincts" and develop his own strengths. Racial self-respect as well as avoidance of acculturation and mixing of races are therefore central to Blyden's type of identity discourse.

The Ground Plan of Identity Discourse

The next step in my investigation, namely, the detection of what I metaphorically called the "genetic code" or the ground plan of the family of identity discourses, can now proceed with the description of Blyden's core ideas. Before embarking on this venture, however, an assumption that may contradict my argument has to be defeated. One could argue that Blyden is in fact not exemplary for an identity discourse because his central notion of race is rather atypical. In addition, the notion of race itself has completely lost credit today because of its connotation with fascist thought. It has lost meaning even in the biological sciences. Interestingly, further inspection shows that there is not a fundamental gulf between a Blydenite discourse on race and today's identity discourse on culture. If we systematically substitute "African culture" for Blyden's "Negro race" and something like "essentially African cultural dispositions" for his "Negro racial instincts," then Blyden's argument remains intact. In fact, it will read like a contemporary text of, for instance, an ethnophilosopher like Anyanwu.[14] The similarity of a discourse on race and one on culture also reveals that the differences between the central notions used are not significant indicators for the ground plan of a discourse.

My conjecture is that a combination of two assumptions determines the ground plan of Blyden's discourse.

Table 6.1
Combination of Two Assumptions of Culturalism

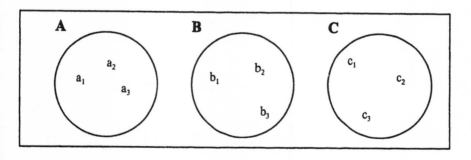

A, B, C	:	cultures
a_1, a_2, a_3	:	individuals with identities deriving from culture A
b_1, b_2, b_3	:	individuals with identities deriving from culture B
c_1, c_2, c_3	:	individuals with identities deriving from culture C

The first assumption is an essentialist idea of culture (or race, or psychological type for that matter). Blyden had a conception of culture as a kind of "body," an entity held together by a strong internal coherence or essence. Such a cultural entity defines a complete "mode of being."

The second assumption concerns the relationship of individuals or groups to the cultural entities. The assumption is that people "belong" to a culture. The mode of being defined by a culture is not something that can be shaken off easily for an individual is anchored in it and can only be "authentic" within his or her culture.

Together, these two assumptions result in a clear picture of the natural interrelation of cultures, groups, and individuals, as represented in Table 6.1. The combination of these two assumptions is essential for an identity discourse. The graphic representation in Table 6.2 shows that by itself the first assumption (cultural essentialism) allows the possibility that people move in and out of these essentially defined units, defining themselves differently at different times, or eclectically combining aspects of different cultures in their own way.

Table 6.2
Only the First Assumption of Culturalism

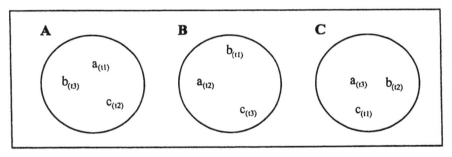

A, B, C	:	cultures
$a_{(t1)}$, $b_{(t1)}$, $c_{(t1)}$	:	individuals with identities deriving from cultures A, B, C respectively, at time t_1
$a_{(t2)}$, $b_{(t2)}$, $c_{(t2)}$	:	individuals with identities deriving from cultures A, B, C, respectively, at time t_1, but from B, C, A, respectively, at t_2
$a_{(t3)}$, $b_{(t3)}$, $c_{(t3)}$	:	individuals with identities deriving from cultures A, B, C, respectively, at time t_1, but from C, A, B, respectively, at t_3

If only the second assumption is maintained (authenticity-within-a-culture), then people are bound up with their culture, but this culture itself does not constitute a solid identity. It permits the possibility that these cultures are multistrained, fluid, mixing, and contextually constructed units, as represented in Table 6.3.[15]

Table 6.3
Only the Second Assumption of Culturalism

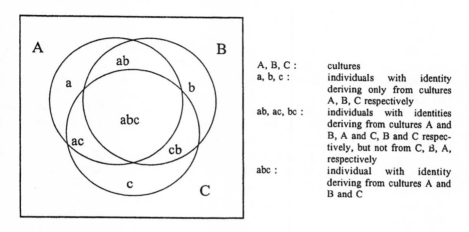

A, B, C :	cultures
a, b, c :	individuals with identity deriving only from cultures A, B, C respectively
ab, ac, bc :	individuals with identities deriving from cultures A and B, A and C, B and C respectively, but not from C, B, A, respectively
abc :	individual with identity deriving from cultures A and B and C

Following the terminology of Samir Amin and others, the discursive logic defined by these two assumptions can be called "culturalism."[16] Culturalism hypostatizes culture while assuming a tight connection between an individual and its culture. This, I claim, is the hidden genetic code of the family of identity discourses that underlies the similarities between Blyden, Anyanwu and Biko. They define cultural (racial) units and perceive the natural place of people to be within their unit.

A number of fundamental features of the identity type of discourse derive logically from the two basic assumptions of culturalism. Together they constitute a consistent model of thought.

1. In the first place, a culturalist ground plan creates a dichotomous worldview, a world divided between "We" and "They" or between what is "indigenous" and what is "alien." Whether it takes the form of the master-slave opposition (Blyden) or that of Negro-African as compared to Hellenic cultures (Senghor), black versus white (Biko) or conqueror versus conquered (Ramose), the "We" is positioned opposite a concrete opponent. Instead of a "We" being marked off from everything else (from an amorphous "They"), "We" and "They" are locked into an opposition where the one defines the other and vice versa. What is African is characterized by stating its differences from what is Western.[17]

The dichotomous worldview is also expressed in the typical line of presentation of culturalist arguments. Mostly they proceed by contrasting Africa with the West. Substantiating factual claims about what is "African" is achieved by sketching its differences from the "Western" model. Where empirical descriptions or references to empirical studies of African cultures are expected, contrasts of stereotypical models are presented.[18]

2. Because cultures are viewed as being defined by their essence, differences between cultures are necessarily perceived as being "deep." Cultural roots are traced back in long historical genealogies.[19] European culturalists search for their roots in ancient Greece, whereas African culturalists search in ancient Egypt. The "We" is projected back into history. In its best representations, this concern with cultural roots has resulted in studies that contradict established views on Africa and uncover Western culturalist bias. Such is the case, for instance, in E. W. Blyden's account of his travel to Egypt, in C. A. Diop's historical and linguistic investigations, and, rather as a negation of Western culturalism, in M. Bernal's *Black Athena*.

3. According to a culturalist view, the elements within each cultural unit are considered to belong "naturally" together thus forming an organic whole. This whole is vulnerable because the intrusion of alien elements can disrupt the organic equilibrium; a unit conceived as a historically fabricated *bricolage* could never be disrupted in such a way. Within a culturalist framework, therefore, penetration by alien elements tends to be perceived as negative while mixing and hybridity tend to be viewed with distrust.

4. The typical way to depict a culturalistically conceived unit is by using a circle to encompass the "We." The boundary that is drawn thus is "overconditioned": it is assumed that racial, cultural, continental, and linguistic boundaries more or less coincide. The human world is thought to be carved up between a limited number of grand units whose boundaries and differences can not be erased. This view of the world as divided into culture-continents induces many reflections upon difference, value and "relativity," such as between the Orient and the Occident, or Africa and the West. It also inspires idealistic ventures aiming at intercultural exchange or understanding that clearly make sense only within such a culturalistic view of a carved-up world.

We see here how the basic assumptions of culturalism lead to the unfolding of a more comprehensive model of viewing the world. Various individual discourses will evolve in their own way within the framework of this model. They can take the form of discourses on race or culture, discourses with cultural revivalist or political ambitions, conservative justifications for authoritarianism or radical inspirations for antiwhite resistance. All, however, are determined by the basic assumptions of the model of thought.

It is interesting to note, as Table 6.4 indicates, that such determinations may also ensue in forms other than the logic of a model of thought. A broader phenomenology of each type could be delineated, tracing its typical imagery, sentiments, philosophical inclinations, favorable words, and aspects of style. It is curious, for instance, to notice how often culturalist publications are given a cover depicting an African mask, or to observe the preference for domestic or rural images to illustrate what is African. Similarly, the choice of Anglo-Saxon mechanicism, rather than, for instance, German romanticism is used to illustrate what is essentially European. The culturalists' preference for philosophical essentialism and holism could also be further investigated. At this point, however, I will not pursue such a phenomenology.

Table 6.4
Identity Model

cultures as circles

basic concern	authenticity (existential)
fundamental features	
POLARITY	indigenous-alien
WORLD	culturalist world order of 1. essentialistically conceived culture-continents 2. people "belonging" in cultures
TO BE DONE	guard and unfold the deeply rooted indigenous identity
METAPHOR	"roots"
EXAMPLE	African family/village meeting
FIELD OF FOCAL AT-TENTION	culture
THEORETICAL KEY WORD	identity
PHILOSOPHICAL INCLI-NATION	holism essentialism

MODERN AFRICA

On the stage of identity discourse, the African predicament is enacted as a world-historical drama of cultures. Identity discourse's loud claim to represent the truly African perspective could make one overlook the fact that there are also other types of discourse in Africa. For many African intellectuals the flagrant development deficit has been a more pressing intellectual challenge than culture. The issue of development puts the practical problem at the top of the agenda of how to catch up, economically and technologically, with the rest of the world.

Looking back at the historical authors discussed so far, the concern with development resounds, although in clearly different ways, among a wide range of authors—such as Horton, Casely Hayford, Azikiwe, Awolowo, Nkrumah, Busia, Chisiza, and the modernizers who have dominated postindependence government administrations. Whether we consider Azikiwe's idea of a renascent Africa, Nkrumah's of the New African, or Busia's of democratic Africa, the intellectual horizon is constituted by the idea of modernity. Their differences concern the details of what this modernity entails and the way to proceed, but not the perspective of working toward a modern Africa.

Next to the family of identity discourses, therefore, a family of, what could be called, modernization discourses can be identified. Modernization is not defined here in the limited sense of a development theory within the structural functionalist tradition of the social sciences, but as an orientation in political thought, provisionally characterized by its concern for development and its ideal of building a modern Africa. The challenge of the present section is to uncover the intellectual ground plan upon which this orientation is built. Let me first take a comprehensive look at the main genealogical lines of the family before attempting to capture its "genetic code."

The optimistic universalism of the mid-Victorian African educated elite of the 1860s and 1870s, exemplified in my discussion in chapter 3 by Africanus Horton, constituted an early start of a modernist type of discourse. The modernist spirit took an interesting turn in the last years of the nineteenth century. Colonial policy and discrimination of the African elite fostered a revaluation of African heritages, for instance, in the Aboriginals Rights Protection Society (ARPS) and among theorists such as J. Mensah Sarbah and J. E. Casely Hayford. Modernization is vital, they argued, but it must come "from our own roots" and not in the form of importing foreign models. African traditions, in their view, are the very basis for development and are not its main obstacle, as Horton had perceived it. The idea of modernization from indigenous roots has been a continuous element, especially in Gold Coast-Ghanaian intellectual life throughout most of the century, with intellectuals such as Danquah, Sekyi, and Busia and today with Boahen, Gyekye, Wiredu, and Ayittey.

Another strand of modernization thought was carried by the young nationalists in the 1940s and 1950s in particular. For Azikiwe, the Nigerian Youth Movement (NYM), and the Zikists, Africa's modern future would be the product of the Young African who has cast off colonial prejudice and the "hat-in-hand-me-too-Sir" submissiveness of the older generation of elite Africans. The Young African is a self-conscious modernizer and a believer in basic liberal democratic values and in rapid industrialization. Together with the very similar, albeit leftist-inspired, modernism of Padmore and Nkrumah, this belief in the Young African making a New Africa has been the major inspiration of the nationalist leaders during the struggles for national independence and the first decade thereafter.

Africanus Horton and the Ground Plan of Modernist Discourse

Exemplary for a modernist orientation is Africanus Horton's view of Africa's marginalization. Africa, which at one time produced glorious civilizations, has landed at the margins of global development because of unhappy historical circumstances. There are no inherent obstacles to its return to prominence because, as Horton (a medical doctor) observed, biologically the races are essentially equal. Psychologically, Africans show great vitality, and because of its material resources Africa has great potential. Escaping current marginalization, therefore, is a practical task. It requires that Africans themselves take the initiative to revolutionize their societies and cultures by absorbing as many beneficial influences as possible, especially scientific and technological expertise, and applying these to the benefit of development.

Horton's basic narrative already contained the ground plan of a modernist model of thought. The centerpiece is a thoroughly universalist view of humanity. Biologically, all humans are equal. Culturally, therefore, no essential differences are expected, so that there is basically one human civilization. When actual differences are observed within humanity, such as differences in development, then these have to be accounted for by factors such as history, human action, and material resources.[20]

From this central universalist assumption a number of views derive.

1. The fact of a single human civilization that is gradually advancing in science and technology implies that for developing countries there is not really a question of development objectives. Since "we know where to go," there can only be questions concerning strategy. The modernization model suggests a pragmatic attitude of identifying the conditioning factors for rapid development and trying to realize such factors.

2. The basic equality of mankind suggests that it does not make sense to dwell too long on questions of race and culture. One can have a critical attitude toward other cultures but finally it is a matter of picking and choosing what is helpful for the "great leap ahead" in one's own development. The model suggests strategies of integration rather than of isolation.

3. As far as political systems are concerned, there is no reason not to learn from experiences anywhere in the world. Being in a relatively weak position, as Azikiwe argued, it may be even less advisable for Africa to experiment. Modernists therefore preferred the modern nation-state and the standard institutions of democratic politics (or those of a socialist polity) as these were said to have worked elsewhere.

Horton's solid universalism can be said to constitute the intellectual "genetic code" of the modernizationist family of theorists. Their shared basic concern with the issue of rapid development matched the universalist view of human progress, thus defining a shared model of thought.

Interestingly, the whole setup of the world in the modernist view is quite different from the one suggested by the identity model. Instead of a partitioned world, characterized by more or less static differences, we have here a single humanity in the process of perpetual development. Where the identity model suggests a graphic representation in the form of different circles, the modernization model (Table 6.5) implies one unit within which a differentiation along a development curve should be depicted.

Table 6.5
Modernization Model

	Development as "take-off"
basic concern	development (pragmatic)
fundamental features	
POLARITY	underdeveloped-developed primitive-modern
WORLD	a single human civilization developing toward universal modernity
TO BE DONE	to make a "great leap ahead" along the universal path of development
METAPHOR	"take-off"
EXAMPLE	modern society in the West
FIELD OF FOCAL ATTENTION	technology/economics
THEORETICAL KEY WORD	modernity
PHILOSOPHICAL INCLINATION	universalism voluntarism

As in the case of the identity model, family members show similarities in quite different areas from that of patterns of reasoning alone. They appear, quite often, to share many aspects of style, person, and background. Horton,

Casely Hayford, and Azikiwe were intensely exposed to cultural plurality at an early age.[21] All were successful, self-confident, and highly competent modern Africans motivated by a practical sense of achievement rather than by indignation over injustices of colonialism or racial discrimination. Being advanced in a Western type of education, they did not conceive of the West as a vague ideal but rather as a concrete complex of institutions and ideas from which one can learn and pick and choose. Even the most Anglophilic of these writers, Africanus Horton, was selective in his preferences.

LIBERATED AFRICA

Even by employing the existential drive of identity discourse as well as the pragmatic drive of modernization discourse, the most pervasive enkindling sentiment of modern African political thought has not yet been identified. The indignation caused by colonialism gave much of African thought a directly political concern, namely liberation.

The basic idea of liberation may be symbolized in Zambia's famous independence statue of a black man standing up and breaking the chains that shackle him. If any specific African is imagined to have been depicted there, then it is probably Kwame Nkrumah. In a way, he is both symbol and spokesman of African liberation. Nkrumah exhibits the essentially political nature of Africa's problems. Underdevelopment and cultural alienation, as he argued, are only symptoms of Africa's seminal problem, namely, its state of subjugation. "Seek ye first the political kingdom, and all things shall be added onto you" was Nkrumah's famous dictum.

The Marxist-inspired nationalism of Nkrumah is probably the best known version of liberation discourse. Africa, in his view, was not simply struggling against European colonialism but also against the more basic force of imperialism as the outgrowth of capitalism. The self-understanding of the struggle has shifted several times, however, in the last 150 years. For the Aboriginals Rights Protection Society (ARPS) in the 1890s Gold Coast, the struggle was that of the indigenous order, ready to adjust in its own ways to the challenges of modernity, versus the imposed order of the colonial intruder.[22] The dominant view of the struggle changed with the full establishment of colonial power around the turn of the century. African resistance was no longer formulated from outside the colonial system but from within. The actors put forth their demands as colonial subjects, referring to citizenship rights and the Wilsonian right to collective self-determination, while describing the struggle as a nationalist one, that is, as the struggle of colonially (not "traditionally") defined "nations."[23] The Pan-Africanist congresses (from 1900) and, to some degree, the National Congress for British West Africa (NCBWA) in the 1920s, proposed a more comprehensive view of the struggle—namely, as one concerned with (parts of) the African continent, the black race as a whole, and even all the colored peoples of the world. Characteristic of radical anti-imperialist thought, from Lamine Senghor, Kouyaté, and Padmore in the 1930s and 1940s, to Nkrumah, Fanon, Cabral, and the (ex-) Marxists of today, is its search for "deeper" historical causes of the African predicament.

The following basic assumptions about such a deeper order can be considered to constitute the ground plan of the liberation type of discourses:

1. The present world is not in its "true," desirable state; it is, so to say, in a state of alienation that should be and will be overcome. Capitalism itself as well as its product, imperialism, will perish.
2. This world is a polarized world divided into the camps of the oppressor and the oppressed (rich and poor, or the colonizer and the colonized).
3. In a way, the system-created polarity already holds the key to its resolution. The oppressed will (and should) force the system to change.

This ground plan of a world order, involving assumptions about types of socioeconomic order, about basic social oppositions and a historicist perspective, sets the stage for a complete model of thought. The ground plan conditions a range of derivative positions.

1. The world is perceived in terms of socioeconomic systems (colonialism, imperialism, capitalism, etc.), which has a number of consequences:

(a) Change is conceptualized as change of system: it is necessarily qualitative, not piecemeal change
(b) The issue of change is a *political* issue, involving changes in relations of power
(c) The horizon of political thought is not open: it consists of a definite alternative politicoeconomic system (mostly a variant of socialism). Universal patterns of systems change have to guarantee success of the struggle. Thus, discussions concerning *ideals* are not relevant: at issue are questions of *strategy*.

2. The "untrue" nature of the present state suggests that liberation equals the establishment of a state where all basic social problems are solved. The new state is either achieved by moving forward (Marxist), by a renaissance of the old (ARPS), or by "returning" to true self-identity or "our own history" (Fanon, Cabral). These variants are expressed in such key metaphors as "breaking the chains," "the Wall Street octopus," "delinking," "de-alienation," and "unfolding."

3. Another consequence of the basic assumptions is that issues of cultural, ethnic, and historical difference do not have a place in the model. The only important differences are those produced by the system itself, such as ones

between imperialist and colonized nations or between internal oppressors, perceived as foreign agents or *compradors*, and the "masses."

As in the case of the identity and modernization models, the liberation model of thought has a determining influence upon discourses built upon its ground plan. Once a theorist starts reasoning from its premises, he or she is induced to follow a specific path of argumentation, thus reproducing the patterns of a liberation model of thought (Table 6.6).

Table 6.6
Liberation Model

center-periphery model

basic concern	liberation
fundamental features	
POLARITY	oppressor-oppressed master-slave
WORLD	a world torn apart by the system of imperialist capitalism
TO BE DONE	revolution
METAPHOR	"breaking the chains," delinking
EXAMPLE	the Chinese Long March (for the ARPS, the Japanese Médji revolution)
FIELD OF FOCAL ATTEN-TION	political economics
THEORETICAL KEY WORD	exploitation, delinking
PHILOSOPHICAL INCLI-NATION	historicism mechanism

TOWARD A GRAMMAR OF MODERN AFRICAN POLITICAL THOUGHT

The present chapter sets out to trace recurring models of thought beneath the great variety of historical discourses in modern African political thought. The result of my analysis thus far provides the outline of what could be called a grammar of African political thought throughout the last 150 years. First of all, I have identified a certain order in the variety of historical discourses in the form of several "families of discourses" (Table 6.7). Subsequently, I have identified basic models of thought underlying the logic of each of these families (Table 6.8). Such a model is said to be conditioned by a basic concern and set of assumptions (I used the metaphors of "genetic code" and "ground plan" for these basics). When thinking within the parameters of the ground plan, a range of related features suggest themselves, making up a comprehensive view of the African condition. Once a theorist is lured into the magic circle of a model of thought, his or her reasoning will unfold along similar lines to those of his accomplices.

The result of this exercise can be summarized in the following two tables:

Table 6.7
Families of Discourse in Historical Perspective

	IDENTITY TYPE	MODERNIZATION TYPE	LIBERATION TYPE
	polarity: indigenous-alien	polarity: primitive-modern	polarity: oppressor-oppressed
1850–1900	Blyden	Horton	ARPS
1900–1940	Keyatta, Danquah (Garvey)	Azikiwe, Zikists	Padmore, Nkrumah
1940–1960	Danquah, Awolowo, (Busia)	Azikiwe	*The Spark*, Nkrumah
1960–1980	African Socialism (Nyerere, Kaunda), Black Consciousness	Development technocrats (Chisiza)	African Marxists (a.o. Amin, Babu, Ake, Nabudere)

Table 6.8
Families of Discourse in Analytical Perspective

MODEL OF THOUGHT	IDENTITY	MODERNIZATION	LIBERATION
basic concern	authenticity (existential)	development (pragmatic)	liberation (political)
fundamental features			
POLARITY	indigenous-alien We-They	underdeveloped-developed primitive-modern	oppressor-oppressed master-slave
WORLD	culturalist world order of 1. essentialistically conceived culture-continents 2. people "belonging" to cultures	a single human civilization developing toward universal modernity	a world torn apart by imperialism and capitalism
TO BE DONE	guard and unfold a deeply rooted indigenous identity	make a "great leap ahead" along the universal path of development	revolution according to the dialectic of historical transformation
METAPHOR	"roots"	"take-off"	"breaking the chains," delinking
EXAMPLE	African family/village meeting	modern society in the West	the Chinese Long March (for ARPS the Japanese Médji revolution)
FIELD OF FOCAL ATTENTION	culture	technology/economy	political economy
THEORETICAL KEY WORD	identity	modernity	exploitation, delinking
PHILOSOPHICAL INCLINATION	holism essentialism	universalism voluntarism	historicism mechanism

At this point in my argument, a final revenue of the analytical exercise in this chapter has to be registered, thus adding an important dimension to the understanding of African political thought. I have focused above on character-istic differences in the basic models of thought, and now I want to show the way they are related. After all, the various discourses address the same African plight and deal with a similar set of basic issues. These issues are, first, political, namely, subjugation; second, economical, namely, underdevelopment and exploitation; and third, cultural, namely, estrangement. Whatever the discourse and its underlying model of political thought, these subjects are always on the agenda. The different models of thought thus share an intellec-tual predicament.

The systematic interrelation between the models of thought expresses both this shared predicament and the essentially different ways in which these concerns are dealt with in the three models. My conjecture is the following: each model shares the problem agenda, comprising political, economic and cultural issues, while the characteristic features of each of the models derive from the basic concern that functions as an anchoring point of the model. I claim that one of these basic concerns always plays a constitutive role in the discourse and conditions the specific way in which other issues are conceptualized. (Table 6.9)

When, for instance, the concern for "modernization" and the connected polarity, primitive-modern, plays a constitutive role, then these condition the specific way in which "liberation" and "authenticity" are conceptualized. Liberation will not be interpreted as a dominantly political concept (such as in the liberation model) but as entailing primarily technological and economic advancement, thereby making the country a strong partner in the world. Authenticity will not mainly refer to the cultural heritage (such as in the identity model) but to the free and open-ended development of individuals and communities.

Table 6.9
Three Basic Types of Discourse (or Models of Thought)

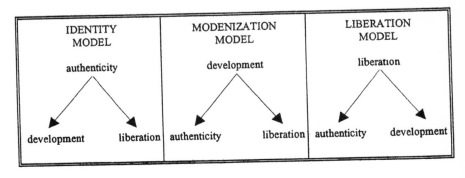

The crux of this conjecture is that all three models of thought deal with all relevant issues of concern (development, liberation, and authenticity). The basic concern of a model, however, conditions the specific way in which the other issues are conceptualized. The concepts "development," "liberation," and "authenticity" have a different meaning in each of the models of thought. The differences between the models of thought are, thus, not a simple difference in the degree of priority given to economic, cultural, or political issues. Blyden, for instance, was not just "more" concerned with authenticity than the early African Marxist Tiémoho Garang Kouyaté and "less" concerned with liberation. It is rather the case that Blyden had a completely different view of what true liberation consists of.[24] For Blyden political independence did not constitute real liberation unless it included the regeneration of African authenticity.[25] Thus, although discourses have certain concepts in common, these concepts have a different meaning in each of the discourses.

From the qualitative differences between the types of discourses, it follows that there is no way of "adding up" the different types to arrive at a complete view of the African condition. Their discursive substances do not mix any better than oil and water do.[26] The logic of the models suggests that consistent alternative political conceptions are only possible when the basic parameters of the three models (their fundamental concerns or polarities) are abandoned. (see chapter 8)

NOTES

1. For example, Shepperson, "Notes on American Negro Influences"; Shepperson, "External Factors in the Development of African Nationalism; Shepperson, "Abolitionism and African Political Thought"; I. Geiss, *Panafrikanismus. Zur Geschichte der Dekolonisation* (Frankfurt am Mein: Europeische Verlagsanstalt, 1968); B. Davidson, *The Black Man's Burden: Africa and the Curse of the Nation-State* (New York: Times Books, 1992).

2. T. S. Khun, *The Essential Tension—Selected Studies in Scientific Tradition and Change* (Chicago: University of Chicago Press, 1977), 10.

3. Another example could be the differences between Anyanwu, Chisiza, and Amin—authors who I will discuss later.

4. I will refer to Ayittey in the next chapter.

5. The accusation of "antimodernism," often directed at movements that are criticizing modernization, can only be conceived within the modernist topology. The "stage" in a nonmodernist conception is simply set differently: it suggests accepting some (e.g., indigenous, or Islamic) but rejecting other (e.g., alien) modernization processes.

6. The proposed method is like Max Weber's method of constructing an ideal-type, that is a "pure form" of an abstract phenomenon. Such a *reines Gedankengebilde* presents a complete and fully consistent image, ignoring contingent and contradictory elements that the real historical case may have, and bringing out a possible internal structure of the phenomenon. See, for example, M. Weber, "Die 'Objectivität'

sozialwissenshaftlicher Erkenntnis," in *Soziologie: Weltgeschichtliche Analysen Politik* (1904; reprint, Stuttgart: Alfred Kröner Verlag, 1956), 186–262, especially 234–244. The use of biological metaphors, such as bone structure or genetic code, does not imply a realistic interpretation of conjectures about deep structures of thought.

7. S. Biko, *I write what I like*. A selection of his writings edited by Aelred Stubbs, C.R. (1978; reprint, London: Heinemann, 1979), 92, in the essay "Black Consciousness and the Quest for True Humanity".

8. K. C. Anyanwu, "African Political Doctrine." In O.E.A. Ruch & K. C. Anyanwu, *African Philosophy. An Introduction to the Main Trends in Contemporary Africa* (Rome: Catholic Book Agency, 1984), 374.

9. H. R. Lynch, ed., *Black Spokesman. Selected Published Writings of Edward Wilmot Blyden* (London: Frank Cass, 1971), 60. Compare also J. E. Casely Hayford, *Ethiopia Unbound. Studies in Race Emancipation* (1911; reprint, London: Frank Cass, 1969), 160: "What shall it profit a race if it shall gain the whole world and lose its own soul?"; and W. E. Blyden, *Christianity, Islam and the Negro Race* (London: W. B. Whittingham & Co., 1887), 71–93: "the African must advance by the methods of his own. He must possess a power distinct from the European."

10. My use of the notion of "family" does not involve the claim that thinkers actually traced back their intellectual ancestry along these lines or were actually influenced by previous generations in that very family.

11. The idea of an "African personality," supported at times by Nkrumah and others, also includes this idea of a phenomenologically coherent *Africanité*.

12. Yet there are definite biological implications of the concept of race used.

13. Ch. A. Diop, *Civilisation ou Barbarie* (Paris: Présence Africaine, 1981). See also, for example, L. Keita "The African Philosophical Tradition," in R. A. Wright, *African Philosophy. An Introduction* (Lanham, New York, and London: University Press of America, 1984), 57–76; J. Vansina, "A Past for the Future?" *Dalhousie Review*, 8–23; J. Vansina "History of Central African Civilization" and "Kings in Tropical Africa," in E. Beumers & H-J. Koloss, *Kings of Africa* (Maastricht: Foundation Kings of Africa, 1992), 13–26, for examples of a discourse that focusses on African cultural traditions.

14. One could argue that the fact that Blyden happened to formulate his views in terms of race and not culture is merely a historical accident caused by the dominance of scientific racism in Blyden's age.

15. The two requirements for the definition of "solid" identities also apply to an essentialist theory of psychological types (certain theories of the African personality) or of historical traditions (concerning the African tradition or the Bantu tradition).

16. S. Amin, *Eurocentrism* (New York: Monthly Review Press, 1989); E. Balibar & I. Wallerstein, eds., *Race, Nation, Class: Ambiguous Identities* (London: Verso, 1991).

17. Examples abound: communalistic versus individualistic, holistic versus analytic, emotion versus reason and so forth. Anyanwu, "African Political Doctrine," 374, for example, stated: "The African escapes upward through the path of the spirit, while the modern man escapes downward by embracing the pathological ego." For a critique, see also S. Koenis & P. Boele van Hensbroek, "Het Westen bestaat niet. Over de implicaties van culturalisme," in D. Pels & G. de Vries, eds., *Burgers en Vreemdelingen* (Amsterdam: van Gennep, 1994), 51–62; P. Boele van Hensbroek "On Cultura-

lism," in H. Kimmerle & F. M. Wimmer, eds., *Philosophy and Democracy in Intercultural Perspective, Studies in Intercultural Philosophy: Vol. 3.* (Amsterdam: Rodopi, 1997), 85–93.

18. See, for example, Anyanwu, "African Political Doctrine," 371, on his method. Argument-by-contrasting is often a simple indicator of a culturalist discourse. Blyden's *African Life and Customs* is a beautiful example but so are I. A. Menkiti, "Person and Community in African Traditional Thought," K. C. Anyanwu, "African Political Doctrine"; and a host of others. A culturalist and a nonculturalist strategy of presentation can be compared well by contrasting Menkiti's and Gyekye's accounts of the concept of person, in R. A. Wright, *African Philosophy. An Introduction* (Lanham, New York, and London: University Press of America, 1984), 171–181, 199–212. Menkiti constantly contrasts "the African view of man" with the Western one; Gyekye simply explains the concept of person in a particular African (namely Akan) culture.

19. The rhetoric of genealogy is analyzed in a magnificent way by David Chioni Moore, starting off from Alex Haley's book *Roots*; see D. C. Moore, "Routes," *Transition* 64 (1994): 4–21.

20. Africanus Horton took such a purely common-sense attitude to this question that sophisticated commentators such as L. C. Gwam accused him of being "too emphatic on the mundane; too materialistic; too bitter in tone; and . . . too silent on the deeper instincts of the native African." L. C. Gwam, "The Social and Political Ideas of Dr. James Africanus Beale Horton," *Ibadan* 19 (1964): 10. For others, however, it may be refreshing to read Horton's statement about women, of over a hundred years ago, that "no arbitrary infringements on their rights should be tolerated." Quoted in D. Nicol, *Africanus Horton. The Dawn of Nationalism in Modern Africa* (London: Longman, 1969), 96.

21. Some call this "detribalized." The case of Danquah or Busia (being in fact neotraditionalist modernizers) is different: the solidity of their tradition was so clearly beyond doubt that culturalist affirmations were rather unnecessary.

22. This perspective is shared by many movements of what is sometimes called "primary resistance" to colonial penetration.

23. As highlighted in chapters 3 and 4, the "nations" of nationalists to a large degree developed into such units during the nationalist struggle itself, such as in the case of Nigeria and the Gold Coast.

24. In principle, Blyden did not object to temporary European political domination (see chapter 3).

25. For Horton, to take another example, development is conceived of as pushing forward along the highway of civilizational advancement. This conditioned his view of liberation as being the casting off of not only external factors hampering such advancement but also of internally African obstacles in the form of "feudal authoritarianism" and "primitive" attitudes.

26. Each model of thought speaks of a different "Africa" and defines a way of seeing the world. The theoretical framework effects the perception of every single major issue under discussion.

7

The Discourse on Democracy
in Africa

This book set out to make a critical inventory of African political thought at the close of the twentieth century. Until this point I have made a long march through history providing interpretations of historical political theorists (chapters 3, 4, 5) and exposing the key models of thought (chapter 6). In this way, I have forged the necessary historical insight as well as the analytical tools for my inventory.

The inventory concerns the contemporary intellectual situation, particularly African political discourses in the 1990s. Before engaging in critical discussions, however, I have to gain an understanding of the relevant discourses. This forces me to return to the role of the hermeneutic before assuming that of the critic. The argument in this chapter thus proceeds in several steps: after understanding the political context and reconstructing the key political discourses of the 1990s, I propose to diagnose the contemporary intellectual situation. The closing chapter can complete the stock taking by providing a critical assessment of standard and alternative intellectual options today.

THE CONTEXT OF AFRICAN POLITICAL THOUGHT IN THE 1990s

African political thought changed radically from the late 1980s onward. The idea of socialism, the key political idea for thirty years, suddenly disappeared from the intellectual stage. In 1987, the Zambian intellectual Henry Meebelo could still publish a book with the title *Zambian Humanism and Scientific Socialism* in order to achieve "greater ideological clarification and a higher revolutionary consciousness among the working people of Zambia."[1] Only a few years later both key terms in the books title, as well as the urge for "ideological clarification" itself, had lost political meaning. There were new beacons on the political horizon, such as democracy, social movements, and civil society.

Several factors contributed to this ideological shift. In the first place, the end of the cold war was a crucial factor. Perceived from the South, the societies of the socialist bloc had appeared as a real alternative road to modernity.[2] This alternative had now evaporated. The change in the aid-policies of the World Bank and other Western donors were another factor. The international institutions introduced new political conditionalities, requiring an end to single-party rule and the fostering of "good governance."[3]

Factors internal to Africa were equally important. There was a sense of complete failure of paradigms in development theory, of development policies, and of the idea of the developmental state.[4] A major positive inspiration for change was the successful National Conference in Benin, in early 1990, declaring itself sovereign and initiating democratic reforms. National confer-ences took place elsewhere in Francophone Africa as well and civil opposition developed in many places. In Arusha in 1990 "The African Charter for Popular Participation in Development and Transformation" was signed: "The burgeon-ing of the informal sector, the flourishing of voluntary associations, and the emergence of new economic, social, and intellectual elites combined to apply multiple pressures on African governments and alter the political calculus in most parts of the continent."[5]

The new political situation changed the idea of who could speak on behalf of Africa. African presidents lost ground to opposition leaders, social movements, and human rights activists, on the one hand, and to donor agencies, on the other.[6] The discourse of the donor world tended to become agenda setting even for African intellectuals.[7]

As the speaker changed so did the words. Single-partyism rapidly lost credit, civil rights were reaffirmed and, more generally, the dominant role of the state in political, economic, and cultural life was criticized. The ideological shift created the curious situation of establishment institutions, such as the World Bank, speaking of "grass roots" and "democratization" and scarcely revolutionary charity organizations, such as the Foster Parents Plan, speaking of "empowerment," while the vocabulary of social movements became enriched with notions such as "human rights," "citizenship," and even "market freedom." Disparate discourses started to conflate. The new wind of change affected intellectuals of all types. We can speak here of a "democratic turn" in African political thought as democracy became the central issue in all traditions of thought.

The "Democratic Turn" and the Idea of Civil Society

Richard Sklar's presidential address to the African Studies Association in 1983 announced a revival of the concern for democracy. Sklar opposed the common view that rapid development requires some form of "developmental dictatorship" and defended, instead, the need for "developmental democracy."[8] Constitutional government would be required, involving effective checks and balances and multiparty systems. In the subsequent decade, "multipartyism" became the dominant shorthand for democracy in publications of international organizations as well as in most academic literature on the issue of democracy in Africa.

Among African intellectuals, the renewed interest in democracy initially took the form of a critique of the single-party system. Its undemocratic record was lifted as well as its claim to conform to African culture.[9] The African critics were, however, far from optimistic because many considered the alternative of multipartyism to be problematic. It was pointed out that most African countries had in fact had multiparty systems after independence so that it would be hard to believe that salvation would come from reintroducing such systems. A number of other objections to multiparty systems were brought up, such as the danger of enhancing tribalism, the need for national unity, and the power of elite interests to subvert multiparty systems. Leftist theorists considered liberal democracy to be the political expression of capitalism and thus it was unattractive. A common position in the ideological deadlock in the second half of the 1980s was to accept the idea of a political plurality while stressing the need for a form appropriate to the particularly African circumstances and cultures.[10]

The rising pressure for democratic reform in many African countries in the early 1990s turned the discourse of African intellectuals wholeheartedly toward the issue of democratization. Meanwhile, the discussion expanded beyond the question of the political system per se to that of a democratic civil society. It was argued that the lifeblood of democratic state institutions is provided by a multitude of civic associations that constitute civil society.[11] Civil associations can be interest groups such as trade unions and student organizations as well as other social actors such as the press, civil rights groups, churches and religious movements, and political, ethnic, and cultural associations.

Halfway through the 1990s a further move away from a state-centrist position could be observed when the idea of the state itself was contested. In some cases the question was raised as to whether the current notions of politics and the state (and related political strategies) were outdated. It was argued that under some conditions more local or more regional or Pan-African "units of accountability" might better serve the move to democratization.[12]

The shifts in African political thought during the 1990s correspond with global intellectual developments. A first example is the academic debate about Africa. While the central position of the state had not yet been called into question in the 1970s and 1980s (such as in the Dar es Salaam debates about the post-colonial African state in the 1970s, or in the debate about the "uncaptured peasantry" in the 1980s), the processes of incorporation and disengagement of state and society became a topical issue in the second half of the 1980s.[13] The state itself was conceived as part of a complex process that acquired different roles at different times. In the 1990s especially, social organization "beyond the state" came into focus.[14] The French Africanist Francois Bayart contributed greatly to the general shift in interest from "high politics" to "low politics" as well as to the introduction of the idea of civil society in the academic debate about Africa.[15]

A second global development was the emergence of the idea of civil society. Initially, civil society captured the political imagination of a number of Eastern European opposition intellectuals. From the late 1980s it became popular among intellectuals in many parts of the globe. The concept of civil society had been part of the main body of history of European political thought and had a number of different meanings.[16] In the influential Hegelian-Marxist tradition, for instance, civil society was equated with social life under capitalism.[17] In the revival of the concept in the 1990s, however, civil society embodied an attempt at defining a new political vocabulary beyond the divide between liberal and socialist traditions. Unlike the Marxist paradigm, class is not considered to be the conditioning factor of civil society; there are many movements and none is licensed as "the subject of revolution." In a similar vein, social movements are viewed primarily from a functional and political point of view as forms of self-organization or as intermediaries between state and society rather than as actors in a socioeconomic power struggle. The idea of civil society expresses "a program that seeks to represent the values and interests of social autonomy in face of both the modern state and the capitalist economy, without falling into a new traditionalism."[18] The notion of civil society, then, refers to 1. a realm of self-regulation of modern societies that cannot be replaced by state action; 2. a realm that is essential for the legitimation and sustainability of the modern state; 3. a realm depending upon the state for its preconditions in terms of the rule of law and protected liberties.

DEMOCRACY DISCOURSES

"The Rules of the Game"

The "democratic turn" of African political thought presents itself, *prima facie*, as the rise of a discourse on liberal democracy. On a range of issues, such as human rights, citizenship, separation of powers (legislative, executive, judiciary), the right to free political association (often confused with multipartyism), and freedom of the press, liberal positions are agenda setting. Also those who hold different views cannot avoid these issues and find themselves in a position where they have to provide arguments for their deviation from the liberal standard.

Some consider the emergence of a liberal vocabulary in Africa as simply a mimic of the West and a deviation from African thought rather than its newest form.[19] Such an accusation has its own problems, however. Why would Africans develop liberal democratic lines of thought only by imitating Europeans and not through their own force of mind? There is no valid reason to assume that African thinkers are intrinsically "unliberal" and can only develop liberal ideas through mimicry or that liberalism is intrinsically "un-African."[20] The liberal orientation in African political thought during the 1990s can, therefore, not be brushed aside. It should be studied.

The dominant strand of liberal democratic thought today stresses the need for a multiparty system. The question of democracy is, in this view, a question of political institutions; democracy is a well-established political system already functioning in the West and intended to be implemented in Africa. The symbol of democracy is the ballot box. Discussions on democracy in Africa in this tradition mainly concern the issue of implementation and result in a rich harvest of studies informing the reader about which countries have turned toward democracy, which are in the process of doing so, and which lag behind. The conditions and "hope" for its successful implantation are contemplated. Frequently used metaphors depict democracy as something that has to "grow," "take root," "come to full flowering," and "bear fruit." The idea of democracy itself is considered universal and thus is not a main focus of discussion. When implementation fails, therefore, the blame is automatically not placed on democracy but on the conditions, the people, or their culture.[21]

A number of African intellectuals, today as well as in history, do not limit the scope of the discussion on democracy to multipartyism. From Horton via Azikiwe and Busia to contemporary authors such as Sithole, Gitonga, Moyo, and Ibrahim, the concept of democracy was not interpreted as referring to a single set of institutions but to the more fundamental idea that in Africa, as anywhere else, modern plural societies can be managed best in a polity involving a system of rights and sophisticated institutions of representation.

The core idea of liberal politics is epitomized by the metaphor of "the rules of the game." This metaphor returns in many of the key passages of the authors previously mentioned, appearing in statements such as "to play the game by the rules" and "politics is a competitive game."[22] The cover of the book *Democratic Theory and Practice in Africa*, edited by W. O. Oyugi and A. Gitongo, shows a huge dice that is used as a ballot box. The "game" represents the institutionalized method of dealing with differences in views and interests. It suggests two levels: playing the game and the rules of the game. Disagreements within the game on social, economic, or cultural issues do not endanger the game itself. The liberal idea of democracy, just like the idea of a game, defines a set of rules that permits a coordinated action among people of diverse backgrounds and opinions. In this way, by defining a political game beyond the level of particular views, interests and identities, liberal democracy has a universalist claim.[23]

The metaphor of the game illustrates another aspect of the liberal idea of democracy as well, namely, that democracy is not about everything. There are various "games." Interactions in the economic market or in the courts of law follow sets of rules different from that of politics. The private sphere sets its own rules and should be largely fenced off from the reach of politics. In the liberal idea democratic rule must always be limited in scope.[24] A system of rights is essential for both the definition of the political game and the limitations of its scope. Liberal conceptions of democracy have to reconcile the idea of participation with that of rights.

Palaver Democracy

The revival of a liberal democratic discourse can characterize only part of the "democratic turn" in African political thought. A number of contemporary democratic theorists in fact reject liberal democracy, arguing that the liberal idea of politics is both unattractive and contradicts African culture. They contend that if the turn toward democracy is to be more than an elite affair, then it has to be rooted in the culture of the people. African traditions involve a rich heritage of democratic culture. Rejecting Western liberal democracy, therefore, is not rejecting democracy as such but rather enriching it with African values and institutional forms that lead to a substantial involvement of the population in public deliberation. "We must . . . move away from the process of moving away from traditional society," Wamba-dia-Wamba stated.[25]

A number of African theorists take such a neotraditionalist stance. Their positions range from general philosophical expositions on the African idea of politics (such as in texts of Anyanwu, Ntumba, Okolo, Momoh, and Ramose) to arguments on specific cultures and institutions (such as those by Ayittey, Gyekye, and Wiredu). Neotraditionalists tend to create a contrast between a "Western" multiparty democracy and an African democracy. The first involves adversarial politics and the power struggle of majority rule whereas the African idea of community politics involves everybody and aims at consensus. A democracy of fractionist battles is contrasted with one where "the elders sit under the big trees, and talk until they agree."[26]

In most cases, a neotraditionalist position is based on the idea of an African identity or a shared African culture. To be an African, one argues, involves more than geographical origin or skin color: it constitutes a particular way of "being-in-the-world." One can speak, therefore, of "the African personality" and "the African precisely as an African," as the Nigerian philosopher Chukwudum B. Okolo elucidates.[27]

The idea of an African identity invariably leads to an affirmation of the communal character of African society and consensus as the basis of its politics. Communalism is then understood to be such "that the group constitutes the main focus of the lives of the individual members of that group."[28] In Mogobe Ramose's holistic formulation, communalism is reflected in a society "guided by the traditional principles of oneness, consensus and openness."[29] The nature of African societies, if not the nature of "the African," thus makes the failure of the "Western" idea of democracy in an African context unavoidable. It "will remain misguided and unsuccessful precisely because it will be unauthentic."[30]

The palaver is often used as an exemplar for this African view of democracy. Palavering or deliberation aimed at reconciling all views is seen as the essence of the political process in African community gatherings, such as the *Kgotla, Ujamaa* and *Mbongi*. The participants in the palaver are not equals, since there are status differences between king (chief), councilors, and ordinary people as well as between men and women, old and young. Nevertheless, everybody can speak out and is listened to attentively. In that sense the palaver goes beyond mere formal representation. It ensures that all views are actually included in the deliberation process, thus realizing a substantive representation of citizens (in Kwasi Wiredu's striking formulation: "on the Ashanti view, substantive representation is a matter of a fundamental human right").[31]

The palaver solution to the question of representation is quite different from the liberal one. Liberalism requires an agreement of citizens on the procedures of democracy, thus indirectly legitimating decisions, even for those citizens who do not agree with a particular decision. The palaver idea of democracy, on the other hand, aims at consensus about the decision itself.

Liberal democracy was described earlier as "limited" (not interfering, as far as possible, in the private sphere, in religious matters, etc.) and "universalist" (in its claim to define the political game beyond the level of particular views, interests and identities). The palaver idea of democracy is its opposite: it is a broad view of democracy that concerns in principle every question relevant to the community, as well as a particularist view, specific to Africa.[32]

The particularly African character of the palaver alternative can be interpreted in different ways. For those who consider the African identity to have deep roots and to represent an authentic way of "being-in-the-world" the choice of a political system is one for or against authenticity; it has a moral dimension. For a number of other authors, however, the particularism of African variants of democracy is a matter of historical contingency. They vindicate democratic forms developed in African societies simply because such forms are more democratic and better understood by the majority of ordinary Africans, thus increasing political participation. The specific political consequences of both the first (the "culturalist") and the second (the "nonculturalist") variants of the discourse on palaver democracy will be discussed later in this chapter.

Popular Struggles for Democracy

The "democratic turn" involves a revival of liberal democratic thought and, for another family of theorists, a reorientation toward indigenous traditions of consensus democracy. The turn entails even more, however. For instance, how do we interpret the statement, "it is the power of the people, unlashed by broad-based movements of a popular alliance type, that can restore democracy" that can "smash the neocolonial state and erect a popular democratic state instead"?[33] The idea of democracy expressed here is clearly not concerned with reestablishing palaver democracy or with clarifying the rules of the democratic game.

The democratic turn of the tradition of revolutionary anti-imperialism (the radical tradition) consisted of a gradual shift within the last ten years from a vocabulary around terms such as "modes of production," "class," and "socialism" to one around the new master-term "democracy." Democracy is discussed here using notions such as "popular forces," "popular struggles," "social movements," and "popular accountability."

A first variant of the democratic turn in the radical tradition is represented by the famous political economist Samir Amin. Amin's work in the field of political economy, focusing on the issue of global dependency relations and the strategy of delinking, was later supplemented by work on such issues as ideology and democracy.[34] His book *Eurocentrism*, for instance, provides a comprehensive historicist conception of society and culture. It identifies liberalism as the ideology and political system of the capitalist "centers" and dictatorial regimes as the political form of dependent capitalism in the periphery. Overcoming authoritarianism in the periphery, therefore, must automatically involve conquering dependent capitalism. True democracy is, in this theory, firmly linked to the idea of socialism (or at least to a noncapitalist social formation).[35]

The shift of Amin's position in the democratic turn is hardly a radical one. The word "socialism" is avoided but his rather complete theory of the world system precludes a major change of position. If the economic order conditions the political and ideological orders and if the economic order is basically that of global capitalism, then there is not much reason to believe in democratization without overturning the global capitalist system (or breaking out of it by delinking). Amin's notions largely duplicate the classical Marxist equivalents. The democratic struggle concerns a "new social formation" (socialism) and has to rely on "national popular movements" (masses). Relevant popular movements are anti-imperialist and share a universalistic and not a parochial, fundamentalist, tribal, or religious ethic (the working class as the universal subject of revolution).

As distinct from the classical position of Samir Amin, one of the focal points of radical discourse today is CODESRIA (The Council for the Development of Social Science Research in Africa).[36] I will use here the position paper for the CODESRIA research network on social movements (the so-called *Green Book* of 1988) and the volume testifying to the state of the discussions after one decade (the massive *African Studies in Social Movements and Democracy* of 1995) to map the development within mainstream radical discourse.[37]

The turn toward democracy from the mid-1980s onward, presents itself here as a self-conscious break with the "statist," top-down paradigm of radical nationalist and developmentalist thought.[38] It wants to "move from a state to a social logic," turning attention to the "subjective factor" and to the "actual forms of organization and participation, democratic or otherwise, that have actually emerged in the historical development of popular movements in Africa." "Appraising movements that set out to change Africa" is what social scientists should do.[39]

An example of this approach is Mamdani's discussion of the development of nationalism in Uganda from the 1940s.[40] Mamdani shows the constant opposition between state nationalism and a popular, social nationalism of diverse social movements. A "rich spectrum of social movements organized in response to a variety of demands—not only national but also social" in the 1940s became subverted by private bourgeois interests due to shrewd colonial reforms in the 1950s and later due to policies of the independent state.[41] Social nationalism thus became state nationalism and bottom-up nationalism became top-down nationalism. In this process the national and modern became opposed to the regional/tribal and the traditional, and the diversity of popular forms of self-assertion became perceived as a threat to national unity.

The new radical discourse on democracy of the late 1980s presents itself as "inventory," "stock-taking," and as "an analytical study, a critical summing up of the positive and negative aspects of these movements."[42] However, the discourse implies a definite political program that can be summarized as follows. The state, which is dominated by neocolonial conditions, is unable to do its job or to change by itself. Popular forces, therefore, have a role in enforcing a "democratic social transformation" and "appropriate development programs": "It is the contending social forces, interested in the implementation of such programs which, after a successful political battle over the control of state power, will use this power to see such programs through." This, if successful, involves "smash[ing] the neocolonial state and erect[ing] a popular democratic state instead." The key to this "popular democratic revolution" is social power: "it is the impatience of left forces to get to positions of political power, rather than first build social power among the people, which remains a plague of revolutionary or potentially revolutionary movements in Africa."[43] The thrust of the new radical discourse is the empowerment of popular movements.

The seminal phrase "popular struggles for democracy" epitomizes the model of the new radical democratic thought. The popular character expresses the idea of broad-based participation as essential for true democracy. This participation, however, is not achieved by simply establishing a range of democratic institutions in the way the liberal democrats hope to implement democracy. In real life, democratization involves struggle: an antagonistic set-up where enemies are confronted.

Mamdani's Ugandan example follows this popular struggles model. It stages basically two kinds of actors: popular forces versus the state (dominated by the property-aspiring middle class) or the democratic versus the antidemocratic forces. The struggle between the two sides constitutes the main story line. For the democratic side, the aim is to transform state and society according to its democratic and social demands. The other side attempts to stop democratization or at least to limit it to the political system, leaving the social question untouched.[44]

Surprisingly, the turn within African radical discourse from a statist to a social perspective in the late 1980s did not change its ground plan.[45] We still have all the fundamentals of the classic Marxist paradigm, namely, a theory of history, a theory of class (popular versus elite, oppressed versus oppressor), the idea of a subject of revolutionary change (popular forces or social movements), and the terminal station in the form of peoples power.[46]

Taking the 1995 CODESRIA volume *African Studies in Social Movements and Democracy* as a guide, it can be seen that the change in radical discourse around the mid-1990s finally affected the theoretical ground plan. Instead of a more-or-less clear project of popular struggles for a popular democratic state, the radicals today tend to identify a variety of social forces, movements, social groups, and autonomous activities with contradictory tendencies and a variety of experiences: "neither social forces nor social movements can be presumed to have an internal consistency and coherence, or to be the agent of realizing a trans-historical agenda."[47] The 1995 volume, edited by M. Mamdani and E. Wamba-dia-Wamba, retains the issue of struggling for popular empowerment and accountable government but the framework of a Marxist-inspired theory of history (socialism) and of class (indicating the social forces that particularly "count" in the struggle) has evaporated.

Significantly, the drift away from the classical radical framework facilitates the elaboration of interesting positions and studies. *African Studies in Social Movements and Democracy* provides a wide range of analyses of movements and political experiences bearing on salient theoretical issues, such as the idea of civil society, the notion of social movements, and the role of party politics. The dominant "liberal" idea of civil society, for instance, is criticized for its exclusive focus on "groups which seek to control the state or seek effective citizenship within the state system."[48] It is pointed out that a number of social movements, such as indigenous women's groups, tend to be state-avoiding, namely, they are orientated toward increasing autonomy rather than toward increased participation. They are not, however, for this reason, irrelevant for democratic struggles. Along a similar line, today's radicals changed their negative view of ethnic and religious movements. If initiative from "below" is taken seriously, then these forms of self-organization can be valued positively. "I don't know a single peasant struggle for emancipation, on this continent, that was not at the same time either ethnic or religious," Mahmood Mamdani states in a discussion with Samir Amin.[49]

The shift in radical discourse around the mid-1990s also provides more room for discussing democratic institutions. Mamdani notes, for instance, that "social movements in Africa are not just about opposing the state, but also about redefining the form of that state." Every successful movement has to shift "away from a demonization of the state to an articulation, both of how state power should be organized and how it should relate to social forces."[50]

In summary, the democratic turn in the radical tradition consists of a gradual shift: first stretching a Marxist theoretical framework and then drifting away from it. In regard to the idea of democracy, however, one basic motivation is maintained, namely, the refusal to limit the issue of democracy to the political sphere alone: "democracy is a concept of society and is about how its resources are used and distributed."[51]

THREE DEMOCRATIC TURNS, THREE DEMOCRACY DISCOURSES

What first appeared to be a single reorientation of African political thought toward a discourse on democracy, turned out to be a multiple event instead. There are three democratic turns and three discourses on democracy. At this point, making use of the archaeological study of African political thought in the previous chapters, I want to obtain a more precise understanding of these discourses in order to proceed to their critical evaluation in the next chapter.

An archaeological view of the three discourses on democracy is somewhat disenchanting at first sight. Perceived from the broad historical perspective that the previous chapters provide, it can be seen that contemporary democracy discourses largely replicate models of thought that have dominated African political thought over the last 150 years.

The first case, mainstream liberal democracy discourse, reproduces the modernization model of thought that was outlined in chapter 6. When modeled upon the idea of "the rules of the game," democracy is conceived as the standard political requirement of universal modernization. The modernization model suggests that the management of any modern society requires a modern state as well as the basic institutions of a liberal polity to handle social plurality and to check state power. For modernizing African societies, with their plurality of interest groups, ethnic groups, and religious groups, liberal democracy appears to be a universal requirement.

The second case, the discourse of palaver democracy (with notable exceptions discussed below), reproduces the basic patterns of the identity model of thought. Democratization, in this conception, is the full realization of African consensus politics in contemporary situations. Finally, the discourse on popular struggles for democracy reproduces the basic pattern of the liberation model of thought. Democracy is conceived here as a phase in the history of social struggle that should ultimately lead to the radical empowerment of the oppressed and the realization of a completely new social order.

Incidentally, although the democracy discourses replicate classical differences, they still involve a certain rapprochement. Within all three discourses today the importance of issues such as accountability, human rights, pluralism, and need for participation is recognized. Protagonists of popular struggles, for instance, do not deny that democratic institutions are important, while multipartyists tend to recognize the importance of popular empowerment, and supporters of palaver democracy (in most cases) do not deny the need for a formal system of rights.

Shared convictions, however, do not imply shared discourses. Even when discourses do not deny each other's agendas, the interpretation and valuation of each of these agenda elements may differ fundamentally. Let me represent these differences in a table that highlights characteristic distinctions without reducing discourses to caricatural stereotypes (Table 7.1). My claim is that the three democracy discourses can be charted with the triangular diagrams of models of thought presented in chapter 6. The triangle indicates that, despite their shared concern for democracy, actual conceptions are conditioned by the specific basic assumptions of each discourse. The discourse covers a range of issues but the way in which these are conceived is determined by the specific basic concern and polarity that is indicated at the top of the triangular diagram.

At first sight, the intellectual specter seems to abound with combinations and intermediate forms of these species of discourse so that my typology of models does not appear very helpful. Mamdani (liberation model) and Biko (identity model), for instance, share a concern for African liberation and both could, therefore, be considered "liberationists." I propose, however, a different approach because a careful examination shows that they were, in fact, talking about quite different things. Mamdani discusses a process of socioeconomic emancipation that overcomes, finally, the basic social distortions deriving from global capitalism. Biko, however, discusses a process of cultural-political liberation of black Africans, conceived of according to a worldview marked by the colorline. Mamdani follows the logic of what I termed the liberation model and Biko follows the identity model. Similarly, both Busia and Azikiwe defended the need for liberal democratic institutions. For Azikiwe, however, this concerned universal requirements of modernity whereas for Busia democratic institutions would have to be tailor-made arrangements for a particular society, closely connected to indigenous political institutions while overcoming their limitations. Azikiwe followed the logic of my modernization model, while Busia followed a variant of the identity model.

Table 7.1
Three Discourses on Democracy

Liberal discourse on democracy	
development authenticity liberation	Primary: democracy is interpreted as an aspect of political **DEVELOPMENT** toward a "modern" polity Secondary: this democracy is considered to express an African IDENTITY because those participating are Africans and because the general idea of democracy is adjusted to suit African conditions; this democracy is considered to be LIBERATING because it is the antidote to any kind of authoritarianism
Palaver discourse on democracy	
authenticity development liberation	Primary: democracy is interpreted as the expression of political/cultural **IDENTITY** Secondary: this democracy is considered to imply DEVELOPMENT because it involves true development from African roots; this democracy is considered to be LIBERATING because it involves true liberation of African potential
Popular Struggles discourse on democracy	
liberation authenticity development	Primary: democracy is interpreted as an aspect of social struggle and **LIBERATION** Secondary: this democracy is considered to be AFRICAN because it is democracy for all Africans; this democracy is considered to be DEVELOPMENTAL because it serves true development for all

My claim for fundamental differences between models also implies that I expect mixtures or additions to these models to remain eclectic combinations that can hardly result in a coherent argument.[52] The logic of the three models suggests that their combination must result in conceptual ambiguity. Key concepts will then be used in two or more meanings in one argument, following the conditioning of their meaning by different models.

My claim that arguments that I allocate to different models do not mix can be illustrated by Basil Davidson's remarkable discussion in *The Black Man's Burden*. In particular his first chapters make an effort to show that the nation-state is a foreign import. Africa has its own alternatives that are indigenous and democratic. The struggle for Africa is therefore to reaffirm its own political identity. Democracy is conceptualized here within an intellectual framework that opposes indigenous and alien political forms. In Davidson's argument, however, this conceptualization has to compete with the notion of democratization as an anti-elite and anti-imperialist struggle. In this second idea, democracy is marked by mass action and the empowerment of the poor. Both lines of argument, while often leading to parallel conclusions, remain remarkably separate (chapters 1, 2, and 3 follow the first line; chapters 8, 9, and the conclusion follow the second line). When it comes, finally, to the question, What should be done? Davidson is a classical radical democrat demanding the empowerment of the masses. The "indigenous" alternative that was so prominent in the first chapters, does not save Africa, but rather the "popular" in the form of the empowered "masses" does.[53] One can combine what I called "identity" and "liberation" models of thought but the resulting argument remains eclectic: paying lip service to one discourse while finally reconfirming another and using key concepts in different meanings.

My charting of discourses through the triangular models has an advantage over the simple comparison of ideas in that it is like identifying species through a DNA test. It is a way to map fundamental differences between discourses while seeing through superficial similarities. It shows that once the thinking about democracy gets trapped in one of the established trails of thought it tends to follow an identical line of argument. Avoiding these established trails of thought requires avoiding its underlying models.

NOTES

1. H. Meebelo, *Zambian Humanism and Scientific Socialism. A Comparative Study* (Lusaka, 1987), 7.

2. Africa had its own experiences with "Marxism-Leninism." The Ethiopian famine of 1984 and the savage war against Eritreans constituted tragic landmarks. In 1981, the book *Afrocommunism* by David and Marina Ottaway could close with "Afrocommunism is still in its infancy. . . . Marxism-Leninism is spreading on the continent and is likely to continue doing so," in their *Afrocommunism* (New York and London: Africana Publishing, 1981), 213. In the 1986 second edition this expectation was clearly tuned down.

3. After the World Bank report *Sub-Saharan Africa: From Crisis to Sustainable Growth* (1989).

4. The belief in liberation through building progressive post-colonial states, expressed at the Bandung conference was lost (L. S. Senghor, *On African Socialism* (1961; reprint, New York: Praeger, 1964), 9. The Ugandan intellectual Mahmood Mamdani called the mid-1980s "the moment of exhaustion of the anti-colonial national project." M. Mamdani, "Introduction," in M. Mamdani & E. Wamba-dia-Wamba, eds., *African Studies in Social Movements and Democracy* (Dakar: Codesria, 1995), 33. Saul spoke of "the decomposition of 'independence ideology.'" J. S. Saul, "Ideology in Africa: Decomposition and Recomposition," in G. M. Carter & P. O'Meara, eds., *African Independence. The First Twenty-five Years* (Bloomington: Indiana University Press, 1986), 326. See also S. Amin, "L'idéologie et la pensée sociale: l'intelligence et la crise du développement" *Africa Development* 19, no. 1 (1994): 12. Carter & O'Meara, *African Independence*, gives some sense of the depressed atmosphere in the 1980s.

5. N. Chazan, "Strengthening Civil Society and the State," *World Policy Journal* 9, no. 2 (1992): 281.

6. A generation of leaders disappeared in the 1980s. Their public image came into disrepute. Significantly, as the new president of Uganda, Museveni spoke out loudly on behalf of Africa, but in the form of a heavy critique of African leaders. Privatization, Structural Adjustment Programs, and large-scale involvement of donors further reduced their power. See, for example, M. Doornbos, "The African State in Academic Debate: Retrospect and Prospect," *Journal of Modern African Studies* 28, no. 2 (1990): 56.

7. Important conferences take place in the context of the donor and international community, and research institutions are funded from aid money. Multipartyism and governance are main topics, since even those who hold a different view of democratization have to participate and refer to these notions.

8. On the idea of developmental dictatorship see A. J. Gregor, "African Socialism, Socialism, and Fascism: An Appraisal," *Review of Politics* 29 (1967); and A. J. Gregor, *Italian Fascism and Developmental Dictatorship* (Princeton: Princeton University Press, 1980).

9. Criticizing the single-party system was the completion of the critique of African Socialism in the previous twenty years. First its socialist and developmental pretensions and then its democratic claims were refuted. See, for example, W. A. Oyugi & A. Gitonga, eds., *Democratic Theory and Practice in Africa* (Nairobi: Heinemann, 1987); P. Meyns & D. W. Nabudere, eds., *Democracy and the One-Party-State in Africa* (Hamburg: Institut für Afrika-Kunde, 1988); and H. G. Mwakayembe, "Democracy or Simple Multi-Partyism? A Contribution to the Debate on Political Pluralism in Africa," paper presented to the conference, "A Generation After; Law and Development in East Africa," Institute of Social Studies, The Hague, November 1990.

10. Mwakayembe, "Democracy or Simple Multi-Partyism?"; C. Ake, "Devaluing Democracy," *Journal of Democracy* 3, no. 3 (1992): 37–44.

11. "Participation of political and social forces in society becomes a crucial element in the democratic process. To grasp this dimension of political change in Africa, 'civil society' has to come to the fore again as a useful analytical concept." Peter Meyns quoted in R. Buitenhuys & C. Thiriot, *Democratization in Sub-Saharan Africa 1992–1995. An Overview of the Literature* (Leiden: Africa Studies Centre, 1995), 112.

12. E. Wamba-dia-Wamba, "Beyond Elite Politics of Democracy in Africa," *Quest: Philosophical Discussions* 6, no. 1 (1992): 29–43; E. Wamba-dia-Wamba, "Africa in Search of a New Mode of Politics," in Ulf Himmelstrand et al., eds., *African Perspectives on Development. Controversies, dilemma's & openings* (London: James Curry, 1994), 249–261; J. Lonsdale, "Political Accountability in African History," in P. Chabal, ed., *Political Domination in Africa: Reflections on the Limits of Power* (London: Cambridge University Press, 1988), 126–157; G. Hawthorn, "Sub-Saharan Africa," in D. Held, ed., *Prospects for Democracy. North, South, East, West* (London: Polity Press, 1993); S. Ellis, ed., *Africa Now: People, Politics & Institutions* (London: James Curry, 1996). Basil Davidson's argument against the nation-state and for federalism are found in his *The Black Man's Burden: Africa and the Curse of the Nation-State* (New York: Times Books, 1992).

13. On the Dar es Salam debates, see Y. Tandon, ed., *The Debate. Debate on Class, State & Imperialism* (Dar es Salam: Tanzanian Publishing House, 1982); on the "uncaptured peasantry," see G. Hyden, *No Shortcuts to Progress: African Development Management in Perspective* (London: Heinemann, 1983), as well as contributions to a debate in the journal *Development and Change* vol. 17, nos. 2 and 4, and vol. 18, no. 4, in 1986 and 1986, by Nelson Kasfir, Goran Hyden, Lionel Cliff and Gavin Williams. On state incorporation and disengagement, see, for example, V. Azarya, "Reordering State-Society Relations: Incorporation and Disengagement," in D. Rothchild & N. Chazan, eds., *The Precarious Balance: State & Society in Africa* (Boulder and London: Westview Press, 1988), 3–25; N. Chazan, "Patterns of State-Society Incorporation and Disengagement in Africa," in Rothchild & Chazan, *The Precarious Balance*, 121–148.

14. For example, Doornbos, "The African State in Academic Debate"; M. Bratton, "Beyond the State. Civil Society and Associational Life in Africa," *World Politics. A Quarterly Journal of International Relations* (1989): 407–414.

15. J-F. Bayart, "Les Sociétés Africaines Face à l'État," *Pouvoirs* 25 (1983): 23–37; J-F. Bayart, "Civil Society in Africa," in Chabal, *Political Domination in Africa*, 109–125. Especially his 1986 article "Civil Society in Africa" and his *L'état en Afrique: la politique du ventre* of 1989 have been pioneering. Also Chabal, *Political Domination in Africa*; and P. Chabal, *Power in Africa. An Essay in Political Interpretation* (Basingstoke: Macmillan, 1992).

16. J. Keane, "Remembering the Dead: Civil Society and the State from Hobbes to Marx and beyond," in J. Keane, *Democracy and Civil Society* (London and New York: Verso, 1988), 31–69; J. Nederveen Pieterse, *Empire and Emancipation: Power and Liberation on a World Scale* (London: Plato Press, 1990); J. L. Cohen & A. Arato, "Politics and the Reconstruction of the Concept of Civil Society," in A. Honneth, *Zwischenbetrachtungen im Prozess der Aufklärung* (Frankfurt am Mein: Suhrkamp, 1989); J. W. Harbeson, D. Rothchild, & N. Chazan, eds., *Civil Society and the State in Africa* (Boulder: Lynne Rienner, 1994). Jean Cohen's important book *Class and Civil Society* (1982) reconstructed several meanings of the term in Marx's work.

17. Several African Marxists followed this use. Amin, for instance, uses "civil society" and "economic life" under capitalism interchangeably. See also, G. Hunt, "Gramsci, Civil Society and Bureaucracy," *Praxis International* 6, no. 2 (1986): 206–219.

18. Quote from J. L. Cohen & A. Arato, "The Contemporary Revival of Civil Society," in J. L. Cohen & A. Arato, *Civil Society and Political Theory* (Cambridge, Ma.: MIT Press, 1992), 30. Exemplary uses of the concept of civil society serving a radical democratization discourse can be found in Latin America. Fernando Calderon, for instance, aimed at strengthening social actors to support democratization as well as strengthen the state itself: "L'état sera fort mais seulement si la société l'est aussi." F. Calderon, "Renforcer la société pour consolider la démocratie," *Africa Development*, 15, nos. 3–4 (1990). Typically for this new use of the concept of civil society, the objective is not formulated in the notions belonging to classical emancipation theory ("smashing of the state" or "establishment of a new gestion sociale"), but in plural terms with a postmodern ring, such as "la production des nouveaux projects historiques" or "des nouveaux chaines émancipatoires."

19. For example, Wamba-dia-Wamba, "Beyond elite politics"; M. Ramose, "African Democratic Tradition: Oneness, Consensus and Openness: A Reply to Wamba-dia-Wamba," *Quest: Philosophical Discussions* 6, no. 2 (1992): 62–83.

20. Note that the accusation itself has roots in the colonial image of Africans, namely that African thinkers do not develop ideas through their own force of mind but through some foreign influence only. The commonplace equations of liberalism with the West, or with capitalism, are rather too facile. Similarly, unless the existence of some unliberal African essence could be assumed (and there is no way to validate statements about such essences), there is no contradiction in being a liberal African intellectual. See also K. A. Busia, *Africa in Search of Democracy* (London, Routledge, 1967), 91–110, on the views of African leaders.

21. For example, R. Sklar, "Developmental Democracy," *Comparative Studies in Society and History* 29, no. 4 (1987); D. Ronen, ed., *Democracy and Pluralism in Africa* (Boulder: Lynne Rienner, 1986); Oyugi & Gitongo, *Democratic Theory and Practice*. The discourse on multipartyism has been especially prevalent in documents of international agencies and international NGO's.

22. M. Sithole, "Is Multi-Party Democracy Possible in Multi-Ethnic African States? The Case of Zimbabwe," in Himmelstrand et al., *African Perspectives,"* 163; and G.B.N. Ayittey, *Africa Betrayed* (New York: St. Martin's Press, 1992), 366.

23. This universalism can involve a *normative claim*. Afrifa Gitongo perceives "a core objective meaning and substance which are at the root of its quasi-universal appeal." Democracy embodies "the great epic of mankind's movement towards civilized political behaviour" expressing values such as equality, liberty, human dignity, and openness to criticism. A. K. Gitonga, "The Meaning and Foundations of Democracy," in Oyugi & Gitonga, *Democratic Theory and Practice in Africa*, 6, 2. For the Zimbabwean Masipula Sithole the universalist claim of democracy is more down to earth: "Democracy's universal character is that those who exercise political authority in society do so with the explicit consent and genuine mandate expressed at regular intervals by the governed through an open, free and fair electoral process." Himmelstrand et al., *African Perspectives*, 152.

24. B. Turok, "No Democracy, No Development?" in *Coalition for Change* (London: IFAA, 1990), 101–112. Page 109 states the opposite view: "Democracy is a concept of society and is about how its resources are used and distributed."

25. Wamba dia Wamba, "Beyond Elite Politics", 32.

26. For instance, K. Gyekye, "The idea of Democracy in the Traditional Setting and its Relevance to Political Development in Contemporary Africa," paper presented at the First International Regional Conference in Philosophy, Mombasa, Kenya, 1988.

27. Ch. B. Okolo, *African Social & Political Philosophy; Selected Essays* (Nsukka: Fulladu Publishing Company, 1993), 4; and N. C. Mangani, *Being-Black-In-The-World* (SPRO-CAS/Ravan, 1973).

28. Gyekye, *Essay on African Philosophical Thought*, 208.

29. Ramose, "African Democratic Tradition," 80.

30. Ibid., 63. See also the discussion of Kofi Baako in chapter 5; and Ramose, "African Democratic Tradition," 75. See T. Ball, "Party," in T. Ball, J. Farr, & R. L. Hanson, eds., *Political Innovation and Conceptual Change* (Cambridge: Cambridge University Press, 1989) on similar discussions about politics in nineteenth-century Europe.

31. K. Wiredu, "Democracy and Consensus: A Plea for a Non-party Polity," in K. Wiredu, *Cultural Universals and Particulars* (Bloomington: Indiana University Press, 1996), 186.

32. Some neotraditionalist views do not share this particularism. Wiredu, "Democracy and Consensus," 190, claims that "there is nothing peculiarly African about the idea itself."

33. P. Anyang' Nyong'o, ed., *Popular Struggles for Democracy in Africa* (London: ZED Press, 1987), 15, 24.

34. S. Amin, "Is there a Political Economy of Islamic Fundamentalism?" *Journal of African Marxists* 3 (1983): 6–29; S. Amin, "The State and the Question of 'Democracy.'" Foreword in Anyang' Nyong'o, *Popular Struggles*, 1–13; Amin, S., *Eurocentrism* (New York: Monthly Review Press, 1989); S. Amin, "L'idéologie et la pensée sociale: l'intelligence et la crise du développement," *Africa Development* 19, no. 1 (1994): 1–16.

35. Amin, "L'idéologie et la pensée sociale." Amin, "La Question," translated in Himmelstrand et al., *African Perspectives*, 332: "the building of true socialism . . . cannot be realized at present. Instead we still have on the agenda what I have called a national popular revolution." The "national popular alternative . . . this transition period, which will be a long transition, a historical phase, in which we have to combine internal social changes with the capacity to master external relations" 334.

36. The continental research network, titled "Social Movements, Social Transformation and the Struggle for Democracy in Africa," was initiated in 1985. CODESRIA publishes books and two house journals *Afrique Developpement* and the *Codesria Bulletin*. As a coordinating continental organization Codesria is closely related to other centers of discussion such as SAPES (Harare) and the Institute of Basic Research (Kampala).

37. M. Mamdani, E. Wamba-dia-Wamba, & T. Mkwandawire, *Social Movements, Social Transformation and the Struggle for Democracy in Africa*, CODESRIA working paper no. 1/88 (Dakar: Codesria, 1988); M. Mamdani & E. Wamba-dia-Wamba, eds., *African Studies in Social Movements and Democracy* (Dakar: Codesria, 1995). Other important works include Anyang' Nyong'o, *Popular Struggles*, resulting from discussions of African scholars on "popular alliances and the state in Africa" in the framework of the United Nations University's African Regional Perspectives Program, in Cairo in 1985. Also, see the *Review of African Political Economy*.

38. Dependency and modes of production schools suffered a "depoliticization of their analysis" by their restriction to the "objective side of reality." This was reflected in the prominence of geographical and mechanical metaphors like center, periphery, and delinking. "(T)he concerns uppermost in the political agenda . . . were national, not social." Mamdani & Wamba-dia-Wamba, *African Studies in Social Movements and Democracy*, 2. "In the absence of organised popular movements of which they may act as organic intellectuals, African intellectuals—even radical ones—tend to be unable to express the demands of the large masses of people" Mamdani et al., *Social Movements*, 8.

39. Quotes Mamdani, "Introduction," 16, 3. Religious, ethnic, women, and youth movements have been investigated by Africanists but the authors of the *Green Book* claim this has been done with a heavily modernist bias.

40. M. Mamdani, "State and Civil Society in Contemporary Africa: Reconceptualizing the Birth of State Nationalism and the Defeat of Popular Movements," *Africa Development* 15 nos. 3–4 (1990): 47–69.

41. Mamdani, "The State and Civil Society," 54–55.

42. Mamdani et al., *Social Movements*, 16.

43. Quotes from Anyang' Nyong'o, *Popular Struggles*, 16, 24, 25, 24 respectively. See also Mamdani, "The State and Civil Society," 63, on smashing the state machinery.

44. Mamdani, "The Social Basis of Constitutionalism," 68.

45. The shift may, in fact, be from one to the other of the two versions of Marxism identified by Alvin Gouldner in *The Two Marxisms*.

46. In fact, Mamdani used the words "social" and "democratic" often interchangeably. Mamdani, "State and Civil Society," 58, 60.

47. Mamdani, "Introduction," 9–10, 32.

48. Ibid., 5. See also the quite massive critique in Mamdani's "A Glimpse at African Studies: Made in the USA," *CODESRIA Bulletin* 2 (1990). Both critiques are directed at what he calls "the discourse of 'civil society.'" Mamdani asks: "is not the discourse of 'civil society' a restatement of an earlier perspective, that of 'modernization' theory, with its notion of the 'traditional' as the problem and the 'modern' as the solution?" Mamdani, "Introduction," 4.

49. M. Mamdani, "Comments on 'Ideology and Social Thought,'" *CODESRIA Bulletin* 3 (1994): 23.

50. Quotes from Mamdani, "Introduction," 34, 33. This point, as well as the discussion of the state in radical discourse, is mentioned in the introduction of the 1995 book as the only point where the agenda of the *Green Book* has been adjusted today. My claim is that much more fundamental differences exist between the 1988 and 1995 versions of radical discourse.

51. Turok, "No Democracy, No Development?" 109.

52. Of course new models of thought may be possible (see also my last chapter).

53. See my "Cursing the Nation-State," *Transition* 61 (1994): 114–122.

8

Assessing Democracy Discourses: A "Critique of Arms"[1]

We cannot change the world simply by evidence and reasoning, but we surely cannot change it without them either.[2]

Kwame A. Appiah

The essential pluralism of the discourses on democracy that I have just demonstrated threatens to jeopardize the whole enterprise of critical assessment. Each discourse presents its own idea of what a democratic society is about and none can claim an objective status that allows it to be used as a gauge in assessment. There is no neutral ground, no "true" conception of democracy, from which to judge.

Should we, therefore, give up the whole idea of critically assessing democracy discourses? I do not think so. I do not even have to revert to the strategy of importing my own favorite conception of democracy as a gauge for others. The solution may be that assessment is possible by measuring each discourse according to its own idea of what a democracy discourse should be. One can assess whether discourses deliver the goods they promise. In fact, when it comes to the promises of the discourses on democracy, they share the basic pledge to provide a viable democratic alternative for contemporary Africa.

In order to pursue the assessment, the heuristics that guide the discourses have to be analyzed. In this way, the assessment can show those issues that come into full focus when following the heuristics of the discourse and those that remain blind spots. Such an analysis can have salutary effects as it indicates inherent contortions and blockades that have to be overcome in order for the discourse to live up to its idea of a good discourse on democracy.

THE SETTING OF THE GAME AND ITS PLAYERS

The liberal discourse involves a focus upon a range of issues that are at the core of current debates on democracy in Africa, such as human rights, citizenship, separation of powers, the right to free political association, and freedom of the press. On many of these issues liberal views have become generally accepted, and even where disputed they still tend to constitute the "received view."[3]

The characteristic focus of a liberal view is on the institutional arrangements for a democratic polity, such as a system of rights, parties, and parliaments as institutions of representation, and separation of powers within the state. When it comes to formulating political alternatives for African societies, the relevance of the issue of political institutions can hardly be denied. The liberal focus is, thus, relevant. It may, however, be too narrow. In Africa the question of the appropriate form, preconditions, and sustainability of institutional arrangements has special relevance. A liberal discourse may not be well prepared to discuss these questions. Let me digress into the presuppositions of a liberal polity.

A liberal polity presumes a particular context. First, it assumes that there is a state embodying supreme power within the territory (the monopoly of legitimate use of force). Second, it assumes that there is a national community that shares a basic solidarity and that comprises individuals who perceive themselves as citizens, accepting the state as "their" state. Third, it presumes that individual citizens have sufficient skills and interest to act their part in the democratic polity. Fourth, it assumes that power and wealth are not distributed so unequally that institutionalized procedures can easily be subverted. Of course a whole range of other presuppositions could be mentioned, such as material and technological ones as well as conditions of "normality"—for instance, freedom from war.

This excursion into some of its presuppositions shows that a liberal polity is a delicate thing. It resembles a modern limousine that needs well-paved roads and a complex infrastructure, rather than a Land Rover that can run under virtually any conditions.[4] The hidden "contextuality" of a liberal polity has consequences for the assessment of African liberal democratic discourse. It leads to the conclusion that questions of infrastructure should be a coherent part of the discourse, and that an institutional setup that fits one context (a particular European one, for instance) will not automatically fit another context (a particular African one).

The heuristics of the liberal discourse are ill prepared, however, to discuss questions of infrastructure. The metaphor of "the rules of the game" suggests a focus on the practice of the game itself. The players remain largely out of scope. An essential, practical fiction of liberal democratic theory is that as players (i.e. as citizens) all are equal.[5] As far as they have outspoken religious, ethnic, or political identities, it is assumed that these can all be accommodated within the game. A further, and more debatable, assumption is that citizens who can play the game have time, interest, no fear, and are sufficiently equipped with "cultural capital" to play effectively, and, on the other hand, that players are never powerful enough to subvert the game. The setting of the game remains out of the scope, as well, in the game model. The modern state is suggested to be the natural unit of the political game. But is this necessarily the case? Could not more comprehensive, transnational or more local frameworks of democratic politics exist? In some cases the role of the national state can be contested. Then the state-political process as locus of coordination has to relate to other processes of coordination that are organized around religious, regional, ethnic, or commercial bonds. In such a situation different games are played, following rules that are not always compatible with that of the official political process. The liberal model may need to be stretched considerably to depict such a multifocal political context.

The main weakness of the "rules of the game" metaphor appears to be that it represents politics as an abstract, decontextualized arrangement that depends on defining the proper rules in order to function. It suggests general solutions to universal problems of political coordination in modern societies. In African realities in particular, however, the great challenge of democratic theorizing is to contextualize democratic arrangements by shaping them to suit historical situations and cultural resources at the individual and collective level.[6] The universalistic modernism inherent in the liberal democratic model thus makes it ill prepared to ask exactly the most challenging questions of democratic theorizing in Africa.

THE MODERN PALAVER

The idea of African communal democracy, exemplified by the palaver, is both classical and topical in African political discourse. It incorporates promises of harnessing the indigenous cultural resources that were too long neglected and suppressed, and promises of overcoming the harrowing exclusion of the majority of Africans from involvement in the political system. The idea of African communal democracy thus coincides perfectly with two global trends, that of a "cultural turn" in the perception of development problems, and a turn to a "bottom-up" view of politics.

The idea of a specifically African democratic alternative builds upon two principles. First, it maintains that there is a distinctly African type of culture, personality and "way-of-being-in-the-world" that corresponds with a mode of political organization. Second, it builds on the idea that such an African mode is essentially democratic. Both contentions (in fact, empirical claims) are hotly debated and will be discussed below. For the moment, however, I will assume that they hold and inquire into the credentials of a democracy discourse built upon these assumptions.

The idea of a palaver democracy for political practice today raises questions of a practical nature. For instance, it introduces questions about the specific political institutions that should be established or about the adaptation of palaver democracy to situations where the size of society is too large for a community gathering. I propose, however, to discuss the question at a more fundamental level as well, namely, by exploring in what significant ways contemporary societies differ from those for which traditional institutions were designed and what consequences political philosophers should derive from these differences.

K. A. Busia is one of the few authors who discussed the question of reviving African political heritages at this level.[7] He noticed, first, that the old systems focused on politics internal to the community whereas the present situation involves primarily the question of organizing political processes between and beyond individual communities.[8] Second, he found that the religious, supernatural aspect of rule was an essential aspect of the traditional system and this cannot be maintained in present-day multireligious and multicultural societies. Other issues could be added, such as the need for formal, juridical structuring of modern political institutions or the possible clash of the "modern" ideal of democratic equality with status differences related to family, age, or sex, such as were basic to "traditional" systems.

In short, it is a requirement for any discourse concerned with reviving the indigenous political heritage to seriously tackle a number of dilemmas concerning the proposed alternative. Among contemporary neotraditionalist authors, however, such discussions are astonishingly rare. These authors are mainly concerned with the more basic issue of defending a legitimate space for a discourse on African democratic alternatives.

The defensive concern with questions of legitimacy is also reflected in the structure of many texts on indigenous democracy. These texts include extensive critiques of other conceptions of democracy, mostly identified as "Western" democracy and reduced to a stereotyped "multipartyism," while giving little attention to discussing the indigenous alternatives themselves. By constructing the intellectual terrain in a completely bipolar way, opposing indigenous with alien, adversarial with consensus variants of democracy, or the "paradigm of the European conqueror" versus "an emancipatory African solution to African political problems," every argument against one pole seems to allocate credit to the other.[9] General expositions of the traditional system and its values are reiterated frequently but the discussion on the implementation of indigenous alternatives is not advanced.[10]

This lack of innovation in most contemporary neotraditional discourse on democracy is puzzling. Why do most authors not include new data and develop more sophisticated and better-argued positions by building on the work of colleagues and by answering criticisms? Historically, the apparent blockades in neotraditionalist discourse are an even more astonishing phenomenon since there have been sophisticated discussions of traditional political systems within the last century by such authors as Mensah Sarbah, Casely Hayford, De Graft Johnson, Kenyatta, Danquah, and Busia.[11]

The blockades in neotraditionalist democracy discourse derive in part from the function of the discourse in political practice. It is often an oppositional discourse challenging hegemonic racist or neocolonial positions.[12] In such situations, the issue is to state a strong counterposition to the hegemonic one whereas a frank discussion of the problems of one's own democratic alternative is reserved for later.[13]

The cause of stagnation may also be sought in the model of thought in which the neotraditionalist position is framed. There are two different ways to frame such a position. In a minority of cases, the position is supported by empirical data and based on an argument specifying why particular indigenous political institutions can provide an appropriate solution to current problems and why these institutions are preferable. In most cases, however, the choice for indigenous alternatives is based on a culturalist argument stating their Africanness and "thus" their appropriateness. Here one finds quite general arguments on types of culture, modes of being, and kinds of political communities.

I will leave the first type of neotraditionalist argument for discussion later. Here I will investigate whether the culturalist model of thought has inherent limits that can be the cause of the noted blockades in culturalist neotraditional discourse. For that purpose, I will first trace some of the most famous criticisms of culturalist assumptions and then try to derive the consequences of culturalist assumptions for a contemporary discourse on democracy. The first step will follow the criticism advanced in some of the highlights of contemporary African philosophy, namely, in Paulin J. Hountondji's discussion of ethnophilosophy, in Valentine Y. Mudimbe's analysis of the invention of Africa and in Kwame A. Appiah's discussions of nativism, ethnophilosophy, and African-American Afrocentrism.[14]

Culturalist thought in its various forms tries to present to the reader the essentially African culture, philosophy, personality, and religious experience. The main point highlighted by the critics is that, far from making up an African discourse, culturalism replicates the patterns of European thought on Africa. As Appiah states, it is a "'reverse discourse': the terms of resistance are already given us, and our contestation is entrapped within the Western cultural conjuncture we affect to dispute."[15]

The criticism of ethnophilosophy by the Beninese philosopher Paulin J. Hountondji is an early example of a critique of culturalist assumptions. Ethnophilosophy holds that there is an essentially African type of philosophy corresponding with traditional African worldviews. Truly African political philosophy, then, expresses the principles of organization of the traditional African polity. In his sophisticated dissection of the idea of ethnophilosophy,

Hountondji showed that ethnophilosophy does not counter but rather reaffirms European influence. Postulating "Africa" and "the West" as generic entities and positioning them as opposites copies the logic of colonial discourse with its racist and culturalist dichotomies. Ethnophilosophy, which explicitly claims to be African and criticizes others for copying the West, turns out to copy European stereotypes itself.

Discussing nativism, Kwame A. Appiah makes similar observations.[16] Nativism uses a vocabulary of Us versus Them, indigenous versus alien, inside (Africa) versus outside (the West), but these entities and oppositions are mythical constructions. The fact is that African intellectuals themselves are marked by Western influences, writing in European languages, participating in European or global debates. So-called "inside" is also "outside." This European imprint counts in particular for nativism itself: "Nativist nostalgia, in short, is largely fuelled by that Western sentimentalism so familiar after Rousseau; few things, then, are less native than nativism in its current forms."[17] The idea of a national philosophy and literature based on African traditions and norms, Appiah argues, follows the old assumptions of Herder about a community or nation having its *Sprachgeist* and about literature and nation (or race) organically belonging together. Like nineteenth-century "scientific" racism, one tends to conflate biological and cultural facts. Trendy Afrocentrism, even C. A. Diop's interpretation of the Negro, black character of Egyptian civilization, suffers from these flaws.[18] "The very invention of Africa must be understood, ultimately, as an outgrowth of modern European racialism," Appiah states.[19]

The origins of culturalist views may be suspect, yet the views can still be correct. Confused parents may have enlightened offspring. The other part of the critique of culturalism is empirical, therefore. This critique argues that the statements of what is essentially African should not be taken for granted. The ideas of "Africa" and "Europe," as if these are entities with a core or essence, are constructions.[20] Cultures, communities, and identities are not just there, but rather they are continuously produced through human actions. Contemporary affirmations of tradition are, therefore, modern affirmations, inventions of tradition that themselves rework and redesign selected indigenous elements often according to foreign designs. "Writing for and about ourselves . . . helps constitute the modern community of the nation." "Ironically, for many African intellectuals, these invented traditions have acquired the status of national mythology, and the invented past of Africa has come to play a role in the political dynamics of the modern state."[21]

The Consequences of Culturalism for a Discourse on Democracy

Let me now proceed to the second step in the assessment of culturalism and try to trace the consequences of culturalist assumptions for a contemporary discourse on democracy. The logic of culturalist thought, as analyzed in chapter 6, is relevant here. Culturalism is characterized by a combination of two ingredients: 1. an essentialist idea of cultures, and 2. the idea that the natural, unalienated state of people is within their culture. The political logic of the culturalist model can be derived at once. First, culturalist thought carves up the world into various cultures (groups) thus creating borders between them. Second, creating domains produces the idea of import and export traffic, the idea of indigenous and alien elements, and the idea of customs and immigration control to protect inside from outside. Third, the geographical metaphor of cultures as domains brings on a "Whig" historiography: by projecting the present view of culture-domains back into history, the multidimensional historical process is streamlined into "the history of" each of the domains.[22] Fourth, the model suggests a difference between purity and hybridity: mixing is abnormal and a bastardization rather than a happy marriage with strong offspring.

The political logic of culturalist thought is fully exposed when the second basic characteristic of culturalism is taken into consideration. If a culture is a positive entity that defines a way of "being-in-the-world" and if the natural unalienated state of people is within their culture then there is no escape. The first assumption constructs a world of separate niches and the second assumption locks people into the niches. Culture sticks and stigmatizes: the political logic of culturalism suggests a system of segregation.

The peculiar political logic of culturalism can also be found in European right-wing politics.[23] Without using the notion of race, right-wing ideology involves a framework of thought suggesting divisions between people that are as ossified as racial divisions. The classical anthropologist Lévy-Bruhl is another case in point. Lévy-Bruhl's works are often considered examples of racist anthropology because they map out a "primitive mentality" that is qualitatively different from the modern, scientific mind. It should be noted, however, that Lévy-Bruhl did not see this primitive mentality as anchored biologically in "primitive" humans. In a long evolution of primitive culture the primitive mentality could advance to the modern form. Yet Lévy-Bruhl's theory has racist implications because, within any practically relevant time span, mentalities are supposed to stick to people.

The analysis of the political logic of culturalism can now be used to assess the credentials of a culturalist discourse on democracy. Can a culturalist discourse on democracy address crucial issues such as those brought forward by K. A. Busia? His first point, the management of intergroup and interculture affairs, is not addressed in culturalist discourse, it is even made into a major problem. From the outset culturalism segregates by defining particularized groupcultures. The possibility of intergroup cooperation can only be based on the vague idea of a universal human brotherhood.[24] The model does not give a clue as to how this brotherhood-in-segregation can be shaped politically.

Busia's second issue, that of handling pluralism within communities, is not addressed either. By stressing the essential unity and coherence of the culture-group matrix, plurality is played down. Even in those culturalist arguments where consensus is not assumed to preexist but to emerge from reconciliation of different points of view, the culturalist conception provides no methods or clues to manage persistent disagreements. They remain an anomaly. It can be expected that, finally, the persistent dissident will have to be excluded due to being unfaithful to the community.[25]

A third crucial issue in the reemployment of traditional political heritages is the question of the need for an institutionalized and legalized framework in complex societies. Here again, the culturalist view gives no clue and, in fact, it even creates obstacles. The monistic idea of cultures, communities, and their politics suggests that the legal-bureaucratic framework can only be an extension of the shared cultural basis of the community. The state should be an organ of the community directly representing its values, mission, and identity. Formalizing a system of rights and political institutions of representation and control can be divisive, disturbing the natural bond linking the community together. The Zairian philosopher Chimalenga Ntumba speaks of the primacy of the "We" (*Wir-Primat*) as the basic principle of an African society.[26]

In conclusion, the identity type of discourse does not provide instruments to tackle several of the most basic issues of democracy in plural and complex societies. The silence of this type of discourse on the dilemmas of the implementation of neotraditional democratic alternatives, that I noted above, may have a very simple reason: it stands empty handed, or handcuffed, in the face of these dilemmas. The "We" and "They" polarity of culturalist discourse does not suggest a fruitful approach to contemporary problems in democratic thought.

At this point I can return to the case of the more empirical and pragmatic nonculturalist neotraditionalists. The above argument, after all, only defeats a neotraditionalist argument involving the assumption of cultural essences. In fact the nonculturalist position produced some of the most interesting arguments on democracy. Examples in the last chapter show that such neotraditionalist arguments can put into question some of the standard ideas about democracy, such as the one that political pluralism necessarily needs adversarial politics or the idea that politics primarily concerns the state.

A number of nonculturalists still defend the idea that the category of "the African political system" makes sense as an empirical generalization. They then point to the phenomenon of politics aiming at consensus in the gathering of elders under the chief, or of chiefs under the paramount chief, where the chief, finally, is only a *primus inter pares*. It is rarely noted, however, that the widespread occurrence of a phenomenon within Africa does not make it typically African. This is only shown to be if the phenomenon does not occur (or rarely occurs) outside Africa. Similar political systems, however, occur and have occurred in many parts of the globe.[27]

POPULAR STRUGGLES FOR WHICH DEMOCRACY?

The turn toward democratization in Africa is easily perceived, especially from outside of Africa, as happening despite Marxist influence. After all, the immediate object of contestation for the democratic opposition, namely, single-partyism, has been part and parcel of radical (revolutionary anti-imperialist) programs of various types.[28] But the fact is that democratic movements as well as democratic thought in Africa have been greatly inspired by radical discourse. Empowerment, popular movements, and the struggle for actual political participation of the populace have been central to radical politics and are an important aspect of the idea of democracy as embodying increased popular accountability.

The focus of radical discourse is on social struggle. It concerns social movements ("those movements that set out to change Africa"), their histories and experiences. Its interest is not in the puzzles of organizing a democratic polity but in attaining it and making it serve popular interests. Radical discourse focuses on attaining power rather than on taming power, that is, on the institutions of a democratic polity. At this point I will investigate whether this idea of democracy can deliver the democratic products it promises.

Within the basic Marxist radical framework, it is logical not to focus on the institutions of a democratic polity. Marxist class theory assumes that all conflicts in civil society are ultimately class struggles. Politics is therefore essentially class struggle. In the coming socialist society the phenomenon of class itself is overcome, so no fundamental social conflicts remain and politics becomes obsolete. Socialist society is a self-managing community.

Already in the *Green Book* of 1988, however, the Marxist assumption that conflict in civil society is merely class struggle is abandoned. Social movements are now considered as movements of various kinds without assuming a priori the primacy of class over other types of social forces. If the class theory is dropped, however, then the expectation of the end of fundamental social conflict in the future society has to be abandoned as well. Furthermore, if fundamental political conflicts will always remain, then the need will always exist for the mediation of conflicts in a political process. Such need for mediation will unavoidably raise a range of questions on how to organize this political process in a democratic way: questions, for instance, on how the usurpation of power can be avoided; how rights and liberties are to be protected; how the government can be controlled; how participation can be organized; and so forth. In summary then, the first step of acknowledging a fundamental pluralism within civil society dictates a second step, namely, discussing how this plurality is going to be mediated democratically.

In the democratic turn of radical discourse, the first step was taken in the *Green Book* of 1988 but not the second step, not even in *African Studies in Social Movements and Democracy* (1995). The question of "how state power should be organized and of how it should relate to social forces" is announced there but not addressed.[29] Without addressing these issues, however, radical discourse can only provide valuable theorizing on liberation but not on democracy. Recognizing the plurality of civil society without discussing a plural political order constitutes a half-way house between the old theory of class (class as the ultimate force in civil society) and of history (as proceeding toward socialism), and the new sense that both theories have to be given up.

A fundamental reason for not addressing these concrete questions concerning political institutions was given by Mamdani himself. In his critique of the "civil society perspective" (i.e., liberal Africanist theorizing), he mentions "the differentiation between the social and the political" as the key to their mistaken position.[30] If my argument above holds then exactly the resistance to this differentiation should be given up. Without recognizing that there are specifically political issues, namely, those that have to do with the institutionalized handling of social, economic, and cultural differences, the basic question of what is involved in framing a democratic society remains. If questions such as "how state power should be organized" or of "how to redefine the form of the state" are considered relevant, as is the case in contemporary radical discourse, then it is necessary to discuss political issues in their own right, distinguished (but not separated) from social ones.[31] After all, the issue of social justice and transformation is not identical with the issue of a democratic society.[32]

A SHARED WORLDVIEW

My critique of arms started with a rather minimal agenda of checking whether the various democracy discourses deliver the products that they promise. For each of them it turned out that their agendas are truncated: a range of relevant issues remain unaddressed making the currently dominant discourses unsatisfactory as vehicles for democratic thought in contemporary Africa. This is not to say that the discussions concerned are not relevant, but rather that the dominant discourses have fundamental deficiencies. They stop just an arms length away (and in the case of the culturalists much more than that) from the most relevant questions concerning a democratic polity in contemporary Africa. To conclude my investigation, this section intends to fathom the specific sources of the limited agendas. Let me quickly review the main points of the criticisms for that purpose.

The modernist liberal democracy discourse, I argued, decontextualizes the issue of democracy. It suggests that the problems of political order in modern societies are universal and that by adhering to the rules of the democratic game, these problems can be handled. The issue of democracy in Africa, consequently, is seen basically as a question of implementation. A whole range of relevant questions do not come into focus from this perspective. I described these as questions concerning the "setting" and the "players" of the democratic game. More specifically, one can think of the question of appropriate democratic institutions for specific African countries and communities and of organizing the empowerment of marginal groups in order for them to become participants in the democratic process. Other relevant questions concern ethnicity as a form of political organization, the issue of the democratization of civil society organizations, and the incorporation of existing traditional modes of political deliberation into a modern democratic polity.

It is essential to note that the limited focus of the liberal democracy discourse is in fact predetermined in its ground plan, namely, the modernization model of thought as discussed in chapter 6. The tradition-modernity polarity involves the idea of universal modernity and thus suggests that there is only a single modern political system. Liberal democracy is perceived as simply the political requirement of universal modernity. The determining influence of the idea of modernity on democratic discourse can be brought out clearly by erasing it. As soon as the idea that something like "modernity" exists is given up, or even if it is used in the plural, as "modernities", then the issue arises of different variants of democratic polity that are contingent upon the historical and cultural context. The idea that there is some specific model of modernity, therefore, is the key to blocking a host of interesting and pertinent questions of democratic thought for Africa.[33]

In the case of culturalist neotraditionalist discourse on democracy, I argued that the two assumptions of culturalism determine a political logic of segregation. Culturalism hypostatizes the idea of cultures, races, or identities, it ossifies differences between cultures, creates "aliens" and suggests, for instance, that purity of the groups and conformity within groups are the normal cases. At the same time, highly relevant and fascinating questions concerning the revival of traditional institutions are not addressed. One could think here of the similarity between the idea of "palaver" and the idea of the "public sphere." Could not the idea of the palaver be incarnated in large-scale societies in the form of a public realm with appropriate values, institutions and guarantees to facilitate the inclusion of all citizens? If such unconventional conjectures are explored, one could ask which institutions (mass-media, social movements, associations) could best facilitate such a public sphere. What would be the appropriate legal and organizational frameworks that could guarantee equal access to this public palaver sphere, which relations of ownership (state, commercial, Church, cooperative, or other) would facilitate best a sustainable, open, and politically relevant palaver? No such questions are explored, however, in contemporary neotraditionalist discourse.

As in the case of modernist liberal discourse, the underlying model of thought predetermines the limitations of neotraditionalist thought about democracy. After establishing the basic culturalist oppositions between "We" and "They" or "Africa" and "the West," a segregated view of political communities follows that directs attention away from relevant questions concerning indigenous democratic alternatives.

In the case of the radical discourse on democracy, I argued that by discussing political issues only in the framework of the struggle of the majority of the people for social transformation, radical discourse can provide theories of liberation but not of democracy. Within a Marxist theory of class and history the absorption of the political into the social belongs to the logic of the discourse. Contemporary radicals distanced themselves from Marxist class theory, however, embracing the idea that the plurality of civil society cannot be reduced to class. A plurality of interests and orientations raises the need for permanent regulation of this plurality, that is the need for politics. The discussion of political issues as distinct from the issue of social struggle thus becomes a necessity if the Marxist theoretical framework is abandoned. A range of questions on shaping a radical democratic polity, on the institutions required for political empowerment, on a system of rights for all, and on democratizing civil society become relevant. Radical authors who refuse to discuss political issues in their own right stop their post-Marxist turn just in sight of such key questions concerning a radical democratic polity.

In the case of the radical discourse, as in the cases of the liberal and culturalist discourses, the limits of its theorizing about democracy derive directly from the liberation model, as discussed in chapter 6. The idea that there is a basic and all-pervading opposition between oppressor and oppressed subsumes the issue of democracy under that of the social struggle. The question of WHO holds power is addressed rather than HOW power can be handled democratically.[34]

The conclusion of my three critiques puts into question not only the dominant democracy discourses but also the key models that shaped African political thought for more than a century. The conclusion should be that the intellectual armory available to think out a political alternative today is comprised of three arms systems that have serious limitations in terms of range, accuracy of fire, and adjustment to the conditions of the field. The critical assessment of democracy discourses leads to the conclusion that the battle cannot be won unless the armory is improved.

The Consequences of Bipolar Models of Thought

Should we resolve at this point that the key models of thought have to be discarded completely and a new paradigm constructed? Such a voluntaristic reshaping of our intellectual world is clearly illusory. After all, to use

Neurath's metaphor, we are intellectually out at sea; if we want to reconstruct our ship, we cannot take it apart to rebuild it without drowning ourselves. The only thing we can do is to restructure and to make adjustments in a piecemeal manner.

There is another reason why the attempt at starting from scratch may be illusory. Each of the three models of thought that were identified in chapter 6 underlines a basic aspect of society: the modernization model focuses on the economical-technological, the identity model on the cultural, and the liberation model on the social. It cannot be expected that such basic orientations can be avoided. Neither, however, are we forced to conclude that such basic orientations should necessarily lead to deficient models of thought.

The conclusion, therefore, should not be to completely eliminate some of the models of thought but rather to track down the specific causes of the handicap within the three models. And in fact the analysis of the three critiques that I have just presented already pinpointed such causes. The truncated agendas of democracy discourses derive right from the basic assumptions of the dominant models of thought.

Remarkably, the analysis allows for an aggravated conclusion at this point. Despite their differences, the three models of thought share the characteristic of a bipolar structure. Each of the models, although in different ways, starts out to create one major division in which all elements of thought are subsequently positioned. For each, "we" and "they" or Africa and the West become the major compartments of this world. In the modernization type, "we" and "they" are the premodern and the modern, where the one has to catch up with the other. In the liberation type the polarity is even clearer. It is a hierarchical order of oppressor versus oppressed, or "they up there (the "center") versus we down here (the "periphery")." In the identity type, the order is a horizontal opposition of cultural difference between Africa and the West or we and they. The polarity, in this case, is not to be eliminated but something that is valued highly.

The bipolarity of the ground plan also involves the introduction of one grand fundamental idea, one could say a myth, in each of the models. In the modernization model this is the idea of a state of modernity (clearly modeled upon the self-image of the West), in the identity model it is the idea of a state of authenticity (modeled upon the negation of the self-image of the West), and in the liberation model it is the idea of a state of complete liberation (in its classical form it is the idea of socialism as a self-managing community of equals).

The bipolarity in the ground plan has far-reaching consequences for discourses built upon such a plan. One consequence is that it radically simplifies our thinking. Where a multitude of differences and resemblances, problems and options could be conceived, only one remains. In the case of the issue of democracy, for instance, it leads to the peculiar view that "basically" one major issue should be resolved for democracy to work. For the modernist liberal, the basic issue of democracy in Africa would be resolved if modernized political institutions were established. For the neotraditionalist, the issue would be resolved if the proper authentic African traditions were revived. For the protagonist of the popular struggles view on democratization, the issue of democracy would be resolved if the poor were empowered. The idea of one grand basic solution leads to the neglect of many challenging specific issues relating to the question of democratization, such as those of empowering citizens in their different roles or of harnessing indigenous cultural resources in institutionalizing democratic practices.

Another consequence of the bipolar models is that they define Africa as something "different from" or "opposed to" something else. The characteristics of Africa are then given in terms of its difference from the stereotypical description of the other rather than by elaborate reference to African realities. The basic point of reference in thinking about Africa is something outside of Africa, namely, modernity, the West, and the exploiting imperialist system.[35]

The suggestion of the depolarization of the models of thought may be discarded as the typical view of an outsider who does not see that the opposition between Africa and the West is a basic fact of life in Africa. Polar models are thus seen as particularly appropriate to the African situation. I do not want to deny that an antithetical relation to the West marks African history in the age of, what I called in the opening chapter, the "great confrontation" involving the epochal events of colonial subjugation and liberation. Even in the lives of many intellectuals the colonial experience has probably been the single most dramatic political event.[36]

For the generations of Africans who grow up in post-colonial states the situation may change, however. Their world is primarily that of African societies. Neocolonial relations have not disappeared and continue to have a strong imprint upon political consciousness, but internal problems, such as misuse of power, state violence, stagnation, and poverty are more visible and prominent. A number of key historical events as well do not necessarily reinforce the idea of a polarity between Africa and the West. For instance, the "development failure" of post-colonial states, the disenchantments of African Socialism and Marxism, the ruthless slaughterings in internal strife, in Liberia, Ruanda, Somalia, Algeria, and elsewhere, the Ethiopian-Eritrean war, and the victory over Apartheid, are primarily events within Africa. There is a problem-shift from issues situated between Africa and the West toward issues that are, at least in important ways, internal to Africa.[37] This shift could have its intellectual counterpart in moving away from bipolar models of thought.

In a way, overcoming the bipolar models is a decolonization of African thought in a fundamental sense. There is nothing particularly European in thinking in terms of we-they oppositions. The specific polarity, however, between the "modern" and the "primitive" ensues from the Enlightenment tradition; the culturalist logic of the various identity discourses, with its *völkische* oppositions between cultures, clearly has its roots in the European Romantic tradition; and the opposition between oppressor and oppressed as the ground plan for a historicist conception of society took its inspiration from the Marxist eschatological tradition. In each case, these traditions suggest forceful representations of political problems but at the same time they are blinding us to contingent facts and the diversity of development options. In order to address the pertinent questions concerning democracy in diverse African contexts and to search for creative solutions it is necessary to overcome the bipolar logic that is inherent in the models of thought that have dominated African political thought in the last 150 years.[38]

FROM BIPOLAR TO DISCURSIVE CONCEPTIONS OF DEMOCRACY

If my argument holds, then the present intellectual situation is a curious one. The main traditions in African political thought, which have been powerful vehicles for addressing relevant issues over the last 150 years, have run out of steam. The issue of democracy is a major invitation to African political thought to reset basic parameters. The conclusion should then be that the more authors distance themselves from the bipolar models of thought, the more relevant and original their contribution to the discussion on democracy in Africa will be.

On the one hand, the issue of African democratic alternatives involves a reorientation toward the specific situations in diverse countries and the actual resources in terms of political heritages in specific African societies. On the other hand, it implies a return to the essential issue of politics formulated by Hannah Arendt as "handling plurality." In fact, the basic issues for African political thought are not essentially different from issues discussed elsewhere in the world among contemporary political theorists. Theoretically, they express a postmodern, post-Marxist, and postliberal era; politically, they concern the question of a political order in highly plural societies.

African political thought may make for an interesting input in contemporary international debates by rethinking a number of its values and institutions for skillfully regulating conflicts. For the most part, a relatively peaceful coordination of actions of many individuals and diverse communities has been achieved from the old commercial cities and long-distance trading networks to the markets, bazaars, and commercial quarters in modern African cities. In many cases, formalized central state structures did not play a dominant role in such coordination. The issue of politics was not primarily that of handling the Weberian absolute monopoly of legitimate use of violence in a definite territory. Probably the current situation of shaky national states with various competing power structures will continue to determine the discussion of state and civil society in political thought in Africa. With issues concerning multicommunity and multicultural states arising in most countries in the world today, African discussions may be of relevance everywhere.

Taking up the challenge to reset basic parameters raises immediate dividends for African political thought. Ernest Wamba-dia-Wamba from Congo, for instance, when addressing the danger of a new elite politics due to democratization, discusses the possible parameters of radical democratic politics. Wamba-dia-Wamba elaborates on the *Mbongi* groups within the Zairian civil society during the struggle in the period of the National Conference in the early 1990s. The *Mbongi* is a type of political meeting of people at workplaces, wards, or villages. In Wamba-dia-Wamba's work, the idea of the *Mbongi* is the beginning of interesting reflections on the concept of "politics" and on what emancipative politics should be. Conventional conceptions of politics, Wamba-dia-Wamba argues, are state centered: politics is either the business of the state itself or of organizations trying to influence or capture state power. In contrast, the *Mbongi* exemplifies a "mode of politics" that allows communities to "deal with their own differences" in terms of sex, origin (immigrants), and minorities. The really democratic state would be

organized around the category, "people of all walks of life" (*gens de partout*). . . . The State must rest on the multiplicity and diversity of the people: old, young, peasants, diverse national or ethnic origins, workers, merchants, intellectuals, professionals, women, men, atheists, believers . . . the State must not be a simple composition or expression of this multiplicity; it must transcend it with new categories. . . . These conditions are required to avoid differences from becoming discriminations.[39]

Interestingly, Wamba-dia-Wamba's discussion concerns palaver democracy while avoiding all cultural essentialism; it concerns radical liberation while avoiding the common reduction of the issue of democracy to that of the social struggle.

A number of authors emanating from the radical tradition also embark on discussions of a democratic polity. The question of democracy is no longer absorbed into the promise of a coming state of liberation (socialism), thus immediately raising a whole range of essential political issues. A SAPES/CODESRIA conference in Harare in 1992 on "Democracy and Human Rights in Africa" affirmed the formal manifestations of democratization in terms of a. plural parties, unions, and mass media; b. constitutional rule; c. observance of human rights; d. accountibility; and e. effective representation, while also raising fundamental issues such as "transforming authoritarian political cultures into democratic ones," "the building of a democratic civil society in which the supremacy of civil institutions has been established," "the expansion of democratic space," and "the construction of effective citizenship capable of demanding and getting more civil, political, social and economic rights."[40] In 1992, the Kenyan scholar Peter Anyang' Nyong'o, whose earlier views were mentioned in chapter 7, defines democracy as the question of "taming the state" and of organized pluralism within a political process.[41] In these three examples, the question of democracy is not reduced to that of empowering the masses. The essential shift has been to abandon the Marxist heritage in terms of a theory of class and a theory of history that promises the coming state of a totally self-managing community (socialism) in which the question of democracy would be resolved. In the absence of classlessness and total liberation, democracy involves the need for a carefully devised institutionalized regulation of differences between social actors.[42]

Quite different from Wamba, the Ghanaian philosopher Kwasi Wiredu addresses the idea of consensus politics while avoiding the standard stereotype of the African communalistic polity where the individual is submerged in the community. Wiredu maintains the Gold Coast/Ghanaian tradition (from Sarbah to Danquah and Busia) of what I called "concrete neotraditionalism" earlier in this book, a tradition that in many cases avoids a bipolar model of thought. Wiredu's "Plea for a Non-party Polity" provides a sophisticated argument for a "consensual nonparty system" as a democratic alternative.[43] Such a system can build on a resourceful African heritage of values and institutions to achieve consensus and reconciliation. Discussing the case of the Akan political system, Wiredu argues for the superiority of a system that negotiates consent by reconciliation of all views presented (a system of "substantive representation") over a system that simply aims at gaining majorities and power (a system of "formal representation").

Wiredu's argument is neotraditional, namely, pertaining to the mobilization of traditional values and institutions, yet it can avoid an essentialistic opposition between African and European culture. Significantly, Wiredu even concludes that "there is nothing peculiarly African about the idea itself" of a consensual nonparty system.[44]

Kwame Anthony Appiah, another Ghanaian, provides an argument for Pan-Africanism that is even further removed from the culturalist identity model of thought. Appiah argues that "an African identity is coming into being. I have argued throughout these essays that this identity is a new thing; that it is the product of history . . . and that the bases through which so far it has largely been theorized—race, a common historical experience, a shared metaphysics—presuppose falsehoods too serious for us to ignore.[45] This does not mean that African or Pan-African identity should always be rejected. The "useless" and often "dangerous falsehoods" that create "tags of disability" or "disabling labels" have to be replaced; "another set of stories will build us identities through which we can make more productive alliances."[46] African identities can thus have different political roles, which makes them a vital issue for debate: "we must argue for or against them case by case."[47] In many contemporary situations in Africa, Appiah argues, "the inscription of difference . . . plays into the hands of the very exploiters whose shackles we are trying to escape"; "there are times when Africa is not the banner we need."[48] The Pan-Africanism that Appiah argues for is a project that needs to be justified as relevant and emancipatory, and preferable over other possible political projects that Africans could engage in, rather than Pan-Africanism considered as an essential requirement of a given African identity.

A number of discussions on the question of democratic governance in situations of ethnic pluralism follow new approaches as well. The Zimbabwean political scientist Masipula Sithole, for instance, argues that ethnic organizations, instead of erecting an obstacle for a pluralist democracy, "historically represent pressures for representation" and cannot be accommodated better, politically, than in a democratic system that "plays the game by the rules" and thereby facilitates "voice" and inclusion.[49] Another interesting discussion is Peter Ekeh's work on the public realm in Africa. The Nigerian Ekeh argues that the perversion of political authority during the era of slavery and colonialism has created an alienation between state and society in Africa. This alienation precludes the emergence of a public sphere on which a democratic system and citizenship can be built. Instead, two public spheres emerged: a realm of the state maintained basically by force, and an ethnic- and community-based sphere where there is, what might be called, local, individual, community citizenship. The two spheres are so far apart, Ekeh argues, that they even maintain their own systems of taxation of public finance.[50] Any political alternative must take note of this situation of what he calls "two publics."

The crucial observation concerning the various examples mentioned here is that they move away from the bipolar models. Such "depolarization" immediately results in interesting and original discussions that go far beyond the ritual restatements of worn out stereotypes on multipartyism, the rule of the community, or the rule of the masses. The invitation to consider the question of Africa's future after the age of "the great confrontation" and beyond the standard bipolar models leads to discussing development without encasing it in the fiction of some specific model of modernity, cultural resources without choking the diversity at hand in culturalist and essentialist stereotypes, and liberation or emancipation without clouding the political horizon with the chimera of a state of complete liberation in a self-managing community, whether defined as socialism or not.

NOTES

1. The expression "Critique of Arms," originally from Marx, is the title of the famous book *La Critique des Armes* (1974) in which Régis Debray, after fighting in Bolivia with Che Guevara, assessed the revolutionary ideology of the struggle.

2. K. A. Appiah, *In My Fathers House, Africa in the Philosophy of Culture* (New York: Methuen, 1992), 179.

3. Presently, Marxists and neotraditionalists tend to accept such liberal concerns, which they had disqualified as typically bourgeois, or Western preoccupations for decades. It is a change of view that remains in most cases unacknowledged.

4. Unlike a liberal democracy, a patrimonial system, for instance, appears to survive under any conditions.

5. This idea of equality-as-citizens is simultaneously one of liberalism's emancipatory missions: the democratic game is self-consciously built upon an egalitarian universalism; whatever your differences in ideology, income, religion, and so forth, you are equal as citizen.

6. In all cases it involves discarding unwarranted claims to universality of any particular form of a democratic polity. Just like we have to give up the idea that there is something like "modernity" in the singular (and secretly model this modernity on contemporary Western societies), we have to learn to think of "democracy" in plural terms.

7. Especially in chapters 1 and 2 of *Africa in Search of Democracy*, where, in the context of an attempt to "examine the problems facing contemporary Africa within the context of the search for democracy," Busia discussed the religious and political heritage.

8. Of course African states and empires involved coordination between and beyond communities, but the actual forms can hardly be described as democratic and are only very rarely propagated as traditional African political systems to be revived.

9. M. Ramose, "African Democratic Tradition: Oneness, Consensus and Openness: A Reply to Wamba-dia-Wamba," *Quest: Philosophical Discussions* 6, no. 2 (1992) 72–73.

10. For instance, M. P. Eboh, "Democracy with an African Flair," *Quest: Philosophical Discussions* 7, no. 1 (June 1993): 92–99; G.B.N. Ayittey, *Africa Betrayed* (New York: St. Martin's Press, 1992); M. Ramose, "African Democratic Tradition"; Ch. B. Okolo, *African Social & Political Philosophy: Selected Essays* (Nsukka: Fulladu Publishing Company, 1993); K. Gyekye, "The Idea of Democracy in the Traditional Setting and Its Relevance to Political Development in Contemporary Africa," paper presented at the First International Regional Conference in Philosophy, Mombasa, Kenya, 1988.

11. See my discussion in the previous chapters. Busia, it should be noted, supported his deliberations on the future of chieftaincy on his sociological and historical investigations in his *The Position of the Chief in the Modern Political System of Ashanti* (1951; reprint, London: Frank Cass, 1968). It is curious that the recent book by G.B.M. Ayittey, *Africa Betrayed*, practically ignores the reflections of his countryman.

12. Neotraditionalist discourse is found especially in the United States and South Africa, where such a struggle makes really sense.

13. Steve Biko, for instance, explicitly considered his struggle to be part of a transitory phase. The new political structure of *Azania* will be different, open, and humanistic. S. Biko, *I Write What I Like*, a selection of his writings edited by Aelred Stubbs, C.R. (1978; reprint, London: Heinemann, 1979), 123. However, even the new situation remains conceptualized in terms of whites and blacks as groups, not in terms of citizens of a democratic community. "Therefore we wish to state explicitly that this country belongs to black people and to them alone." Biko, *I Write What I Like*, 121.

14. P. J. Hountondji, *African Philosophy. Myth and Reality* (1976; reprint, Bloomington: Indiana University Press, 1983); and P. J. Hountondji, "Occidentalisme, élitisme: Réponse à deux critiques," *Recherche, Pédagogie et Culture* 57 (1982): 58–67, translated as "Occidentalism, Elitism: Answer to Two Critiques," *Quest: Philosophical Discussions* 3, no. 2 (1990); V. Y. Mudimbe, *The Invention of Africa* (Bloomington: Indiana University Press, 1988); K. A. Appiah, *In My Fathers House, Africa in the Philosophy of Culture* (Methuen: New York, 1992); K. A. Appiah, "Europe Upside Down; Fallacies of the New Afrocentrism," *Sapina Newsletter* 5, no. 1 (1993).

15. Appiah, *In My Fathers House*, 59.

16. Appiah defines nativism as "the claim that true African independence requires a literature of one's own." Appiah, *In My Fathers House*, 56. He equates it some pages later with "the rhetoric of ancestral purity," 61.

17. Appiah, *In My Fathers House*, 59–60.

18. See Appiah's magnificent "Europe Upside Down."

19. Appiah, *In My Fathers House*, 62.

20. S. Koenis & P. Boele van Hensbroek, "Het Westen bestaat niet. Over de implicaties van culturalisme," in D. Pels & G. de Vries, eds., *Burgers en Vreemdelingen* (Amsterdam: van Gennep, 1994), 51–62; E. Hobsbawm & T. Ranger, *The Invention of Tradition* (Cambridge: Cambridge University Press, 1983).

21. Appiah, *In My Fathers House*, 55–56, 61. The fact, as such, that identities are situational constructs does not disqualify them. The struggle for an identity simply needs a political justification, just like any political objective. The justification for such a struggle cannot, finally, rely on a claim for intrinsic value.

22. The pitfalls of this culturalism in historiography are shown in the heated debate about the origins of Western culture. M. Bernal, *Black Athena: the Afroasiatic Roots of Classical Civilization* (1987; reprint, London: Vintage Press, 1991). Do the origins of Europe lie in Greece (Europe, as Western culturalists say) or in Egypt (black, as African culturalists say)? Present-day categories are applied to partition a world of 2,500 years ago in which these categories made no sense. Historically, there was one cultural space involving West Asia and the eastern Mediterranean basin. W.M.J. van Binsbergen, "Black Athena and Africa's Contribution to Global Cultural History," *Quest: Philosophical Discussions* 9, no. 2 and 10, no. 1 (1996): 101–137. Such questions of origins are culturalist artifacts.

23. This New Racism melts together concepts such as "culture," "nation," "natural home," "tradition," and "way of life" into a framework that can effectively stigmatize (minority) groups. The message is that there are essential differences between cultures, defining a way of life and eventually also a nation. Every culture should be respected, guarded, and protected against outside influences. It is therefore necessary to limit immigration and repatriate nonindigenous elements to where they naturally belong. This is in the natural interest of both sides. M. Barker, *The New Racism* (London: Junction Books, 1982); and E. Balibar & I. Wallerstein, eds., *Race, Nation, Class: Ambiguous Identities* (London: Verso, 1991).

24. For instance, Nyerere's idea of *Ujamaa* implies familyhood at the national level but again a kind of super-familyhood at the level of humanity as a whole.

25. This is not to deny that, as political values, consensus and compromising are certainly basic to managing plurality within a community. They are just not enough, not by far.

26. T. Ntumba, "Afrikanische Weisheit. Das dialectische Primat des *Wir* vor dem *Ich-Du*," in W. Oelmüller, *Philosophie und Weisheit* (Baderhorn: F. Schöningh, 1988).

27. Polynesian, American Indian, and African examples can often be used interchangeably. See, for example, E. A. Hoebel, *Anthropology* (1949; reprint, New York: McGraw-Hill, 1972). Hoebel states on p. 459 that "the universal instrument of government is the council." The attempt to return to a supposedly unique indigenous source for shaping an alternative development path is also a familiar political strategy. G. Kitching, *Development and Underdevelopment in Historical Perspective: Populism, Nationalism and Industrialization* (London: Oxford University Press, 1982) calls this strategy "populism."

28. Even today discussion of the single-multiparty issue does not excel in unambiguous statements. See, for example, Mamdani, "Introduction," in M. Mamdani & E. Wamba-dia-Wamba, *African Studies in Social Movements and Democracy* (Dakar: Codesria, 1995), 8.

29. Ibid., 33.

30. Ibid., 4.

31. For quotes, see ibid., 33. Failing to do so when considering political issues, can lead to curious arguments, like Mamdani's when he argues that "the demand for democracy . . . is not always progressive" (ibid., 68); and, there is "the need to underline the class content of every demand for democracy in a specific situation" (ibid., 68). The concept of democracy is here analytically so unspecified that conservative claims can be distinguished from progressive ones only by reference to WHO puts forward the claim (not why certain demands in the name of democracy are deficient). The suggestion to distinguish movements struggling for "rights" from those struggling for "privileges" can neither be of much help here (ibid., 57).

32. Radical intellectuals in Latin America as well as in the West took this step and thereby blurred the distinction between socialist and liberal positions in a fundamental way. Pursuing their new agenda, questions can be asked such as what could be a "socialist civil society" (Keane) or a "liberal socialism" (Mouffe). By this move a wide range of issues in political thought are raised that have hitherto received attention primarily in liberal and social democratic thought.

33. An individual liberal thinker can give such questions attention but the modernization model as an intellectual framework does not suggest them.

34. Of course individual radical thinkers can address such typically political issues but dominant radical discourse cannot be a heuristic guide for them. An interesting example of the truncated radical agenda is Claude Ake's recent book on democracy *Democracy and Development in Africa* (Washington: The Brookings Institution, 1996). His first-class presentation of the problem of African emancipation in the form of democracy takes no more than one page (p. 132) to discuss the required democratic institutions! Finally, it is not a book on democracy but one on social change. It stops exactly where relevant issues on a democratic polity start.

35. The clearest example is culturalism. See also Appiah, "Europe Upside Down." On the chimera of "the West," see Koenis & Boele van Hensbroek, "Het Westen Bestaat Niet"; and P. Boele van Hensbroek, "On Culturalism," in H. Kimmerle & F. M.

Wimmer, eds., *Philosophy and Democracy in Intercultural Perspective*. Studies in Intercultural Philosophy: Vol. 3. (Amsterdam: Rodopi, 1997). On defining a position in terms of the position it opposes, see Dick Pels, *Property and Power in Social Theory: A Study in Intellectual Rivalry* (London: Routledge, 1998).

36. This leaves what Basil Davidson termed "the deep and lasting sense of injury, above all of moral injury." B. Davidson, *The Black Man's Burden: Africa and the Curse of the Nation-State* (New York: Times Books, 1992) 297.

37. This problem of politics, or of democracy, does not immediately suggest a bipolar order, in the way that the problems of identity or imperialism do. It is a problem of "construction," namely, that of regulating political processes in society. It is a problem for all human societies.

38. The result of such changes would not be the end of a neotraditionalist, liberationist, or liberal political discourse, since they would be built upon a different ground plan.

39. E. Wamba-dia-Wamba, "The State of All Rwandese: Political Prescriptions and Disasters," 9. Wamba's version of a palaver discourse constitutes an interesting answer to the issue of handling intracommunity pluralism. Other issues, such as that of managing inter-Mbongi matters, practically managing the state of the *gens de partout*, and institutions and rights involved, are hardly dealt with.

40. J. Ibrahim, report of the conference, "Democracy and Human Rights in Africa: The Internal and External Contexts," held in Harare, Zimbabwe, 11–14 May 1992, in *CODESRIA Bulletin* no. 4 (1992): 2–8.

41. P. Anyang' Nyong'o, "Democratization Processes in Africa," *Review of African Political Economy* 54 (1992): 98. See also A. Imam, "Democratization Process in Africa: Problems and Prospects," *Review of African Political Economics* 54 (1992): 102–105. Harry Goulbourne was more concrete on what participatory democracy could mean already in Anyang' Nyong'o, *Popular Struggles for Democracy in Africa* (1987): 26–47.

42. This is the direction in which political discourse around CODESRIA develops. The theoretical statements of several of the "new" leaders in Africa, such as Museweni (Uganda) and Afworki (Eritrea), seem not to follow new directions here. They are rather repeating discourses from the 1960s.

43. Wiredu, "Democracy and Consensus."

44. Ibid., 190.

45. Appiah, *In My Fathers House*, 174.

46. Appiah, *In My Fathers House*, 176. "They are . . . disabling labels; which is, in essence, my complaint against a racial methodology—The Africa of Crummell and Du Bois (from the New World) and of the *bolekaja* critics (from the Old); against Africa as a shared metaphysics—the Africa of Soyinka; against Africa as a fancied past of shared glories—the Africa of Diop and the "Egyptianists."

47. Quotes from Appiah, *In My Fathers House*, 175, 178.

48. Appiah, *In My Fathers House*, 179, 180.

49. M. Sithole, "Is Multi-Party Democracy Possible in Multi-Ethnic African States? The Case of Zimbabwe," in Himmelstrand et al., eds., *African Perspectives on Development. Controversies, Dilemmas & Openings* (London: James Curry, 1994), 162. Compare, for example, with K. A. Busia, *Africa in Search of Democracy* (London: Routledge, 1967), 106, and N. Azikiwe, "Tribalism: A Pragmatic Instrument for

National Unity," in *President Azikiwe: Selected Speeches 1960–1964* (Lagos: The Daily Times of Nigeria, 1964).

50. P. P. Ekeh, "The Public Realm & Public Finance: In Africa," in Himmelstrand et al., eds., *African Perspectives*, 234–248.

Bibliography

Ahuma, Atto. (1911) *The Gold Coast nation and national consciousness.* Liverpool: Marples. Reprinted: (1971). London: Frank Cass.

Ajayi, J.F.A. (1961). Nineteenth century origins of Nigerian nationalism. *Journal of the Historical Society of Nigeria, 2*(2), 196–210.

Ajisafe, A. K. (1924). *The laws and customs of the Yoruba people.* London: Routledge.

Ake, C. (1991). Rethinking African democracy. *Journal of Democracy, 2,* 32–44.

———. (1992). Devaluing democracy. *Journal of Democracy, 3*(3), 37–44.

———. (1993). The unique case of African democracy. *International Affairs, 69*(2), 239–244.

———. (1996). *Democracy and Development in Africa.* Washington, DC: The Brookings Institution.

Akpan, M. B. (1973). Liberia and the universal Negro improvement association: The background to the abortion of Garvey's scheme for African colonization. *Journal of African History, 14*(1), 105–127.

Amin, S. (1983). Is there a political economy of Islamic fundamentalism? *Journal of African Marxists, 3,* 6–29.

———. (1987). The State and the question of "Development." Preface in P. Anyang' Nyong'o, ed., *Popular Struggles for democracy in Africa.* London: ZED Press, 1–13.

———. (1989). *Eurocentrism.* New York: Monthly Review Press. Translation of *Eurocentrisme: critique d'une idéologie.* Paris: Anthropos, 1988.

———. (1989). La Question démocratique dans le tiers monde contemporain. *Afrique Développement. 14*(2), 5–25. Translated as The issue of democracy in the contemporary Third World in U. Himmelstrand et al. (1994), *African perspectives on development. Controversies, dilemma's and openings* (pp. 320–335). London: James Curry.

————. (1994). L'idéologie et la pensée sociale: l'intelligence et la crise du développement. *Africa Development, 19*(1), 1–16.

Anderson, B. (1983). *Imagined communities. Reflections on the origins of nationalism.* London: Verso.

Anyang' Nyong'o, P. (ed.). (1987). *Popular struggles for democracy in Africa.* London: ZED Press.

————. (1988). African intellectuals and the state. *CODESRIA Newsletter, 5*(3), 6.

————. (1992). Democratization processes in Africa. *Review of African Political Economy, 54,* 97–102.

Anyanwu, K. C. (1984). African political doctrine. In O.E.A. Ruch & K. C. Anyanwu, *African philosophy. An introduction to the main trends in contemporary Africa* (pp. 369–383). Rome: Catholic Book Agency.

Appadurai, A. (1990). Disjuncture and difference in the global cultural economy. *Theory, Culture & Society, 7,* 295–310.

Appiah, K. A. (1992). *In my father's house, Africa in the philosophy of culture.* New York: Methuen.

————. (1993). Europe upside down: Fallacies of the new Afrocentrism. *Sapina Newsletter, 5* (1).

Arato, A. (1990). Revolution, civil society and democracy. *Praxis International, 10* (1–2), 24–38.

Asante, S.K.B. (1977). The Politics of confrontation: The case of Kobina Sekyi and the colonial system in Ghana. *Universitas, 6*(2), 15–38.

Asante, M. K., & Asante, K. W. (1985). *African culture: The rhythms of unity.* Westport, CT: Greenwood Press.

Auroi, C. (ed.). (1992). *The role of the state in development processes.* London: Frank Cass.

Awolowo, O. (1947). *Path to Nigerian freedom.* London: Faber and Faber.

————. (1961). A critique of one-party systems. In *The Autobiography of Chief Obafemi Awolowo.* New York: Cambridge University Press. Partly reprinted in P. Sigmund (ed.) (1963), *The ideologies of developing nations* (pp. 223–228). New York: Praeger.

————. (1968). *The people's republic.* Ibadan: Oxford University Press.

Awoonor, K. (1990). *Ghana: a political history.* Accra: Sedco.

Ayandele, E. A. (1968). Introduction to the Second Edition. In Africanus B. Horton, (1970), *Letters on the political condition of the Gold Coast* London: Frank Cass & Co., 1970 (pp. 5–35).

————. (1970). *Holy Johnson. Pioneer of African nationalism, 1836–1917.* London: Frank Cass.

————. (1971). James Africanus Beale Horton, 1835–1883: Prophet of modernisation in West Africa. *African Historical Studies, 4*(3), pp. 691–707.

Ayittey, G.B.N. (1991). *Indigenous African institutions.* New York: Transnational Publishers.

————. (1992). *Africa betrayed.* New York: St. Martin's Press.

Azarya, V. (1988). Reordering state-society relations: Incorporation and disengagement. In D. Rothchild & N. Chazan (ed.), *The precarious balance: State and society in Africa* (pp. 3–25). Boulder, Co & London: Westview Press.

Azikiwe, N. (1961). Parliaments and parties. Speech delivered on March 10, 1952. In

Zik: A Selection of Speeches of Nnamdi Azikiwe. New York: Cambridge University Press. Partly reprinted in P. Sigmund (ed.). (1963), *The ideologies of developing nations* (pp. 212–215). New York: Praeger.

———. (1962). The future of Pan-Africanism. *Présence Africaine, 40*(12), 7–29.

———. (1964). Tribalism: A pragmatic instrument for national unity. In *President Azikiwe: Selected speeches 1940-1964.* Lagos: The Daily Times of Nigeria.

———. (1968). *Renascent Africa.* London: Frank Cass. (Reprint from 1937).

Baako, K. (1961). Nkrumaism—Its theory and practice. *The Party* (CPP Journal, Accra), 4–7. Reprinted in P. Sigmund (ed). (1963), *The ideologies of developing nations* (pp. 188–195). New York: Praeger.

———. (1970). Nkrumahism—African Socialism: Ghana's concept of socialism. In T. P. Omari (1970), *Kwame Nkrumah, the anatomy of an African dictatorship.* London: Hurst.

Babu, A. M. (1981). African socialism or socialist Africa? London: ZED Press.

———. (1982). Introduction. In Y. Tandon (ed.) (1982), *The debate. Debate on class, state & imperialism.* Dar es Salam: Tanzanian Publishing House.

Balibar, E. & Wallerstein, I. (eds.) (1991). *Race, nation, class: Ambiguous identities.* London: Verso.

Ball, T. (1989). Party. In T. Ball, J. Farr, & R. L. Hanson (eds.) (1989), *Political innovation and conceptual change* (pp. 155–176). Cambridge: Cambridge University Press.

Ball, T., Farr, J., & Hanson, R. L. (eds.). (1989). *Political innovation and conceptual change.* Cambridge: Cambridge University Press.

Barker, M. (1982). *The new racism.* London: Junction Books.

Bauman, Z. (1990). Modernity and ambivalence. In M. Featherstone (ed.) (1990), *Global Culture.* Special issue of *Theory, Culture & Society, 7*(2–3), 143–169.

Bayart, J-F. (1983). Les Sociétés Africaines Face à l'État. *Pouvoirs, 25,* 23–37.

———. (1983). La Revanche des Sociétés Africaines. *Politique Africaine, 11,* 95–122.

———. (1986). Civil society in Africa. In P. Chabal (ed.) (1986), *Political domination in Africa: Reflections on the limits of power* (pp. 109–125). London: Cambridge University Press.

———. (1986). Populist political action. Historical understanding and political analysis in Africa. In B. Jewsiewicki & D. Newbury, *African historiographies: What history for which Africa?* (pp. 261–268). Beverley Hills: Sage.

———. (1989). *L'état en Afrique: la politique du ventre.* Paris: Fayart.

———. (1991). La problématique de la démocratie en Afrique noire: La Baule, et puis après. *Politique Africain, 43* (October).

Bénot, Y. (1972). *Idéologies des Indépendences Africaines.* Paris: Maspero. (Reprinted from 1969)

Bernal, M. (1991). *Black Athena: The Afroasiatic roots of classical civilization.* London: Vintage Press. (Reprinted from 1987)

Bernstein, H., & Campbell, B. K. (eds.). (1985). *Contradictions of accumulation in Africa: Studies in economy and state.* Beverley Hills: Sage.

Beumers, E., & Koloss, H-J. (1992). *Kings of Africa.* Maastricht: Foundation Kings of Africa.

Bienen, H. (1977). State and revolution: The work of Amílcar Cabral. *The Journal of Modern African Studies, 15*(4), 555–568.

Biko, S. (1979). *I write what I like*. A selection of his writings edited by Aelred Stubbs, C.R. London: Heinemann. (Reprinted from 1978)

Binsbergen, W.M.J. (1996). Black Athena and Africa's contribution to global cultural history. *Quest: Philosophical Discussions, 9*(2), *10*(1), 101–137.

Binsbergen, W.M.J., Reyntjes, F., & Hesseling, G. (eds.). (1986). *State and local Communities in Africa*. Brussels: CEDAF.

Blyden, E. W. (1857). *A vindication of the Negro race: Being a brief examination of the arguments in favour of African inferiority*, with introduction by A. Crummell. Monrovia: n.p.

———. (1862). *Liberia's offering*. New York: n.p.

———. (1869). *Liberia past, present, future*. Washington, DC: n.p.

———. (1869). *The Negro in ancient history*. Washington, DC: n.p.

———. (1887). *Christianity, Islam and the Negro race*. London: W. B. Whittingham & Co. Reprinted: (1967) Edinburgh: Edinburgh University Press.

———. (1901). *The African society and Miss M. Kingsley*. London: n.p.

———. (1903). *Africa and the Africans, Proceedings on the occasion of a banquet*. London: n.p.

———. (1908). *African life and customs*. London: C. M. Phillips.

Boahen, A. A. (1987). *African perspectives on colonialism*. Baltimore and London: John Hopkins University Press.

Boele van Hensbroek, P. (1994). Cursing the nation-state. *Transition, 61,* 114–122.

———. (1997). On culturalism. In H. Kimmerle & F. M. Wimmer (eds.) (1997), *Philosophy and democracy in intercultural perspective* (pp. 85–93). Studies in Intercultural Philosophy: Vol. 3. Amsterdam: Rodopi.

Bratton, M. (1989). Beyond the state. Civil society and associational life in Africa. *World Politics. A Quarterly Journal of International Relations*, 407–414.

———. (1994). *Civil society and political transition in Africa*. Boston: Institute for Development Studies.

Buijtenhuijs, R. (1990). Democratization and participation in Africa south of the Sahara. In *Beyond adjustment: Subsaharan Africa*. The Hague: Ministry of Foreign Affairs.

Buijtenhuijs, R., & Thiriot, C. (1995). *Democratization in Sub-Saharan Africa 1992–1995. An overview of the literature*. Leiden: Africa Studies Centre.

Burke, F. G. (1964). Tanganyika: The search for Ujamaa. In W. H. Friedland & G. G. Rosberg (1964), *African socialism* (pp. 194–219). Stanford: Stanford University Press.

Busia, K. A. (1962). *The challenge of Africa*. New York: Praeger.

———. (1967). *Africa in search of democracy*. London: Routledge.

———. (1968). *The position of the chief in the political system of Ashanti*. London: Frank Cass. (Reprinted from 1951)

Bwalya, R.M.K. (1987). On Kaundaism. *Quest: Philosophical Discussions, 1*(1), 31–38.

Cabral, A. (1966). The weapon of theory. Presuppositions and objectives of national liberation in relation to social structure. Speech to the First Solidarity Conference of the Peoples of Africa, Asia, and Latin America (Havana, 3–12 January 1966). Reprinted in A. Cabral, *Unity and struggle* (pp. 119–137). London: Heinemann.

———. (1969). *Revolution in Guinea: An African peoples' struggle. Selected texts by Amilcar Cabral*. London: Stage 1.

————. (1970). National liberation and culture. Mondlane Memorial Lecture, Syracuse University. Reprinted in A. Cabral, *Unity and Struggle* (pp. 138–154). London: Heinemann.

————. (1980). *Unity and struggle: Speeches and writings.* London: Heinemann. The English text contains about two-thirds of the French volumes: (1975). *Unité et Lutte* (textes reunis par Mario de Andrade). Paris: Maspero.

Calderon, F. (1990). Renforcer la société pour consolider la démocratie. *Africa Development, 15*(3/4).

Campbell, H. (1987). *Rasta and resistance: From Marcus Garvey to Walter Rodney.* Trenton, N J: African World Press.

Carter, G. M., & O'Meara, P. (eds.). (1986). *African independence. The first twenty-five years.* Bloomington: Indiana University Press.

Chabal, P. (1983). *Amilcar Cabral: Revolutionary leadership and people's war.* London: Cambridge University Press.

————. (1992). *Power in Africa. An essay in political interpretation.* Basingstoke: Macmillan.

Chabal, P. (ed.). (1986). *Political domination in Africa: Reflections on the limits of power.* London: Cambridge University Press.

Chazan, N. (1982). The new politics of participation in tropical Africa. *Comparative Politics,* 169–189.

————. (1987). Patterns of state-society incorporation and disengagement in Africa. In D. Rothchild & N. Chazan (eds.) (1988), *The precarious balance: State & society in Africa* (pp. 121–148). Boulder, CO and London: Westview Press.

————. (1992). Strengthening civil society and the state. *World Policy Journal, 9*(2), 279–307.

Chilote, R. H. (1968). The political thought of Amilcar Cabral. *The Journal of Modern African Studies, 6*(3), 373–388.

Chisiza, D. K. (1961). *Africa—what lies ahead.* Indian Council for Africa (1–10). Reprinted in J. A. Langley (1979) *Ideologies of liberation in black Africa 1856–1970: Documents on modern African political thought from colonial times to the present* (pp. 573–580). London: Rex Collings.

————. (1961) *Realities of African Independence.* London: The African Publications Trust.

Clapham, Ch. (1970). The context of African political thought. *The Journal of Modern African Studies, 8*(1), 1–13.

Clarke, J. H. (1988). Pan-Africanism: A brief history of an idea in the African world. *Présence Africaine, 145*(1), 26–57.

Cohen, J. L. (1982). *Class and civil society: The limits of Marxian critical theory.* Amherst: University of Massachusetts Press.

Cohen, J. L., & Arato, A. (1989). Politics and the reconstruction of the concept of civil society. In A. Honneth 1989, *Zwischenbertachtungen im Prozess der Aufklärung.* Frankfurt am Mein: Suhrkamp.

————. (1990). The contemporary revival of civil society. Chapter 1 of Cohen, J. L. & Arato A., *Civil society and political theory.* Cambridge: MIT Press.

Cohen, R., & H. Goulbourne (eds.). (1991). *Democracy and socialism in Africa.* Boulder, CO: Westview Press.

Coleman, J. S. (1958). *Nigeria: Background to nationalism.* Berkeley: University of

California Press.

Condé, M. (1984). *Segu. Les murailles de terre*. Paris: Ed. R. Laffront.

Crummell, A. (1862). *The Future of Africa: Being addresses, sermons, etc., etc., delivered in the Republic of Liberia*. New York: Charles Scribner. Republished (n.d.), Scholarly Press.

———. (1891). *Africa and America: Addresses and discourses*, Springfield, MA: Republished: (1969), Negro University Press.

Curtin, P. D. (1960). "Scientific" racism and the British theory of empire. *Journal of the Historical Society of Nigeria, 2*(1), 40–51.

———. (1964). *The image of Africa: British ideas and action, 1790–1850*. Madison: University of Wisconsin Press.

Danquah, J. B. (1928). *Gold Coast: Akan laws and customs and the Akim Abuakwa constitution*. London: Routledge.

———. (1932). Introduction. In M. I. Sampson (1932), *Gold Coast men of affairs* (pp. 9–38). Reprinted: (1969). London: Dawson of Pall Mall.

Davidson, B. (1969). *The liberation of Guinea: Aspects of an African revolution*. Harmondsworth. Penguin.

———. (1987). Du Nationalisme Révolutionaire: L'héritage d'Amilcar Cabral. In *Pour Cabral*, International Symposium, Amilcar Cabral in Praia Cap-Vert (1983). Paris and Dakar: Presence Africaine.

———. (1987). *African nationalism and the problem of nation building*. Lagos: Nigerian Institute of International Affairs. (1989). *Black star. A view of the life and times of Kwame Nkrumah*. Boulder, CO: Westview Press. (Reprinted from 1974)

———. (1992). *The black man's burden: Africa and the curse of the Nation-State*, New York: Times Books.

Debray, R. (1974). *La Critique des Armes*. Paris: Ed. du Seuil.

Dewitte, Ph. (1985). *Les Mouvements Nègres en France 1919–1939*. Paris: L'Harmattan.

Dia, M. (1960). Independence and neocolonialism. In P. Sigmund (1963), *The Ideologies of developing nations* (pp. 232–238). New York: Praeger. A section of M. Dia (1960), *The African Nations and World Solidarity*. Translated by M. Cook. New York: Praeger.

Diagne, S. B. (1993). The Future of Tradition. In M. C. Diop (1993), *Senegal. Essays in Statecraft*. (pp. 269–290). Dakar: Codesia.

Diaw, A. (1993). Democracy of the literati. In M. C. Diop (1993), *Senegal. Essays in statecraft* (pp. 291–323). Dakar: Codersia.

Diemer, A. (1985). *Africa and the problem of its identity*. Frankfurt am Mein: Lang.

Diop, Ch. A. (1959). L'unité culturelle Africaine. *Présence Africaine, 24*(25), 60–65.

———. (1981). *Civilisation ou Barbarie*. Paris: Présence Africaine.

Diop, M. (1958). *Contribution à l'Étude des Problèmes Politiques en Afrique Noire*. Paris: Présence Africaine.

Diop, M. C. (1993). *Senegal. Essays in statecraft*. Dakar: Codersia.

Diouf, M. (1993). Beyond patronage and "technocracy." In M. P. Diop (1993), *Senegal. Essays in statecraft* (pp. 221–268). Dakar: Codersia.

———. (1994). L'Échec du Modèle Démocratique du Sénégal, 1981–1993. *Afrika Spectrum, 29*(1), 47–64.

Dixon-Fyle, M. (1989). The Saro in the political life of early Port Harcourt, 1913–49. *Journal of African History, 30,* 125–138.

Doornbos, M. (1990). The African state in academic debate: Retrospect and prospect. *Journal of Modern African Studies, 28*(2), 179–198.

———. (1991). Linking the future to the past: Ethnicity and pluralism. *Review of African Political Economy, 52,* 53–65.

———. (1994). State formation and collapse: Reflections on identity and power. In M. van Bakel, R. Hagestein, and P. van der Velde (1994), *Pivot politics: Changing cultural identities in early state formation processes.* Amsterdam: Het Spinhuis.

Eboh, M. P. (1993). Democracy with an African flair. *Quest: Philosophical Discussions, 7*(1), 92–99.

Echeruo, M.J.C. (1992). Edward W. Blyden, W.E.B. Du Bois, and the "color complex." *The Journal of Modern African Studies, 30*(4), 669–684.

Economic Commission for Africa (1990). The African charter for popular participation in development and transformation. Arusha: Economic Commission for Africa.

Edwards, P. N. (1996). *The closed world: Computers and the politics of discourse in cold war America.* Cambridge: MIT Press.

Ekeh, P. P. (1975). Colonialism and the two publics in Africa: A theoretical statement. *Contemporary Studies in Society and History, 17*(1), 91–112.

———. (1994). The public realm & public finance in Africa. In U. Himmelstrand et al. (eds.) (1994), *African perspectives on development. Controversies, dilemmas & openings* (pp. 234–248). London: James Curry.

Ellis, S. (ed.). (1996). *Africa now: People, politics & institutions.* London: James Curry.

Ergas, Z. (ed.). (1987). *The African state in transition.* London: MacMillan.

Esedebe, P. O. (1969, July). Edward Wilmot Blyden (1832–1912). As a Pan-African theorist. *Sierra Leone Studies, New series,* no. 25, 14–23.

Essien-Udom, E. U. (1962). *Black nationalism: The search for identity.* Chicago: University of Chicago Press.

Eze, E. (ed.). (1997). *Postcolonial African philosophy. A critical reader.* Cambridge: Blackwell Publishers.

Fage, J. D. (1995). *A History of Africa.* London: Routledge. (Reprinted from 1978)

Fanon, F. (1959). Fondement réciproque de la culture nationale et des luttes de libération. *Présence Africaine, 24*(25), 82–89.

———. (1967). *Black skin, white masks.* New York: Grove Press. English edition of *Peau Noire, Masques Blancs.* Paris: Ed. du Seuil. (Reprinted from 1952)

———. (1967). *The wretched of the earth.* Harmondsworth: Penguin. English edition of *Les damnés de la Terre.* Paris: Maspero. (Reprinted from 1961)

———. (1988). *Toward the African revolution. The revolutionary thought of Frantz Fanon.* New York: Grove Press. English edition of *Pour la Révolution Africaine.* Paris: Maspero. (reprinted from 1964)

———. (1989). *Studies in a dying colonialism.* London: Earthscan. English edition of *L'an cinq de la révolution algerienne.* Paris: Maspero. (Reprinted from 1959)

Featherstone, M. (ed.). (1990). *Global Culture.* Special issue of *Theory, Culture & Society, 7* (2–3).

Federici, S. (1994). Journey to the native land. Violence and the concept of the self in Fanon and Gandhi. *Quest: Philosophical Discussions, 7*(2), 47–70.

Fortes, M., & Dieterlen, G. (eds.). (1965). *African systems of thought*. London: Oxford University Press.

Fortes, M., & Evans-Pritchard, E. E. (1940). *African political systems*. Oxford: Oxford University Press.

Foucault, M. (1984). Nietzsche, Genealogy and History. Reprinted in P. Rabinov *The Foucault reader* (pp. 76–100). New York: Pantheon Book.

Friedland, W. H., & Rosberg, C. G. (1964). *African socialism*. Stanford: Stanford University Press.

Fyfe, C. (1962). *A history of Sierra Leone*. Oxford: Oxford University Press.

———. (1970/71). Contrasting themes in the writings of Africanus Horton, James Johnson and Edward Blyden. *Africana Research Bulletin, 1*(3), 3–18.

———. (1972). *Africanus Horton, 1835–1883, West African scientist and patriot*. New York: Oxford University Press.

———. (1988). Africanus Horton as a constitution-maker. *Journal of Commonwealth and Comparative Politics, 26* (2).

Garvey, A. J. (ed.). (1977). *Philosophy and opinions of Marcus Garvey, or Africa for the Africans*. London: Frank Cass. (Reprinted from 1923)

Geiss, I. (1968). *Panafrikanismus. Zur Geschichte der Dekolonisation*. Frankfurt am Mein: Europeische Verlagsanstalt.

Giddens, A. (1976). *New rules of sociological method*. London: Hutchinson.

Gitonga, A. K. (1987). The meaning and foundations of democracy. In W. O. Oyugi & A. Gitonga (1987), *Democratic theory and practice in Africa* (pp. 4–23). Nairobi: Heinemann.

Glaser, D. (1991). Discourses of democracy in the South African Left: A critical commentary. In R. Cohen & H. Goulbourne (eds.) (1991), *Democracy and socialism in Africa* (pp. 93–121). Boulder, CO: Westview Press.

Goody, J. (1977). *Domesticating the savage mind*. Cambridge: Cambridge University Press.

———. (1980). *Technology, tradition, and the state in Africa*. London: Hutchinson.

Goulbourne, H. (1986). The state, development and the need for participatory democracy in Africa. In P. Anyang' Nyong'o (ed.) (1987), *Popular struggles for democracy in Africa* (pp. 26–47). London: ZED Press.

Gouldner, A. W. (1980). *The two Marxisms: Contradictions and anomalies in the development of theory*. London: Macmillan.

Graft Johnson, J. W. de (1971). *Towards nationhood in West Africa*. London: Frank Cass. (Reprinted from 1928)

Grégoire, A.H.B. (1991). *La Littérature des Nègres, ou recherches sur leur facultés intellectuelles, leur qualités morales, et leur littérature*. Paris: Perrin. (Reprinted from 1808)

Gregor, A. J. (1967). African socialism, socialism, and fascism: An appraisal. *Review of Politics, 29*.

———. (1980). *Italian fascism and developmental dictatorship*. Princeton: Princeton University Press.

Grohs, G. (1967). *Stufen Afrikanischer Emancipation. Studie zur Selbstverständnis West Afrikanischer Eliten*. Stuttgart: Kohlhammer.

Grohs, G. (Hrsg.). (1971). *Theoretische Probleme des Sozialismus in Afrika: Negritude und Arusha Deklaration*. 2e Tagung der Vereinigung der Afrikanisten

Deutschlands, 1970. Hamburg: Bruske.

Gugler, J. (1994). How Ngugi wa Thiong'o shifted from a class analysis to a neo-colonialist perspective. *Journal of Modern African Studies, 32*(2), 329–339.

Gutting, G. (ed.). (1980). *Paradigms and revolutions.* Notre Dame: University of Notre Dame Press.

Gwam, L. C. (1964). The social and political ideas of Dr. James Africanus Beale Horton. *Ibadan, 19,* 10–18.

Gyekye, K. (1978). The Akan concept of a person. *The International Philosophical Quarterly, 18,* 277–287. Reprinted in R. A. Wright (1984), *African philosophy. An introduction* (pp. 199–212). New York, Lanham, and London: University Press of America.

———. (1987). *Essay on African philosophical thought: The Akan conceptual scheme.* Cambridge: Cambridge University Press.

———. (1988). The idea of democracy in the traditional setting and its relevance to political development in contemporary Africa. Paper presented at the First International Regional Conference in Philosophy (Mombasa, Kenya).

———. (1992). Traditional political ideas, their relevance to development in contemporary Africa. In K. Wiredu & K. A. Gyekye (1992), *Person and community. Ghanaian philosophical studies, I.* (pp. 241–255). Washington, DC: The Council for Research in Values and Philosophy.

Hacking, I. (ed.). (1981). *Scientific revolutions.* London: Oxford University Press.

Hadjor, K. B. (1988). *Nkrumah and Ghana: The dilemma of post-colonial power.* London: Keagan Paul International.

Hair, P.E.H. (1967). Africanism: The Freetown contribution. *Journal of Modern African Studies, 5*(4), 521–539.

Hallen, B. & Sodipo J. O. (1986). *Knowledge, belief & witchcraft: Analytic experiments in African philosophy.* London: Ethnographica.

Hallett, R. (1986). Theories of Race and Culture: 'The Negro's Place in Nature.' In *Cambridge History of Africa V, 1790–1870* (Chpt. 13). Cambridge: Cambridge University Press.

Hanson, E. (1977). *Frantz Fanon: Social and political thought.* Columbus: Ohio State University Press.

Hara, F. (1904) The Secret Doctrine of Racial Development. *The Theosophist,* July, 596–604; August, 660–669.

Harbeson, J. W., Rothchild, D., & Chazan, N. (eds.). (1994). *Civil society and the state in Africa.* Boulder, CO: Lynne Rienner.

Hargreaves, J. D. (1963). *Prelude to the partition of West Africa,* London: Macmillan.

———. (1969). Blyden of Liberia. *History Today, 19,* 568–578.

Hawthorn, G. (1993). Sub-Saharan Africa. In D. Held (ed.), *Prospects for democracy: North, south, east, west.* London: Polity Press.

Hayford, J. E. Casely (1969). *Ethiopia Unbound. Studies in race emancipation.* London: Frank Cass. (Reprinted from 1911)

———. (1970). *Gold Coast native institutions. With thoughts upon a healthy imperial policy for the Gold Coast and Ashanti.* London: Frank Cass. (Reprinted from 1903)

———. (1971). *The Truth about the West African land question.* London: Frank Cass. (Reprinted from 1913)

Hill, R. (ed.). (1987). *Marcus Garvey: Life and lessons, a centennial companion to the Marcus Garvey and UNIA papers*. Berkeley: University of California Press.

Himmelstrand, U., Kinyanjui, K., & Mburugu, E. (eds.). (1994). *African perspectives on development. Controversies, dilemmas & openings*. London: James Curry.

Hobsbawm, E., & Ranger, T. (1983). *The invention of tradition*. Cambridge: Cambridge University Press.

Hodgkin, T. (1961). A note on the language of African nationalism. *African Affairs*, 22–40.

Hoebel, E. A. (1972). *Anthropology*. New York: McGraw-Hill. (Reprinted from 1949)

Hoffmann, G. R. (1988). Materialistisches Credo und Revolutionaire Utopie: zu Kwame Nkrumah and Philosoph. *Zeitschrift für Afrika Studien, 3*, 25–45.

Holden, E. (1966). *Blyden of Liberia: An account of the life and labours of Edward Wilmot Blyden, LL.D., as recorded in letters and in print*. New York: Vantage Press.

Hollis, M., & Lukes, S. (eds.). (1982). *Rationality and relativism*. Oxford: Basil Blackwell.

Honneth, A. (1989). *Zwischenbetrachtungen im Prozess der Aufklärung*. Frankfurt am Mein: Suhrkamp.

Horton, J.A.B. (1868). *West African countries and peoples, British, and native. With the requirements necessary for establishing that self-government recommended by the Committee of the House of Commons, 1865; and a vindication of the Negro race*. London: W. J. Johnson. Reprinted: 1970. Nendeln, Lichtenstein: Kraus Reprint.

———. (1970). *Letters on the political condition of the Gold Coast: since the exchange of territory between the English and Dutch governments, on January 1, 1868; together with a short account of the Ashanti War, 1862–4, and the Awoonah War, 1866*. Africana Modern Library. London: Frank Cass. (Reprinted from 1870)

Horton, R. (1967). African traditional thought and Western science. *Africa, 34*, 50–71, 155–187.

———. (1982). Tradition and modernity revisited. In M. Hollis & S. Lukes (eds.) (1982), *Rationality and relativism* (pp. 201–260). Oxford: Basil Blackwell.

Hountondji, P. J. (1982). Occidentalisme, élitisme: Réponse à deux critiques. *Recherche, Pédagogie et Culture, 57*, 58–67. Translated in (1990): Occidentalism, elitism: Answer to two critiques. *Quest: Philosophical Discussions, 3*(2), 3-29.

———. (1983). *African philosophy. Myth and reality*. Bloomington: Indiana University Press. (Reprinted from 1976)

———. (1986). The master's voice—remarks on the problem of human rights in Africa. In A. Diemer (1986), *Africa and the problem of its identity* (pp. 319–332). Frankfurt am Mein: Lang.

———. (1987) What Philosophy can do. *Quest: Philosophical Discussions, 1*(2), 3–30

———. (1992). The crisis of the African state. In C. Auroi (ed.) (1992), *The role of the state in the development process* (pp. 239–246). London: Frank Cass.

Howe, R. W. (1967). Did Nkrumah favour Pan-Africanism? *Transition 27*, 13–15.

Hunt, G. (1986). Gramsci, civil society and bureaucracy. *Praxis International, 6*(2), 206–219.

Hyden, G. (1983). *No shortcuts to progress: African development management in perspective*. London: Heinemann.

————. (1988). *State and nation under stress*. Oslo: Forum for utviklingsstudier.

Ibrahim, J. (1992). Report of the conference, "Democracy and Human Rights in Africa: The Internal and External Contexts," Harare, Zimbabwe, 11–14 May 1992. In *CODESRIA Bulletin*, 4, 2–8.

Ikoku, S. G. (Julius Sago). (1971). *Le Ghana de Nkrumah: autopsie de la 1re Republique (1957–1966)*. Trad. Y. Bénot. Paris: Maspero. (Originally published as *Mission to Ghana*. Benin City: Ethiope Ed.)

Imam, A. (1992). Democratization process in Africa: Problems and prospects. *Review of African Political Economics*, 54, 102–105.

James, C.L.R. (1982). *Nkrumah and the Ghana revolution*. London: Allison & Busy.

James-Quartey, K.A.B. (1965). *A Life of Azikiwe*. Harmondsworth: Penguin.

Janssen, P. L. (1985). Political thought as traditionary action: Critical responses to Skinner and Pocock. *History and Theory*, 24, 115–146.

Jewsiewicki, B., & Newbury, D. (1986). *African historiographies: What history for which Africa?* Beverley Hills: Sage.

Johnson, G. W. (1966). The ascendency of Blaise Diagne and the beginning of African Politics in Senegal. *Africa*, 36(3), 235–253.

July, Robert W. (1964). Nineteenth century Negritude: Edward Wilmot Blyden. in *Journal of African History*, 1, 73–86.

————. (1966, January). Africanus Horton and the idea of independence in West Africa. *Sierra Leone Studies*, new series no. 18, 2–17.

————. (1968). *The origins of modern African thought: Its development in West Africa during the nineteenth and twentieth centuries*. London: Faber & Faber.

————. (1968). Review of H. R. Lynch (1967). *Edward Wilmot Blyden: Pan-Negro patriot 1832–1912*. London: Oxford University Press. *Journal of African History*, 9, 486–487.

————. (1980). *A history of the African People*. New York: Faber & Faber.

————. (1981). The artist's credo: The political philosophy of Whole Soyinka. *Journal of Modern African Studies*, 19(3), 477–498.

Kalb, M. G. (1982). *The Congo cables: The cold war in Africa, from Eisenhower to Kennedy*. New York: MacMillan.

Kandeke, T. K. (1977). *Fundamentals of Zambian humanism*. Lusaka: Neczam.

Karp, I., & Bird, Ch. S. (eds.). (1980). *Explorations in African systems of thought*. Bloomington: Indiana University Press.

Keane, J. (1987). *Socialism and civil society*. London and New York: Verso.

————. (1988). *Democracy and civil society*. London and New York: Verso.

————. (1988). Remembering the dead: Civil society and the state from Hobbes to Marx and beyond. In I. Keane (ed.) (1988), *Civil society and the state* (pp. 31–69). London and New York: Verso.

Keane, J. (ed.). (1988). *Civil society and the state*. London and New York: Verso.

Keita, L. (1984). The African philosophical tradition. In R. A. Wright (1984), *African philosophy: An introduction* (pp. 57–76). Lanham, New York, and London: University Press of America.

————. (1987). Africa's triple heritage: Unique or universal? *Présence Africaine*, 143, 91–100.

Keita, M. (1960). Le Parti Unique en Afrique. *Présence Africaine*, 30. Partly reproduced and translated as The Single Party in Africa. In P. Sigmund (ed.) (1963), The ideologies of developing nations (pp. 170–182). New York: Praeger.

Kenyatta, J. (1979). *Facing Mount Kenya. The traditional life of the Gikuyu*. London, and Nairobi, Ibadan: Heinemann. (Reprinted from 1938)

Kimble, D. (1963). *A political history of Ghana: The rise of Gold Coast nationalism, 1850–1928*. Oxford: Clarendon Press.

Kimmerle, H. H. (1990). *Philosophie in Afrika und Afrikanische Philosophie heute*. Frankfurt am Mein: Kautis Verlag.

Kimmerle, H. H. & F. M. Wimmer (eds.). (1997). *Philosophy and democracy in intercultural perspective*. Studies in Intercultural Philosophy: Vol. 3. Amsterdam: Rodopi.

King, J. K. (1969). Africa and the southern states of the USA: notes on J. H. Oldham and American Negro education for Africans. *Journal of African History, 10* (4), 659–677.

Kitching, G. (1982). *Development and underdevelopment in historical perspective: Populism, nationalism and industrialization*. London: Oxford University Press.

———. (1985). Politics, method, and evidence in the "Kenya Debate." In H. Berstein, & B. K. Campbell (eds.) (1985). *Contradictions of Accumulation in Africa: Studies in economy and state*. Beverley Hills: Sage.

Koenis, S., & Boele van Hensbroek, P. (1994). Het Westen bestaat niet. Over de implicaties van culturalism. In D. Pels & G. de Vries (eds.) *Burgers en Vreemdelingen*. (pp. 51–62). Amsterdam: van Gennep.

Kolakowski, L. (1981). *Main currents of Marxism*: Vol. 2. *The Golden Age*. Oxford: Oxford University Press.

Kuhn, T. S. (1969). *The structure of scientific revolutions (2nd ed.)*. Chicago: University of Chicago Press.

———. (1970). Reflections on my Critics. In I. Lakatos & A. Musgrave, *Criticism and the growth of knowledge*. Cambridge: Cambridge University Press.

———. (1977). *The essential tension—selected studies in scientific tradition and change*. Chicago: University of Chicago Press.

Laett, J., Kneifel, T., & Nürberger, K. (eds.). (1986). *Contending ideologies in South Africa*. Report to the South African Council of Churches. Cape Town: Philip.

Langley, J. Ayo (1969). Garveyism and African Nationalism. *Race, 11*(2), 157–172.

———. (1969). Pan-Africanism and nationalism in West Africa 1923–1936. *Journal of Modern African Studies, 7*(1).

———. (1970). Modernisation and its malcontents: Kobina Sekye 1892–1956 and the restatement of African political thought. *Research Review*, 6 (University of Ghana), 1–61.

———. (1973). *Pan-Africanism and nationalism in West Africa: A case study in ideology and social classes*. Oxford: Clarendon Press.

———. (1979). *Ideologies of liberation in black Africa 1856–1970: Documents on modern African political thought from colonial times to the present*. London: Rex Collings.

Legum, C. (1962). *Pan-Africanism. A short political guide*. London: Pall Mall Press.

———. (1964). Socialism in Ghana. A political interpretation. In W. H. Friedland & C. G. Rosberg, *Africa socialism* (pp. 131–159). Stanford: Stanford University Press.

————. (1986). Democracy in Africa: Hope and trends. In D. Ronen *Democracy and pluralism in Africa* (pp. 175–187). Boulder, CO: Lynne Rienner.

Lemarchand, R. (1988). The changing structure of patronage systems. In D. Rothchild & N. Chazan (eds.), *The precarious balance: State and society in Africa* (pp. 1988), 149–170. Boulder, CO and London: Westview Press.

————. (1992). Uncivilized states and civil societies: How illusion became reality. *Africana, 30*(2), 177–191.

Leys, C. (1975). *Underdevelopment in Kenya: The political economics of neo-colonialism.* London: Heinemann.

Lonsdale, J. (1988). Political accountability in African history. In P. Chabal, *Political domination in Africa: Reflections in the limits if power* (pp. 126–157). London: Cambridge University Press.

Ly, A. (1956). *Les Masses Africaines et l'actuelle condition humaine.* Paris: Présence Africaine.

Lynch, H. R. (1963). E. W. Blyden: Pioneer West African nationalist. *Journal of African History, 4*(3), 373–388.

————. (1964). The Native Pastorate controversy and cultural ethno-centrism in Sierra Leone, 1871–1874. *Journal of African History, 5*(3) 395–413.

————. (1967). *Edward Wilmot Blyden: Pan-Negro Patriot 1832–1912.* London: Oxford University Press.

Lynch, H. R. (ed.). (1971). *Black spokesman. Selected published writings of Edward Wilmot Blyden.* London: Frank Cass.

————. (1978). *Selected letters of Edward Wilmot Blyden.* New York: Kto Press.

Mair, L. (1971). New elites in East and West Africa. In V. Turner (ed.), *Colonialism in Africa, 1870–1960* (pp. 167–193). Cambridge: Cambridge University Press.

Mamdani, M. (1986). The agrarian question and the democratization struggle. *Bulletin of the Third World Forum, 6.*

————. (1987). Contradictory class perspectives on the question of democracy: The case of Uganda. In P. Anyang' Nyong'o (ed.), *Popular struggles for democracy in Africa* (pp. 78–95). London: ZED Press.

————. (1990). The social basis of constitutionalism in Africa. *Journal of Modern African Studies, 28*(3), 359–374.

————. (1990). A glimpse at African studies: Made in the USA. *CODESRIA Bulletin,* 2.

————. (1990). State and civil society in contemporary Africa: Reconceptualizing the birth of state nationalism and the defeat of popular movements. *Africa Development, 15* (3/4), 47–69.

————. (1992). Conceptualizing state and civil society relations: Towards a methodological critique of contemporary Africanism. In C. Auroi (ed.), *The role of the state in development processes* (pp. 7–24). London: Frank Cass.

————. (1994). *Academic freedom in Africa.* Dakar: CODESRIA.

————. (1994). Comments on "ideology and social thought." *CODESRIA Bulletin, 3,* 23.

————. (1995). Introduction. In M. Mamdani & E. Wamba-dia-Wamba (eds.) *African studies in social movements and democracy* (pp. 1–34). Dakar: CODESRIA.

————. (1995). A critique of the state and civil society paradigm in Africanist studies. In M. Mamdani & E. Wamba-dia-Wamba (eds.) *African studies in social movements and democracy* (pp. 602–616). Dakar: CODESRIA.

———. (1996). *Citizen and subject. Contemporary Africa and the legacy of late colonialism.* Princeton: Princeton University Press.

Mamdani, M., & Wamba-dia-Wamba, E. (eds.). (1995). *African studies in social movements and democracy.* Dakar: CODESRIA.

Mamdani, M., Wamba-dia-Wamba, E., & Mkwandawire, T. (1988). *Social movements, social transformation and the struggle for democracy in Africa.* CODESRIA working paper, no. 1/88. Dakar: CODESRIA.

Mandaza, I. (1994). The state and democracy in southern Africa: Towards a conceptual framework. In E. E. Osaghae, *Between state and civil society* (pp. 249–270). Dakar: CODESRIA.

Mandela, N. R. (1994). *Long walk to freedom. The autobiography of Nelson Mandela.* London: Little Brown and Co.

Mangani, N. C. (1973). *Being-black-in-the-world.* SPRO-CAS/Ravan.

Marshall, T. H. (1965). *Class, citizenship and social development.* London: Anchor Books.

Mazrui, A. A. (1963). On the concept "We are all Africans." *American Political Science Review, 57,* 88–97.

———. (1964). Pluralism and national integration. In L. Kuper & M. G. Smith (1963), *Pluralism in Africa.* (pp. 333–350). Berkeley: University of California Press.

———. (1966). Nkrumah: The Leninist czar. *Transition, 26*(3), 9–17.

———. (1967). *Towards a Pax-Africana: A study of ideology and ambition.* London: Weidenfeld & Nicleson.

———. (1969). Borrowed theory and original political practice in African politics. In H. J. Spiro, *Patterns of African development: Five comparisons.* Englewood Cliffs: Prentice Hall.

———. (1984). *Nationalism and the new states in Africa.* London: Heinemann.

———. (1986). Africa between ideology and technology: Two frustrated forces of change. In G. M. Carter & P. O'Meara (eds.) *African independence. The first twenty-five years* (pp. 275–300). Bloomington: Indiana University Press.

Mbembe, A. (1988). Etat, Violence et Accumulation. *Foi et Développement, 164/165,* 1–8. Paris: Centre Lebret.

———. (1990). Provisional notes on the postcolony. *Africa, 62*(1), 3–37.

Mbinimpa, M. (1989). *Idéologies de l'independence Africain.* Paris: L'Harmattan.

Mbiti, J. S. (1969). *African religions & philosophy.* London: Heinemann.

Mboya, T. J. (1963). *Freedom and after.* London: Deutsch.

———. (1970). *The challenge of nationhood: a collection of speeches and writings.* London: Heinemann.

McCaskie, T. C. (1990). Inventing Asante. In P. F. De Moraes Farias & K. Barber, *Self-assertion and brokerage: Early cultural nationalism in west Africa* (pp. 55–67). Birmingham: University of Birmingham Centre for West African Studies.

Meebelo, H. (1987). *Zambian humanism and scientific socialism. A comparative study.* Lusaka: n.p.

Menkiti, I. A. (1984). Person and community in African traditional thought. In R. A. Wright, *African philosophy. An introduction* (pp. 171–181). Lanham, New York and London: University Press of America.

Meyns, P., & Nabudere, D. W. (eds.). (1988). *Democracy and the one-party-state in*

Africa. Hamburg: Institut für Afrika-Kunde.

Milne, J. (1990). *Kwame Nkrumah: The Conakry years: His life and letters.* London: Panaf.

Molteno, R. (1977). Zambian Humanism: The way ahead. In T. K. Kandeke *Fundamentals of Zambian humanism* (pp. 212–239). Lusaka: Neczam.

Moore, D. C. (1994). Routes. *Transition, 64,* 4–21.

Moraes Farias P. F. de, & Barber, K. (eds.). (1990). *Self-assertion and brokerage: Early cultural nationalism in West Africa.* Birmingham: University of Birmingham Centre for West African Studies.

Mosley, A. G. (ed.). (1995). *African philosophy: Selected readings.* Englewood Cliffs: Prentice Hall.

Mudimbe, V. Y. (1988). *The invention of Africa.* Bloomington: Indiana University Press.

———. (1991). *Parables & fables: Exegesis, textuality and politics in Central Africa.* Madison: University of Wisconsin Press.

Mudimbe, V. Y. (ed.). (1992). *The surreptitious speech. Présence Africaine and the Politics of Otherness (1947–1987).* Chicago: University of Chicago Press.

Mutiso, G. C., & Rohio, S. W. (1975). *Readings in African political thought.* London: Heinemann.

Mwakayembe, H. G. (1990, November 26–28). Democracy or simple multi-partyism? A contribution to the debate on political pluralism in Africa. Paper presented at the conference, A Generation After: Law and Development in East Africa, Institute of Social Studies, The Hague.

Nabudere, D. W. (1989). The one-party state in Africa and its assumed philosophical roots. In P. Meyns & D. W. Nabudere (eds.), *Democracy and the one-party state in Africa* (pp. 1–24). Hamburg: Institute für Afrika-Kunde.

Nauta, L. W. (1985). Historical roots of the concept of autonomy in Western philosophy. *Praxis International, 4*(4), 263–279.

———. (1986). Heuristischer Wert und Unwert der Dialektik. In A. Honneth & A. Wellmer (Hrsg.), *Die Frankfurter Schule und die Folgen* (pp. 299–312). Berlin and New York: de Gruyter.

———. (1987). Marx in Afrika. In L. W. Nauta, *De factor van de kleine c. Essays over culturele armoede en politieke cultuur* (pp. 133–158). Amsterdam: Van Gennep.

Nederveen Pieterse, J. (1990). *Empire and emancipation: Power and liberation on a world scale.* London: Plato Press.

Neuberger, B. (1977). State and nation in African political thought. *Journal of African Studies, 4* (no. 2, Summer), 198–205.

Neugebauer. Chr. (1989). *Einführung in die afrikanische Philosophie.* München: Afrikanische Hochschulschriften.

———. (1997). Against culture and the aliens of modernization: The case of Africa. In H. Kimmerle & F. M. Wimmer (eds.), *Philosophy and democracy in intercultural perspective* (pp. 95–113). Studies in Intercultural Philosophy: Vol. 3. Amsterdam: Rodopi.

Ngugi wa Thiong'o (1981). *Writers in politics.* London: Heinemann.

———. (1993). *Moving the centre: The struggle for cultural freedoms.* London: Curry; Nairobi: East African Educational Publishers.

Nicol, D. (1969). *Africanus Horton. The dawn of nationalism in modern Africa.* London: Longman.

Ninsin, K. A. (1985). The Nkrumah government and the opposition on the nation state: Unity versus fragmentation. Contribution to a symposium on the life and work of Kwame Nkrumah. Legon: Institute of African Studies.

Nkrumah, K. (1961). *I speak of freedom. A statement of African ideology.* London: Mercury Books.

———. (1962). *Towards colonial freedom.* London: Heinemann. (Reprinted from 1945)

———. (1965). *Neo-colonialism: The last stage of imperialism.* London: Nelson.

———. (1967). Reply to Nkrumah: The Leninist czar. *Transition, 26*(3). *Transition 27,* 5.

———. (1969). *Handbook of revolutionary warfare.* London: Panaf.

———. (1970). *Class Struggle in Africa.* London: Panaf.

———. (1970). *Africa must unite.* New York: International Publishers. (Reprinted from 1963)

———. (1970). *Consciencism. Philosophy and ideology for decolonization.* New York: Monthly Review Press. (Reprinted from 1964)

———. (1971). *Ghana: The autobiography of Kwame Nkrumah.* London: Nelson; New York: International Publishers. (Reprinted from 1957)

Ntumba, T. (1988). Afrikanische Weisheit. Das dialectische Primat des *Wir* vor dem *Ich-Du.* In W. Oelmüller, *Philosophie und Weisheit.* Baderhorn: F. Schöningh.

Nyerere, J. (1961, November). One-party Rule. In *Spearhead.* Reprinted in P. Sigmund (ed.) (1963), *The ideologies of developing nations* (pp. 197–211). New York: Praeger.

———. (1968). *Freedom and unity: A selection from writings and speeches, 1952–1965.* Dar es Salam: Oxford University Press.

———. (1968). *Freedom and socialism: A selection from writings and speeches, 1965–1967.* Dar es Salam: Oxford University Press.

———. (1969). *Arusha Declaration.* Dar es Salam: The Government Printer.

———. (1973). *Freedom and development: A selection from writings and speeches, 1968–1973.* Dar es Salam: Oxford University Press.

Nyongoro, J. E., & Shaw, T. M. (1989). *The state and capitalist development in Africa.* New York: Praeger.

Okadigbo, Ch. (1985). *Consciencism in African Political Philosophy.* Enugu: Fourth Dimension Publishers.

Okolo, Ch. B. (1993). *African social & political philosophy: Selected essays.* Nsukka: Fulladu Publishing Company.

Okonkwo, R. L. (1980). The Garvey movement in British West Africa. *Journal of African History, 21,* 105–117.

Okoth, A. (1979). *A History of Africa: 1855–1914.* Nairobi: Heinemann.

Oladipo, O. (1996). *African philosophy and the African experience. The contributions of Kwasi Wiredu.* Ibadan: Hope Publications.

Oliver, R., & Atmore, A. (1994). *Africa since 1800.* Cambridge: Cambridge University Press. (Reprinted from 1967)

Omari, T. P. (1970). *Kwame Nkrumah, the anatomy of an African dictatorship.* London: Hurst.

Omoniyi, B. (1908). *In defence of the Ethiopian movement*. Edinburgh. Fragments reprinted in J. Ayo Langley (1979), *Ideologies of liberation in black Africa 1856–1970. Documents in modern political thought from colonial times to the present* (pp. 173–187). London: Rex Collings.

Omwony-Ojwok (1982). Review of the debate on imperialism, state, class and the national question. In Y. Tandon (ed.), *The debate. Debate on class, state of imperialism* (pp. 283–299). Dar es Salam: Tanzanian Publishing House.

Orizu, A.A.N. (1944). *Without bitterness. Western nations in post-war Africa*. New York: Creative Age Press.

Oruka, H. O. (1976). *Punishment and terrorism in Africa*. Nairobi: East African Literature Bureau.

———. (1990). *Sage philosophy*. Leiden: Brill.

Oruka, H. O., & Masolo, D. A. (eds.). (1983). *Philosophy and cultures*. Nairobi: Bookwise.

Osaghae, E. E. (ed.). (1994). *Between state and civil society*. Dakar: CODESRIA.

Ottaway, D., & Ottaway, M. (1981). *Afrocommunism*. New York and London: Africana Publishing.

———. (1987). The crisis of the socialist state in Africa. In Z. Ergas (ed.), *The African state in transition* (pp. 169–190). London: MacMillan.

Oyugi, W. O., & Gitonga, A. (eds.). (1987). *Democratic theory and practice in Africa*. Nairobi: Heinemann.

Padmore, G. (1953). *The Gold Coast revolution: The struggle of an African people from slavery to freedom*. London: Dobson.

———. (1956). *Pan-Africanism or communism? The coming struggle for Africa*. London: Dobson.

———. (1959). *A guide to Pan-African socialism*. In W. H. Friedland & C. G. Rosberg, *African socialism* (pp. 223–237). Stanford: Stanford University Press.

———. (1972). *Africa and world peace*. London: Frank Cass. (Reprinted from 1937)

Pels, D. (1998). *Property and power in social theory: A study in intellectual rivalry*. London: Routledge.

Pelszynski, Z. A. (1988). Solidarity and the 'rebirth of civil society' in Poland, 1976–81. In J. Keane (1988), *Civil society and the state* (pp. 361–380). London and New York: Verso.

Plaatje, S. T. (1916). *Native life in South Africa*. London: P. S. King. Reprinted by Longman in 1987.

Pour Cabral. (1987). International Symposium, Amilcar Cabral in Praia Cap-Vert, 1983. Paris and Dakar: Presence Africaine.

Prah, K. K. (1989). The rise and fall of CCP populism in Ghana 1947–1966: A critique of populist nationalism. In P. Meyns & D. W. Nabudere (eds.), *Democracy and the one-party state in Africa* (pp. 43–56). Hamburg: Institut für Afrika-Kunde.

Ramose, M. (1992). African democratic tradition: Oneness, consensus and openness: A reply to Wamba-dia-Wamba. *Quest: Philosophical Discussions, 6*(2), 62–83.

Rigsby, G. N. (1987). *Alexander Crummell: Pioneer in nineteenth-century Pan-Africanist thought*. Westport, CT: Greenwood.

Riseeuw, C. (1998). Thinking culture through counter-culture: The case of the Theosophists in India and Ceylon and their ideas on race and hierarchy (1875–1947). In A. Copley, & H. Rustau (eds.), *New religious movements*.

London: Oxford University Press.

Rodney, W. (1982). *How Europe underdeveloped Africa*. Washington, DC: Howard University Press. (Reprinted from 1972)

Ronen, D. (ed.). (1986). *Democracy and pluralism in Africa*. Boulder, CO: Lynne Rienner.

Rooney, D. (1988). *Kwame Nkrumah: The political kingdom in the Third World*. London: Tauris.

Rothchild, D., & Chazan, N. (eds.). (1988). *The precarious balance: State & society in Africa*. Boulder, CO and London: Westview Press.

Rotberg, R. I. (1970). *Strike a blow and die*. London: Heinemann. (Reprinted from 1967)

Rouveroy van Nieuwaal, E.A.B. & Ray D. I. (1996). *The new relevance of traditional authorities to Africa's future*. Special Issue of *Journal of Legal Pluralism, 37*(38).

Ruch, O.E.A., & Anyanwu, K. C. (1984). *African philosophy. An introduction to the main trends in contemporary Africa*. Rome: Catholic Book Agency.

Sampson, M. J. (1932). *Gold Coast men of affairs*. London: n.p. Reprinted: (1969). London: Dawsons of Pall Mall.

———. (1951). *West African leadership*. Ilfracombe: n.p. Reprinted (1971). London: Frank Cass.

———. (1969). *Makers of Modern Ghana*. Accra: n.p.

Sandbrook, R., & Barker, J. (1985). *The politics of Africa's economic stagnation*. Cambridge: Cambridge University Press.

Sarbah, J. Mensah (1968). *Fanti customary law*. London: Frank Cass. (Reprinted from 1897)

———. (1968). *Fanti national institutions*. London: Frank Cass. (Reprinted from 1906)

Saul, J. S. (1986). Ideology in Africa: Decomposition and recomposition. In G. M. Carter & P. O'Meara (eds.), *Africa independence. The first twenty-five years* (pp. 301–329). Bloomington: Indiana University Press.

Sekyi, K. (1925). *The parting of the ways*. Cape Coast: n.p. A fragment reprinted in J. Ayo Langley, *Ideologies of liberation in black Africa 1856–1970: Documents on modern African political thought from colonial times to the present* (pp. 251–254). London: Rex Collings.

Senghor, L. S. (1964). *On African socialism*. New York: Praeger. (Reprinted from 1961)

———. (1978). Foreword. In H. R. Lynch (ed.) *Selected letters of Edward Wilmot Blyden*. New York: Kto Press.

Shepperson, G. (1960). Notes on American Negro influences on the emergence of African nationalism. *Journal of African History, 1*(2), 299–312.

———. (1961). External factors in the development of African nationalism, with particular reference to British Central Africa. *Phylon, 22*(3).

———. (1964). Abolitionism and African Political Thought. *Transition, 3*(2), 22–26.

Shivji, I. G. (1991). The democracy debate in Africa: Tanzania. *Review of African Political Economy, 50*, 79–91.

Sigmund, P. (ed.). (1963). *The ideologies of developing nations*. New York: Praeger.

Simone, A. M., & Pieterse, E. (1993). Civil societies in an internationalized Africa. *Social Dynamics, 19*(2), 41–69.

Sithole, M. (1984). Class and factionalism in the Zimbabwean Nationalist movement.

African Studies Review, 27(1), 117–125.

———. (1994). Is multi-party democracy possible in multi-ethnic African states? The case of Zimbabwe. In U. Himmelstrand et al. (eds.), *African perspectives on development. Controversies, dilemmas & openings* (pp. 152–165). London: James Curry.

Sithole, N. (1959). *African nationalism*. Cape Town and New York: Oxford University Press.

Skinner, Q. (1969). Meaning and understanding in the history of ideas. *History and Theory, 8*, 3–53. Reprinted in J. Tully (ed.) *Meaning & context. Quentin Skinner and his critics* (pp. 27–67). Cambridge: Polity Press.

———. (1974). Some problems in the analysis of political thought and action. *Political Theory, 23*, 277–303. Reprinted in J. Tully (ed.) (1988), *Meaning & context. Quentin Skinner and his critics* (pp. 97–118). Cambridge: Polity Press.

———. (1988). Reply to my Critics. In J. Tully (ed.) (1988), *Meaning & context. Quentin Skinner and his critics* (pp. 231–288). Cambridge: Polity Press.

Sklar, R. (1983). Democracy in Africa. *African Studies Review, 26*(3–4), 11–24.

———. (1986). Reds and rights: Zimbabwe's experiment. In D. Ronen (ed.) *Democracy and pluralism in Africa* (pp. 135–144). Boulder, CO: Lynne Rienner.

———. (1986). The colonial imprint on African political thought. In G. M. Carter & P. O'Meara (eds.), *African independence. The first twenty-five years* (pp. 135–144). Bloomington: Indiana University Press.

———. (1987). Developmental democracy. *Comparative Studies in Society and History, 29*(4).

Soyinka, W. (1985). The African world and the ethnocultural debate. In M. K. Asante & K. W. Asante, *African culture: The rhythms of unity* (pp. 13–38). Westport, CT: Greenwood Press.

———. (1994). Democracy and the cultural apologia. *Afrika Spectrum, 29*(1), 5–13.

Staniland, M. (1986). Democracy and ethnocentrism. In P. Chabal (ed.), *Political domination in Africa: Reflections on the limitations of power* (pp. 52–80). London: Cambridge University Press.

Tandon, Y. (ed.). (1993). *In defense of democracy*. (Reprinted from 1979)

———. (1982). *The debate. Debate on class, state & imperialism*. Dar es Salam: Tanzanian Publishing House.

Tempels, P. (1959). *Bantou Philosophy*. Paris: Présence Africaine. (Reprinted from 1947)

Thuku, H. (1970). *Harry Thuku. An Autobiography*. With assistance from Kenneth King. Nairobi: n.p.

Todorov, T. (1982). *La conquête de l'Amérique: La question de l'autre*. Paris: Ed. du Seuil.

Tomlinson, J. (1991). *Cultural imperialism. A critical introduction*. London: Pinter.

Towa, M. (1973). Consciencism. *Présence Africaine, 85*, 148–177.

Tully, J. (ed.). (1988). *Meaning & context. Quentin Skinner and his Critics*. Cambridge: Polity Press.

Turner, V. (ed.). (1971). *Colonialism in Africa, 1870–1960*. Cambridge: Cambridge University Press.

Turok, B. (1990). No democracy, no development? *Coalition for Change*, 101–112. London: IFAA.

Ugonna, F. N. (1966). Introduction to the second edition. In J. E. Hayford, *Ethiopia unbound. Studies in race emancipation* (pp. v–xxxvi). London: Frank Cass. (Reprinted from 1911)

Vansina, J. (1990). *Paths in the Rainforest*. London: James Curry.

———. (1992). A past for the future? *Dalhousie Review*, 8–23.

———. (1992). History of Central African civilization and Kings in tropical Africa. In E. Beumers & H-J. Koloss, *Kings of Africa* (pp. 13–26). Maastricht: Foundation Kings of Africa.

Walraven, K. van. (1997). *Dreams of power. The role of the Organization of African Unity in the politics of Africa 1963–1993*. Leiden: n.p.

Wamba-dia-Wamba, E. (1984). Struggles for democracy in Africa: The case of the People's Republic of Congo. *Philosophy and Social Action, 10*(1–2).

———. (1992). Beyond elite politics of democracy in Africa. *Quest: Philosophical Discussions, 6*(1), 29–43.

———. (1994). Africa in search of a new mode of politics. In U. Himmelstrand et al. (eds.), *African perspectives on development. Controversies, dilemmas, openings* (pp. 249–261). London: James Curry.

———. (1995). The state of all Rwandese: Political prescriptions and disasters. Unpublished paper.

Wauthier, C. (1966). *The literature and thought of modern Africa—a survey*. London: Heinemann. English translation of *L'Afrique des Africains* (1964). Paris: Ed. du Seuil.

Weber, M. (1956). Die "Objectivität" sozialwissenshaftlicher Erkenntnis. In *Soziologie: Weltgeschichtliche Analysen Politik*. (pp. 186–262). Stuttgart: Alfred Kröner Verlag. (Originally printed in 1904).

Wilson, B. R. (1979). *Rationality*. Oxford: Blackwell.

Wilson, H. S. (1969). *Origins of West African nationalism*. London: MacMillan; St. Martin's Press.

Wiredu, K. (1984). How not to compare African thought with Western thought. In R. A. Wright *African philosophy. An introduction* (pp. 149–162). Lanham, New York, and London: University Press of America.

———. (1986). The question of violence in contemporary African political thought. *Praxis International, 6*(3), 373–381.

———. (1996). *Cultural universals and particulars*. Bloomington: Indiana University Press.

———. (1996). Democracy and consensus: A plea for a non-party polity. In K. Wiredu, *Cultural universals and particulars* (pp. 182–190). Bloomington: Indiana University Press. Originally in *The Centennial Review, 39*(1), 1995; also reproduced in E. Eze (ed.), *Postcolonial African philosophy* (pp. 303–312). Cambridge: Blackwell.

Wiredu, K., & Gyekye K. A. (1992). *Person and community. Ghanaian philosophical studies*, Vol. I. Washington, DC: The Council for Research in Values and Philosophy.

Woods, D. (1992) Civil society in Europe and Africa: Limiting state power through a public sphere. *African Studies Review, 35*(2), 77–100.

Wright, R. A. (1984). *African philosophy. An introduction*. Lanham, New York, and London: University Press of America.

Wyse, A. (1989). *The Krio of Sierra Leone: An interpretative history.* London: C. Hurst & Co.

Yohmed, B. B. (1964). Pour et contre le parti unique. *Jeune Afrique,* 166. Reprinted in P. Sigmund (ed.) (1963). *The ideologies of developing nations* (pp. 184–186). New York: Praeger.

Young, C. (1982). *Ideology and development in Africa.* New Haven and London: Yale University Press.

Zahar, R. (1974). *Colonialism and alienation: Concerning Frantz Fanon's political theory.* New York: Monthly Review Press. Originally published in German, *Befreiung und Entfremdung* (1969). Frankfurt am Mein.

Index

About the Author

PIETER BOELE van HENSBROEK is Coordinator, Interuniversity Cooperation programs between the University of Groningen in the Netherlands and universities in Africa and Asia. Dr. Boele van Hensbroek has taught at several institutions, including three years at the University of Zambia. He is co-founder and editor of the African journal of philosophy *Quest*.

ISBN 0-275-96494-9

90000>

EAN

9 780275 964948